Ian Mutch was born in London in 1952, and bought his first motorcycle (a 500cc BSA sidecar outfit) in 1969. After leaving school in 1970, he took a number of jobs before joining the merchant navy in 1971 in the employ of the British India Steam Navigation Company, as a Navigation Officer cadet, graduating eventually to Second Officer. Leaving the sea in 1983 he pursued a career in journalism, which alternated with work as a motorcycle courier in London until 1991 when, following a motorcycle trip to Israel, he gained full-time employment working on the motorcycle lifestyle titles *Heavy Duty* and *Back Street Heroes*. The summer of 1995 was spent photographing Harley Owners Group rallies around Europe, before taking up a retainer to produce a newspaper for The Motorcycle Action Group (MAG), of which he is a founder member. The trip about which this book is written, represents the fulfilment of a 20-year dream to ride a Harley-Davidson from coast to coast across the USA.

A firm believer in God, he has no idea if the creator rides a motorcycle or not, but if he does, then it sure as hell has to be a Harley.

LOOKING FOR AMERICA

IAN MUTCH

Proofing by:–
John Birdsall
Barbara Mutch • Craig Carey-Clinch • Dave French

Design – Be Jaye
Illustration – Stu Garland
Photography – Ian Mutch
Cover picture – Corbis

First published July 2001

Published by Ian Mutch
PO Box 18519, London E11 4HF

ISBN 09541136-0-8

Printed and bound in Great Britain
by Cox & Wyman Ltd, Reading
Copies available from: ne-mag@ukonline.co.uk
Tel: (UK) 0044 (0)191 2711 746

This is not a book about motorcycles. It's a book about
Americans, and about life. BUT, if you can watch a
Harley-Davidson loaded up with a bedroll and saddlebags,
rumble toward the horizon like thunder on vacation, and feel
nothing, then this book is not for you.

If I have to explain to you why I ride a
motorcycle, and you still don't understand,
then I must be inarticulate.

ARRIVAL

Port Authority on Forty-Second Street is a desperate place to be. Alone, anxious, hungry and exhausted, at one in the morning, it feels like the worst place in the world. Sitting in the neon cafeteria on a plastic stool with a cardboard carton of orange juice cradled between my hands, I thought back to my conversation on the aircraft.

'How are you planning to get from New York to Ashtabula,' asked the robust American tourist in the next seat.

'I'm going to take a Greyhound bus,' I replied. 'I know I could fly but I don't like flying. I don't want to fly any more than I have to. I don't want to fly one mile more than I need to. Besides, I want to see what it's like riding on a Greyhound bus; my father's thinking of riding around America on a Greyhound and he asked me to find out what it's like.' I nodded, short positive nods, lips pursed shut like Kermit the frog, a confirmation of my certainty that what I had just said was exactly what I meant. I'd picked up this confidence boosting mannerism from a host of contemporary American movies. Dustin Hoffman uses it, Woody Allen uses it, even Kermit the frog uses it, especially Kermit the frog, maybe Kermit the frog invented it. A friend once remarked that he knew I was about to impersonate Kermit the frog even before I started talking because of the cranial reciprocations which he hadn't consciously noted when watching the Muppet Show. There is about Kermit's assertive endeavours, an amusing indication of insecurity that endears one to the character. Did Americans acquire the habit from Kermit. There was an amusing thought: a nation, an entire continent of people, taking its cue from an amphibian, and an amphibian puppet at that. Why not? The greatest military force on earth took its orders from an actor for many years, why not its mannerisms from a frog?

My fellow traveller sustained a steady unsmiling gaze throughout the course of my protracted reply, his face a dramatic exaggeration of concern. 'Have you ever travelled by Greyhound before?' His tone was serious, sympathetic, almost schoolmasterly. In the seat to his left a small child began squawking petulantly. 'Daddy daddy, I want a drink, I'm thirsty, I have to have a drink.' 'Quiet a minute honey, daddy's talking.' The resolution with which

9

the girl's father subordinated his daughter's petulant request to the superior concern of my travelling arrangements, added a gravity to the situation which bordered on the theatrical. I felt as some naive explorer, venturing ashore in nineteenth-century Africa, with a straw hat and a walking stick to investigate the uncharted interior. The American beside me was a hardened trader with enough sense to venture no farther, a man whose advice would be rejected at one's peril.

'Do you know where to pick the bus up?' he asked.

'Port Authority' I replied, cheerfully implying a cognizance of New York geography that was illusory. He nodded his confirmation, leaving me with a well-intentioned caution. 'That is the worst place in Manhattan. Port Authority is the very worst place in the whole of New York.'

I nodded for want of some kind of response, I nodded with the certainty of a man who hears confirmation of something he already knew. Sure, Port Authority is the worst place in the whole of New York, everyone knows that, what am I a spring chicken? A green twig? The worst place in New York, of course it is, bloody obvious isn't it. As I sat wondering what could be so terrible about a bus station, an exquisitely manicured hand pushed my dining tray shut as the cheery ding of the cabin's PA system sprang into life. 'Ignore that red illuminated sign ordering me to belt up,' I thought, you must wait at least thirty seconds before moving a muscle to comply with a machine's instructions; only amateurs and freshmen of the air respond to these warnings with an infantile enthusiasm. There is something undignified, unseemly, about responding with alacrity to instructions delivered by a machine. Better to stay cool, act indifferent, maintain the blasé identity of the seasoned campaigner who deals with all things in his own time, on his own terms, yes that's much more adult, much more mature, much more confident. I checked the view through the window, a tidy maze of detached homes with spacious gardens, rather like some extravagant London satellite new town, the comfortable middle class suburbia of Long Island. The reassuring soft thud of the wheels locking out provided my excuse to buckle up as the aircraft angled for the approach to JFK International Airport.

I looked up at the cabin ceiling as the hiss of the air conditioning changed note, an anxious time for the nervous flier, though for me, a different source of concern presented itself. What was so terrible about Port Authority?

PORT AUTHORITY

'Right over there,' replied the laconic cop, his ostentatious hardware glittering against the matt blue of the police officer's uniform.

'Right over there,' I repeated, setting out tentatively in the direction indicated. Outside the terminal building, the exact location of 'over there,' was less clear. The world was a mass of buses and cabs going in contrary directions on a number of lanes, the overall impression of confusion being compounded by airport service vehicles chicaning every which way to fill in all the angles not already adopted by the buses. 'Over there,' I repeated to myself, 'over there.'

'Excuse me, can you tell me where I can catch a bus to Port Authority?' This time I asked a porter of Latin origin who, being occupied in the outdoor environs of what was known from inside the building as, 'over there,' might, I thought, be better acquainted with the finer details of unqualified description.

'You see that line of people over there?'

'Over there?' I asked, staring in the direction of at least three rows of people facing every which way. 'No no, over there,' he repeated, springing up on to tip toe and arching his arm in a vertical curve to pinpoint the exact location. I followed the curve of his arm, assuming it to be describing the parabolic course of an arrow, judging its target to lie somewhere in the middle of the fleshy face of a large black woman contemplating our unintentioned scrutiny with some curiosity.

'Oh, over there!' I exclaimed, with a mixture of feigned enlightenment and gratitude. I set off hopefully, the heavy hold-all unbalancing me as it threatened the steadiness of my course. Fifty yards and two cab horn blasts later, I was, at last, 'over there,' and set down my load to await the bus. Thinking it wise to check I was in the right queue, I asked the assembled people for confirmation.

'No no no' they cried with the harmonious unity of a gospel choir as their black hands fluttered horizontally for corroborative emphasis like an enthusiastic congregation at an evangelical meeting. A brief conference ensued, during which all those participating revolved several times on the spot, pointing with a collective mass of conjectural digits in every direction of the compass. As is the way with these situations, one voice of decision had been spontaneously distilled by the process of the great consult, and now, with calm resolution, the faces of his fellows looking on, and heavy with concern, he spoke.

'You want to go to Port Authority?' We were back to first principles.

'Yes,' I replied.

'You must go...' a pause for thought, like a javelin-thrower preparing himself for the ultimate fling. 'Over there.' Stretching his arm at full length for definition as one might use a long barrelled rifle for maximum accuracy, he turned his head at right angles to this human plumb line, staring over his shoulder at me to ensure my appreciation of his directive. The eyes of all involved in the preceding conference followed the course directed by his limb with a comical uniformity reminiscent of the painting by Scobely of a crowd awed by the sight of Halley's Comet, their heavenly gaze directed by the eccentric person of the mad astronomer desperately pointing skyward with ecstatic vindication.

I could not help noticing that the spot to which I was directed, bore an uncanny resemblance to the one from which I had collected my last set of instructions from the Latin porter; never mind.

The bag was becoming heavy now, as I retraced my steps less hopefully to the spot from where I observed my earlier instructor had conveniently absented himself. Not only was there no bus there, there was no hint of a bus stop, and as if further discouragement were needed, the fat yellow paint at the curbside spelled out the words, 'CABS ONLY.' I was not encouraged, and set out on my own at random amidst the confusion of cabs, cops, baggage trolleys and buses bearing destination details of everywhere in the Eastern United States bar Port Authority. In the distance, I caught sight of the huddle of well intentioned navigators who'd last directed my efforts. Rooted to the spot, their arms waved vigorously in an effort to guide my feet, like figures in an epic tapestry stitched permanently to the canvas whilst filled with enthusiastic endeavour. I pointed to various locations with what I imagined could be identified as an attitude of enquiry, thus prompting the collective organism of advisors to behave in a manner resembling something akin to a demented Medusa. Seeking a second, or rather, fourth, opinion, I enquired of a woman police officer.

'Stay here,' she advised me. 'The bus for Port Authority leaves from right here.'

'Not over there?' I double checked.

'Here,' she repeated, pointing with smiling confidence vertically downwards at the ground. Dropping my bag I massaged an aching shoulder. Meanwhile, 'over there', the clutch of navigators was boarding a bus bearing the world famous legend 'Harlem.'

The hydraulic hiss of the doors opening, broke the reverie into which I'd fallen as I stood in line; checking the destination on the front of the vehicle, I climbed aboard.

'Will you tell me when we arrive at Port Authority?' I enquired of the driver.

'I certainly will, I will tell you when we get to Port Authority.' Very emphatic these New Yorkers, plenty of emphasis, plenty of repetition, no equivocality about their responses, like well disciplined seamen.

Behind me on the bus sat two airline stewardesses, their conversation loaded with the inevitable colour of what might be critically described as geographical name dropping. Exotic place names slipped off their tongues as they described the experiences of what to them, was probably an average week's work. As their conversation progressed, so too did the bus, bringing the magnetic Manhattan skyline clearly into view. My enjoyment of the dramatic sight was, however, diminished by the anxious warnings of my fellow traveller on the aircraft, so that it was with some trepidation that I awaited the conclusion of the journey at the city's central bus terminal.

With the exception of aircraft travel and motorcycle journeys in the rain, I don't like journey's-end. I have an infinite capacity for travel and, like a well-fed dog, am more or less content whenever scenery is rolling by me. The hiss of the brakes accompanied by the driver's announcement, 'Port Authority folks,' unleashed a wave of apprehension that rippled through my body like a shudder. I had now to leave my seat, to jostle with the other passengers, to regain my luggage, and then negotiate the hazards of the unfamiliar streets which separated this point from the infamous depot. Why the airport bus could not set its passengers down at Port Authority was a mystery to me, perhaps the muggers union demanded a gap into which they could insinuate themselves in order to ply their nefarious trade. Such cheerful speculation consumed my imagination as I joined the muddle of passengers struggling amidst the mound of bags fast accumulating on the pavement. I spotted my own long-hinged sausage of a grip and made a grab for it, but my effort was pre-empted by another, and long black fingers curled around the handles ahead of me.

'This your bag?' asked a gravelly voice with a familiarity that implied an earlier acquaintance.

'Yes,' I replied, with an unintentional but implicit acceptance of his assistance. As is often the way in third world countries, and downtown Manhattan feels very much like one, I had, without request, acquired the services of a porter, a guide, a minder, to see me through the urban gauntlet of Manhattan's Lower East Side.

I strolled along a half pace behind the gaunt dark figure preceding me into the labyrinth of human hazard of which I had been forewarned. Though I could see skyscrapers in the distance, the feel of the area down here at street level was positively third world. As a 'Whitey,' I was in a very small minority. Latinos, Puerto Ricans, Mexicans, and Blacks ruled the roost, blending chameleon-like into the seedy sweatiness of the sidewalks, against which I felt myself to be spotlit like a luminous Jew in a mosque. Having unloaded most of my gear on the entrepreneurial bearer, I had a hand free to stuff nonchalantly into my pocket; look casual, that's the trick. Human predators, in common with their canine counterparts, can smell fear, and the smell of fear encourages attack. I scratched my jaw with a hasty irritation which I hoped did

14

not look affected, and wiped my nose crudely with the back of my hand. The shops and kiosks that lined the street seemed reminiscent of a thousand streets in India, Latin America, or the Middle East. It seems that the more desperate a retail enterprise, the greater the variety of goods on offer. While at the other end of the scale, an up-market Kings Road fashion shop might feature a few pairs of poncey shoes at stupid prices, and a single suited mannequin in the window, these down-town mini bazaars are cluttered with a kaleidoscopic variety of small artifacts, all of which are doubtless of some use, but none of which I ever seem to need immediately. Pens, cards, cigarette lighters, nail clippers, safety razors, hair clips, combs, cheap sunglasses, chewing gum and paper handkerchiefs in pocket size packs, a jumble sale of miscellanea sprouting like the accumulated debris of an untidy bird's nest.

Besides the optimistic vendors, peering out of their doors in search of custom like hungry congas in their aquatic lairs, there are the lurkers, loiterers and lamp post lingerers whose presence seems gratuitous, whose existence suggests superfluity. It is this species of resident locust that gives New York its dangerous air, its predatorial threat. In groups of two, three or more, they cluster at doorways and corners like oily flotsam in the nooks and crevices of ill kept docks and shadowed urban waterways. You don't get this in London in the same way or on the same scale, and certainly not so close to the centre of the hive. Perhaps we don't have as much unemployment, or maybe it's the weather; but here in New York these threatening cliques of malingerers are part of, if not the essence of, the street life for which the city is famous.

I was glad of the porter I had unintentionally acquired, he knew where he was going and he was the right colour, two factors which gave his employment the edge over a DIY effort on my part. Notwithstanding his support, I felt, in my over anxious condition, that our progress was accompanied by the sharpening of carnivorous teeth as the malevolents, grinning and fidgeting in the shadows, eyed the pale intruder that was myself, creeping along with my hired collaborator. Stoats and weasels, secure in their numbers, plotting from their hedgerow hideouts. I worked hard at looking relaxed, tried not to react to the jungle squawks, imprecations and sudden commotions emanating from the spitting, whooping, hand slapping serpents of the sidewalk. Perhaps I do them an injustice, maybe they all have loving wives and families, clean homes and worthwhile jobs, but if that is the case, what the hell were they doing lurking on the street making me feel nervous? My observation of these pavement piranha lent me an understanding of why police in the movies are forever urging them to 'keep moving.' Just as an unstable government fears the orchestration of opposition that grows from public meetings, so the small time threat to domestic peace is nurtured by these festering coagulations of ill intent, fouling the arteries of urban progress.

I had assumed, of course, that my St Christopher of the suitcases was what he appeared to be, and not some Judas agent of 'muggers incorporated.' It was as my mind toyed with this cheerful doubt that we turned sharp left under a sign which brought instant relief: 'Port Authority.'

You can't book Greyhound tickets in advance, it's first come first served, and I joined a queue for mine which cost a surprisingly hefty ninety dollars for a one way ticket that would take me about five hundred miles, considerably more expensive than a British equivalent coach, despite the fuel costs being a fraction of those in Britain. Given the perception of Greyhound travel as the economical, working class facility that I thought it to be, this charge seemed to me perplexingly steep. Ticket firmly ensconced in wallet, I followed my guide into the catacombs of this maligned terminus, his long loping form ploughing through the scurrying bodies with the reassuring resolution of a nonchalant ice breaker. Dumping my baggage at the door of an almost violently lit cafe, the professional Samaritan pointed out to me where I must queue for my bus, and where I could wait in the meantime. Thanking him for his help, I fished around awkwardly for the means to pay him. As fate would have it the whole wad of ten dollar bills bulged unintentionally into sight with the hazardous provocation of a Hasidic handkerchief in a Beirut bazaar, an indiscretion which earned me some street level advice.

'Don't do that in here, never do that around this place, just take out the money you need, keep the rest of your stash out of sight, you understand what I'm saying to you?'

It was well intended advice, though my gratitude for it was tempered by the irritation I felt at the neglect of a simple precaution of which years in foreign countries should have taught me the necessity. I extracted two dollar bills and offered them up as payment for the man's labours.

'It's err.. seven dollars,' he replied, scratching his wiry scalp and staring down at the inadequate reward dampening in his sweaty palm. This seemed a great deal to me for ten minutes' effort, but I was in no mood to argue, and was happy to have completed one of the more dangerous stages of my marathon without sustaining loss or injury. I handed over a further five dollars, suspecting the fee reflected an inflation that was both local and transient in character, tailor-made in fact to my particular requirements or rather, potential. What the hell, the old fellow wasn't going to get rich, even at that rate, and he did not look like a man upon whom the bounty of life was about to spontaneously descend. I thanked him and he reciprocated my gratitude with interest.

'God bless you,' declared the ragged bearer, in a tone of convincing sincerity as he folded the money before thrusting it deep into the recesses of his tattered clothing. I watched as his stooped figure cut a slow chicane through the pimps, pushers and gun toting cops who rub shoulders in this desperate terminus.

Inside the blinding chandelier of the cafe, I ordered orange juice; there was a good quart of sweat to be replaced before I moved anywhere. Before I'd made it to my seat I was accosted by a pale character of dubious intent, who promptly invited me to commit acts of criminal indulgence.

'You want crack, you want speed, hash, pills – what you want?' It's always best, in my opinion, to respond to unwanted attention of this kind with a reasonable mouthful; a monosyllabic grunt, an embarrassed 'No thank you,' just aren't good enough; that's too English, it isn't the American way, there have to be more words. I've watched Woody Allen films, I was ready for him.

'You see this orange juice? This is what I want, this is all I want, I don't need anything else, I don't want anything else. I am here to catch a bus, and right now I am going to sit down, right there, and drink this orange juice – OK?'

A toothless grin was the mute response to my theatrics. 'Hey it's my birthday man, make my day for me man, it's my birthday.' The trouble with some people is that they just cannot take 'no' for an answer. I sat down in the corner at a plastic table, my bag close to me, zipped my wallet into the inside pocket of my jacket and opened the book I'd bought in the airport lounge at Heathrow.

Porterhouse Blue, a humorous account of life at a Cambridge University college during the sixties; very English.

Over by the food counter, a wretched character was trying to extract money from customers in the queue. His manner was loathsome, shuffling up to potential benefactors and jabbing at them with a hand from which most of the digits had decayed by means no doubt of some leprous malady, if not the savage retribution of a vengeful society which had rewarded his nefarious misdeeds with Islamic severity. The fingerless palm was turned upward in anticipation of some financial assistance, whilst a blister fringed mouth worked at some barely audible plea.

Sadly for him the proprietor was not sympathetic to this luckless leech, and made his feelings clear in a manner as characteristically New York as the Empire State Building.

'Hey you! What the hell are you doing in here again? I've told you before, stay out of this place, you're a bum, I don't need bums in here, we got more bums than we need, we don't need you too, you hear what I'm saying to you, no one wants you in here, get the fuck out of this place and take your frigging fingers with you.'

Leaving aside the curious irony of the 'frigging fingers', it has to be said that the target of this criticism was left in no doubt as to the kind of reception he might expect on a future visit. That's the great thing about American speech, particularly New York speech, it's the repetition that lends it an air of theatrical emphasis. You never need to say 'pardon,' because not only is every statement spelt out to you several times, but confirmation that you understand what is being said to you is sought at intervals along the way, 'you understand what I'm saying to you?' It's so very considerate.

A man who looked as if he understood very little of what was being said, and definitely did not want to be involved, was sitting opposite me. Chinese, small of stature, and defective in the sight department, he sat bespectacled before me, avoiding all eye contact, his nose pointed between the pages of a paperback book. This man was not going to give me a problem, I liked this fellow; I even toyed with the idea of talking to him so that I might see evidence of someone more apprehensive than myself. The idea remained stillborn, however, as a drama was unfolding before me into which I was to be recruited like the shy clot who takes a stall seat at a magic show.

A young, tarty looking white woman, accompanied by a small bewildered child, marched in, her high heels clip-clopping noisily on the hard, tiled floor. The distraught looking creature cast her eyes about the assembled travellers as if seeking someone she expected to meet. Fixing her anxious eyes on me, she strode over, dragging the infant behind her like Christopher Robin with Winnie the Pooh. 'This woman is trouble,' I thought, as soon as I looked at her. Why did I look at her I wondered? She must have detected some element of sympathetic humanity in my face that prompted her to steer so determined a course for my limited territory; yes, I predicted, 'this woman is trouble.' This is the kind of woman who will always be in trouble, always be stumbling from one crisis to the next like a lame horse that upon stumbling into the edge of a swamp, heads instinctively for its middle. I didn't want to know this woman. I didn't need any trouble right now. I did not want any problems or complications in my life at this time. I wanted to sit quietly reading my book until the bus came. 'Don't come over here,' I thought, don't head this way, veer over there a bit, sit over there, go and bother that guy in the corner, I mean, what is wrong with him, what is it that I have that he doesn't?

'Excuse me sir.'

AAAAARRGH!

'Yes?'

'Would you please look after my suitcase, I have to go looking for my purse, I've lost my purse, my purse had all my money in it, my ticket everything, I've lost everything.' 'Hell', I thought, this is the ruse, she's lost her purse so she needs money, she is certain to ask me for money. The woman strutted out the door, the child, a girl of about three, lingering behind.

'Come on, come on, you want to come with me or you want to stay here, you want to come with me or you want to stay with the man?'

'No! No she doesn't', I sent desperate telepathic messages across the floor as the child's eyes surveyed me with a speculative innocence. I felt panicky, half an hour in New York City and I become responsible for a child whose crazy mother is obviously going to desert her. 'Go with your mummy there's a good girl, go with mummy, the man is guarding the suitcase already, he doesn't want to guard small children as well, off you go now – for Christ's sake, go!'

19

'Bye bye.' This was the woman speaking. 'Bye bye.' She was on the far side of the open doorway now, amidst a group of huge black youths pacing slowly by like cruising sharks, slowing to peer at the unravelling domestic drama.

'You staying here, you staying here with the man till I get back?'

'Like hell you are, you get over there with your mummy, for Christ's sake woman, come and take a hold of this child and drag it wherever you have to, only don't leave it here with me.' Finally the woman departed, dragging the squawking child, much in the manner that I had mentally indicated. Meanwhile a fresh horror had belched onto the stage.

This was another woman, but of a different breed, a gross pasty creature, the kind of frightful travesty of womanhood that sends shudders through your body as perverse notions of enforced physical contact loom before the fertile imagination like ghoulish possibilities from the darkest gulleys of tortured speculation; self inflicted injuries of psychological masochism.

Edgar Allen Poe describes such sensations as his 'theory of the perverse.' In any given situation, the colourful imagination contemplates the worst scenario that might evolve from the available ingredients. Stand on the edge of a cliff and you can't help imagining stepping off, ditto railway platforms. I looked at the woman and shivered.

This wretch suffered from a particularly unpleasant form of obesity, in that the translucence of her skin suggested an inability to contain the blubber around which it was tautly stretched. Huge red blotches shining waxily in the artificial light, stood out against the ghastly pallor of her flesh like splodges of jam on fresh rolled pastry. The woman made for the chair at the next table to mine – she would – and threatened to sit down. Leaving aside the unpleasantness of her proximity, I felt certain that the strain on her skin would split it as the blubber beneath reassembled itself. Like a hissing pork sausage, plump to bursting point, over-filled and over stressed, splits would surely appear, and raw globular tissue like cod's roe, would spill out in the manner of a macabre spectacle from a graphic medical documentary. 'Please don't sit down, oh please...' Too late, she'd landed, the lard arsed colossus was planted on the wretchedly inadequate plastic stool whose up-curved edges flattened out under her weight like a defeated mushroom; it practically sighed. Worse yet, the contents had breached their sack and a preliminary stream of steaming wax was running down one jellyfish forearm. 'Surreal,' I thought, 'positively surreal.' She pulled back the cuff to lick up the waxy stream; a cow eating its afterbirth.

'She's devouring herself,' I thought, sharks do the same when they have feeding frenzies. These predators, when torn open by their colleagues, have been seen to gorge themselves on their own trailing intestines, but even these killer fish, in their sense-numbed obsession fall short of the horror before my eyes.

It was at this point in my reflections, that I noticed the presence of a brace of hot dogs grasped in the fat woman's paw, the kind of cheap low meat items, half unwanted blubber, half offal and fried in copious lard. If they hadn't been placed in a thick absorbent tissue they would have shot out of the glistening paw holding them, like a couple of well oiled torpedoes. 'Slurp!' The swollen red tongue dragged the resinous scum back into its diseased grotto of un-brushed yellow fangs, pegs of neglected enamel shrouded in copious plaque like the weed clad legs of some seaside pier. A human lug worm, the beast's reptilian tongue slithered between the carbuncular lips and scouted around the shapeless orifice in quest of straggling remnants of grease to consume. No more was to be had, but the roving organ, searching on sightless spec, collided with the pregnant peak of a ripe sore, which promptly split, spawning a lava-like effluent to trickle from this biological Vesuvius.

Turning my way and gesturing toward the door through which the unfortunate mother had now reappeared, the ogre belched a sentence of surprising coherence.

'What's with her?' she demanded.

The notion that anyone on the planet could have been worse off than this thing struck me as extraordinary, and I was momentarily numbed by the irony of her concern.

'She's lost her purse,' I replied, relieved that the creature was actually capable of speech, and fortifying my faith that I had not drifted into an improbable nightmare.

'Lost her purse, what she do, leave it some place?'

'I expect so,' I replied somewhat lamely.

'Jesus, in a place like this, she leaves her purse, what is she, crazy?'

I nodded my tacit agreement, complementing the gaggle of colleagues further along the wall, who provided a chorus of agreement. 'Crazy, crazy and crazy,' yes, by unanimous decree the spontaneous panel of celebrated judges had declared her totally and irredeemably, crazy.

The young mother had returned, more distraught than before.

'Any luck?' I ventured optimistically. The response was predictably negative, this was a luckless place, lucky people didn't belong here. Here there was no such thing as luck, here things could only be lost, never found.

Fortunately, sincere and sympathetic counselling was close at hand.

'OK lady; take a seat,' the fat woman was in charge. 'Now where did you leave your purse?'

'I left it outside the bathroom when I went inside, when I came out it was gone,' wailed the young woman.

'Hang on, let's get this straight, you went into the bathroom, you left your purse outside, and when you came out it was gone?' The wretch nodded tearfully, a pupil in the throes of remorse being consoled by a sympathetic teacher applying balm after a necessary scolding. The woman was a natural mother figure, gross but kindly; advice followed the establishment of the facts.

'Lady, this is a public place, you cannot do things like that in a public place,' the voice was rising now, 'you do something like that in a place like this, you have to be totally, I mean totally, crazy! You hear what I'm saying to you? Crazy!'

The young woman's acquiescent nodding was mirrored in that of the muppet congregation, sagaciously reciprocating their heads in unison from the plastic pews to the right, where they sat double handedly clutching their polystyrene prayer books of steaming coffee.

'Listen lady,' Counsellor Huge had the stage again. 'Go over to the ticket office, explain your situation to them, maybe they'll give you another ticket. OK you go along now dear.' Mother and child dutifully tottered off, whilst the large one sought corroboration of her analysis of the situation. A thin woman, a silent stooge to her sister in suet, had opened the voting by nodding assent to her companion's verdict. 'Crazy, definitely crazy;' but more opinions were needed. 'Hey Frank, Frank, get over here.' A gaunt elderly Negro languidly sweeping a debris of crumbs, wrappers and crunched hypos into a long-handled dustpan, looked up, a cigarette hung limply from his mouth, the smoke made him squint as he peered through the cloud at the dictatorial conductor. She waved him over petulantly with the baton of her remaining hot dog, spraying a circle of waxen droplets on the floor before the sweeper's eyes. Viewing the mess dispassionately, this grim reaper of the bus stop slouched toward the centre stage where an excited story teller awaited him. Outside the window, the groups of tall athletic black youths continued drifting by, peering in menacingly, faces anonymous behind needless mirrored black shades. A ghetto blaster woke up a dosser with a raucous cacophony of mindless rap as a drunk slipped on a puddle of vomit. Inside the expostulations continued.

'Frank, you see that young woman, the one with the little girl?' Frank nodded. 'Get this. She goes into the lady's room, but she leaves her purse outside. When she comes out, it's gone. What you make of that?' The old man's lined face creased itself into an aspect of deep concentration as he struggled with the facts.

'The woman goes into the bathroom right?'

'Right,' confirmed the blubber.

'She leaves her purse outside?'

'Right.'

'When she comes out her purse is gone.'

'Right,' squealed the woman, evidently delighted by the clarity of her pupil's perception. 'What you make of that?'

Frank's mouth moved mechanically, the remaining features of his face remaining undisturbed. Slowly he raised his head, eyes turned heavenward, a judge pronouncing sentence.

'She's crazy,' he declared sombrely.

'That's what I told her!' shrieked the blubber triumphantly, thumping a plump paw on the table. A further drop of grease from the hot dog spat over the table, streaking across the lens of the Chinaman's glasses and obstructing his reading. Putting down his book, he removed the spectacles with stoic calm, studied the pollution for a moment without a trace of emotion, and then wiped them on an unused paper napkin. The pusher who'd accosted me earlier, floated in, grinned at me, and arched his eyebrows in a manner which suggested he thought I might have changed my mind. I shook my head and he swam off into a shoal of desperados pacing the concourse outside the cafe. Inside, the fat woman was repeating her story of the unfortunate mother to a fresh companion, the hot dogs were finished now, the waxy papers that

23

had cradled them lying crumpled on the table like the debris of a whaling station. The word 'crazy' overflowed from the bowl of conversation as the story climaxed with the now familiar team of nodding heads confirming uniform agreement with the popular diagnosis.

Over by the service counter the leprous beggar had returned, and was plying his miserable trade on some late arrivals to the pantomime.

'Hey you, you!' yelled the man in charge, pointing from behind a steaming tea urn. 'I told you once before, you're a bum, we don't need bums, you're not wanted in here, get out of here or I'll call the cops.'

The Chinaman sank further into his coat as if willing himself into invisibility, passive contempt for his environment subtly reflected in every element of his understated demeanour. From a tape deck in the accumulating bus queue outside the cafe, a familiar line from a David Bowie hit drifted poignantly across the tragic concourse; 'this...is not A–m–er–i–ca.'

I hoped he was right.

THE GREYHOUND

Two and a half hours after arriving at the bus station, I decided it was time to get in line for a bus to Buffalo, and so joined a queue with the town's name at its head. Another queue, a longer one, largely composed of people sitting on rucksacks with their backs to the wall, led to an adjacent door over which the same legend, 'Buffalo', extended. I asked around to make sure I was in the right line. (Americans use the word 'line,' rather than 'queue' which many of them don't understand.) At this point, a man with a hat appeared, unlocked the door at the head of my queue and declared, 'Passengers for Buffalo, this way.' A riot of protest now erupted in the adjacent, older queue, where protestations of injustice greeted the announcement.

'Hey what is this? We've been here longest. We've lined up here for over two hours!'

'What's the matter with these people,' I thought, surely they've all got tickets, tickets can't have been sold for seats that don't exist. Just the same, there did seem to be a lot of people waiting, and I began to wonder if I was going to spend the entire night in the bus depot.

'I wish to protest,' shouted a particularly vocal chap in a lumberjack shirt.

'This is grossly unfair; I am going to complain, this is grossly unfair!' I had to agree with the protester but as I seemed to be an innocent beneficiary of the injustice, I kept my mouth shut and shuffled along toward the door with the discreetly silent column. After more protests and explanations, a second door was unlocked, and the other queue surged forward like a stampede from *Rawhide*.

Once on the bus I looked around for a place to sit, preferably

25

not next to some garrulous soul who was going to bend my ear all the way to Buffalo. The Chinaman from the cafe seemed a safe bet, he hadn't uttered a word so far, and I could see no reason why he should start now. I dumped myself in the vacant seat next to him and sat back with relief as the diesel fired into life, the doors swung shut, and the bus lurched out of the terminus into the pre-dawn chill of a Manhattan morning.

I was glad to be away from the big city with its squalor and hysterics, and my spirits rose as the urban lights diminished and our bus was absorbed into the rural environment of forest-cloaked up-state New York.

Sleeping on buses isn't easy. The chap across the aisle seemed to have achieved it, by collapsing across his girlfriend's lap. The Chinaman too, appeared to have achieved a state of sublime unconsciousness. But then Orientals are capable of many extraordinary feats that they perfect in order to astonish Westerners, of which this self motivated somnolence was but a modest example.

After an hour or two of uncomfortable insomnia, I dwelt on the power of sleep deprivation as a device of torturers for eliciting confessions from the wretches in their power. An interrogator, climbing aboard the bus I was travelling on, would have needed no lamps to shine in my eyes, no bamboo splinters to poke under my fingernails, or thumb screws to squeeze my digits. I'd been awake and travelling, somewhat stressfully, for 24 sleepless hours. I'd have unloaded any amount of incriminating details in return for a few cushions and a blanket. I'd even have thrown in some speculative embroidery and incriminated a few innocents for the sake of an air bed to make life really pleasant. As it was, unable to sleep in the seat, I decided to stretch out on the floor in the aisle. This was a little undignified but I was past caring, and I doubted if any of my fellow passengers could have given a damn. Taking off my coat to make a pillow I stretched full length to await the administrations of the sandman. Sadly, the whine of the prop shaft, now at ear level, exercised an insomniac rather than soporific influence. Twenty minutes after attaining the horizontal, the driver announced a stopover.

'Twenty-five minutes' break folks,' he hollered, as the coach lurched into a service area.

At four in the morning, the enthusiasm of the staff was not at peak level. I don't believe I heard anyone sing out the obligatory, 'have a nice day,' as notes and coins changed hands with a minimum of conversation. I bought a polystyrene beaker of coffee, which operated initially as a hand warmer as I paced around the parking lot, my palms curled around its regular contours, blowing vapour into the crisp dark air, and sipping tentatively at the scalding contents. I felt tired, greasy, itchy, petulant and insecure, the demoralising influence of sleeplessness against a background of anxious uncertainty, had unravelled the fibre of my dwindling confidence. I felt like a threadbare shirt with its buttons missing.

Time up, we re-boarded the bus, a dreary straggle of sleepy dissidents resuming their journey to some appalling *gulag*, after an obligatory rest stop under the watchful eyes of the guards. The reassuring rumble of the engine, the hiss and fangled flapping of the doors, and we were off again. I'd passed the period of worst sleeplessness now, and was feeling better as the sun rose and dozing passengers, awakened by the lightening sky, wiped condensation from the windows to peer curiously out into the Ohio dawn.

At Buffalo I changed buses at a depot worlds apart from the one at New York. Only a fraction of the size, it was clear of the scavenging ponces that polluted the New York terminus. Furthermore, I was at ground level and could see outside to where the sun was shining, a sharp contrast to the permanent artificial night of the subterranean ghetto in the Big Apple where I'd spent several nervous hours earlier. Here all seemed pleasant.

A pretty teenage girl was kissing her grandfather goodbye, hands were being shaken, cheeks pecked. This seemed a more normal area of human interaction, the only thing anyone tried to sell me was a ticket, and then only when I asked for it. There were however, still too many tall people around for my liking. This is so even in England, but here in America the complaint is more prevalent. It was whilst deliberating on this, however, that I noticed the fellow selling newspapers. He was little more than four feet in height, but exhibited nonetheless, a heartening enthusiasm for his modest responsibilities. There was so much life and pride in the way he took coins, folded papers, and handed them to their new owners that I felt strangely humbled. Here was a chap who was not about to oust Schwarzenegger from his Hollywood perch. No talent scout was going to lift him out of this humble role, and put him in a blockbuster, and he wasn't likely to be turning down interviews with David Frost; not this week. That said, he impressed me as is the way when one sees someone so much less fortunate than oneself making an effort, a real effort. In consequence, I registered dual emotions of guilt and gratitude that bolstered my confidence and inspired me with optimistic resolve. I had the opportunity to ride a Harley-Davidson across America, and though I was only five-foot five, that was just enough, and when all is said and done, it's a hell of a lot more than four-foot nothing.

ASHTABULA

The bus-ride to Ashtabula took me through a multitude of small towns arranged roughly along the southern bank of Lake Erie. Embarkations and disembarkations fell into a monotonous pattern that was abruptly disturbed by an announcement that, though heard for the first time, sounded familiar, like one's own name heard for the first time over a PA system: 'Ashtabula.' Again that sense of misgiving at journey's-end, my name called out in court, my name read out in school assembly, 'Will the following boys report to the headmaster's office.' On a more humorous level, I used to have the same experience when I was studying for my Second Mate's Certificate at a college in Kent, only there the headmaster's office had been replaced by the central office, and the reason was always the same, I hadn't paid the rent for my room in the residential complex. It was hardly my fault, I was broke. Off the company payroll, *fiscus desperandum*. No matter, every day at the end of morning lectures, my name would be tagged on the end of the list of paupers and miscreants. So predictable was its inclusion, that the rest of the class would precede the tannoy system with the anticipated 'and I Mutch,' just as the secretary on the microphone was drawing breath to pronounce the final, predictable name. Now it was the name 'Ashtabula' that woke me from my reverie, and I scrambled down the steps to the ground where I retrieved my bag. As the bus pulled away into the distance I looked around for a phone. I'd told my friend Chip, who had arranged a motorcycle for me, that I would be coming and when, a monumental piece of preparation on my part, so I reasoned, there should not be a problem. But what if I rang and there was no answer? I would feel the identity of a lemon rapidly overtake me. I'd been awake for 34 hours now, I would be a tired lemon.

I'd been deposited at the end of a parade of shops, along which I trotted to a department store where I noticed a telephone through the window. Buying a soft drink to break a five dollar bill, I took my change in quarters and approached the phone. Chip was at home, this was too much to hope for, a plan actually unfolding as anticipated! I waited for Chip's battered Oldsmobile, as stationwagons, Cherokee Chiefs, Dodges and Pontiacs barrelled up the slip road where I stood. It came. Chip Bugansky was at the wheel, his brother Frank, one leg in plaster, sat beside him. It was mid afternoon and we had still to register the bike and arrange insurance before five-thirty. After that it was shut-down time for the Thanksgiving weekend, which would mean I wouldn't be able to set out on my journey for another four days, by which time, if things went well, I intended to be at least a third of my way across the United States.

The registration of the bike was no big problem, and I left the office two dollars lighter with a large piece of floppy cardboard which passed as a State of Ohio registration plate. The insurance was a little trickier. Chip had a mate whose dad was a big wheel in an insurance company, he was supposed to have smoothed everything over so that on my arrival, all I should have had to do was sign a piece of paper, make a payment and everything would be sweet. The son of the big wheel would sort it all, only he hadn't, and we had to phone around. The first quote we got was out of this world. I gave the man all the facts he asked for, make of motorcycle, Harley-Davidson, year 1985, engine capacity 1340 ccs. 'Three hundred and forty ccs?' asked the voice on the other end of the phone. 'No thirteen hundred,' I corrected him, 'one thousand three hundred and forty ccs.' The voice '*ummd*' as remote eyes scanned a table of rates. 'Right, take a seat,' warned the distant voice. 'That will be two-thousand, two-hundred and thirty dollars.' I was pole-axed; gobsmacked. 'What is this?' I thought. I felt like Sir Edmund Hilary, who, having climbed all the way to Everest base camp is then told there is a million-dollar fee for those wishing to climb further. This was the kind of feeling I remember experiencing as a child, the kind of devastating disappointment that deflates infantile aspirations with a sudden and unassailable finality that adult life metes out less often. Like the time I went to see a film version of Jules Verne's *Journey to the Centre of the Earth*, at the local cinema. I must have queued for an hour before I reached that box office with the one-and-threepence which my mum had given me, gripped tightly in my paw, only to discover when I reached the window of that little glass box, the altar of my greatest ambitions, that there were no more seats downstairs, only seats in the circle remained, and they cost one and ninepence. I didn't have one and ninepence. Over a quarter of a century later, I found myself in a similar position, only this time I did have two thousand two hundred and thirty dollars but I was damned if I was going to spend it on motorcycle insurance for one lousy month! 'Oh, if you only want it for a month then you'll get a rebate when you leave the country,' the voice on the other end of the line assured me. This was not what I wanted to hear. I wanted to hear about decimal points migrating westward on that figure, and then some divisions being made, before I was going to feel remotely mollified. Thank you for playing the game sir. Next caller please. All play ended for Thanksgiving at five-thirty; I had little time left to manoeuvre. We finally tracked down a company who dealt in real numbers which became even more sensible when I explained that I was thirty-seven, not as he had thought, about twenty-one. There are advantages to growing older, and one of them is to be found in motor insurance rates. I was running desperately short of time now, however, and with minutes only to spare, I walked through the door of a local broker's office, handed him eighty dollars, collected some paperwork, shook hands, and stepped outside, as the manager turned the 'open' sign around to show 'closed'. It was five-thirty-two.

The bike was at a local dealers and it was time to collect. I knew what an FXR looked like, but every Harley is different. This one had clearly been owned by an atypical Harley owner, not a 'righteous bro.' The exhaust system was a Kerker high performance item, with dual silencers upswept like the ones on old Norton Commandos. Proper Harleys have horizontal staggered 'shotguns' that terminate more than a foot apart, accentuating the *potato-potato* sound that Harley were shortly to endeavour patenting. Some people thought it was a joke at first, but it wasn't. Harley-Davidson has the most valuable and distinctive heritage of any motorcycle in history, and the company guard it as jealously as the Greek monster that guarded the Golden Fleece that Jason had to nick. As the Japanese began building ever more convincing Harley clones, they really tried to emulate the distinctive, irregular heartbeat of the Harley-Davidson engine and so Harley-D headed straight for the patent office, where the unique exhaust-note took form on paper as *potato-potato*. Quite right too!

I wasn't keen on the exhausts, the clocks on the bars didn't look right with risers, the colour wasn't black, it was a little high for my length of leg, and it had a screen! Proper Harley riders do not have screens; you take the wind and the flies or you get an automobile. All of this was easily remedied however. What was important was that I had an absolutely immaculate, Evo-engined, rubber-mounted, belt-driven, big twin Harley-Davidson, with a mere 7000 miles on its clock for a ridiculously modest $6000. I'd been offered the same model in similar trim back home for £6,200 which at the prevailing exchange rate of $1.71 to £1, was $10,260 and I didn't have to ship it to America to begin the trip, it was here waiting for me. I had a bargain; yes sir I did good!

I was legitimate and ready to go! But not tonight. I needed some sleep first, and before that was to come to me there were a couple of bars to be visited. I couldn't think of anything I wanted to do less. I had now been awake longer than ever in my life, but Chip wanted to visit some bars and I reckoned I owed him. He'd got me one hell of a buy, so being a little sociable for a few hours was hardly out of order.

I rode my new bike, Chip rode his old one, a rakish looking Shovelhead. It was more my kind of bike to look at, but once you've tasted the smoothness of a rubber-mounted Evo engine there's no going back and style is easily changed. The first Evolution-engined Harley that I'd ridden belonged to Steve Myatt, the publisher of *Back Street Heroes*, and after riding it for five minutes I was sold on Evos. So, to Annie's Bar. It was a ten-mile ride to Annie's, a single storey wooden building, with creaking floorboards that made you feel heavy, and a clientele that reminded you that you weren't. We sat on stools by the bar, and ordered up some food – the first for me since my dinner on the aircraft half a lifetime away. Furthermore, I hadn't slept now for forty-two hours, I was in need of every kind of sustenance available. I didn't feel I could order a soft drink, after all I had pulled up outside on a Harley-Davidson, besides which, American beer is about half the strength of British, so I reckoned one wasn't going to make a lot of difference either way. I suppose most people make a big thing out of not drinking and driving, certainly by the end of the eighties it was becoming unfashionable to boast about alcoholic excess in the same breath as you mentioned motor vehicles. I've never mixed the indulgence with the responsibility more than three or four times in my life, and those occasions all back in my teens, which are a long time past. It isn't a moral motivation that restrains me, but just plain fear of being caught and losing my licence. I have always had a great fear of the omnipresence of the police, which probably stems from having grown up within a hundred yards of a large police station. Police were always around in my youth, police on foot, police in cars, police on motorcycles, police on bicycles, police on horses, police on dogs – no that can't be right – police with dogs, yes with dogs. Police were everywhere, they could see anything, they could do anything, you couldn't fool the police, you might as well try and out-swim a porpoise or out-fly an eagle. Some things in life are just impossible, and in my mind, getting one up on the police has always been listed among them. I think retrospectively, that my conviction may have something to do with my deep seated belief in the ultimate exercise of justice. Whilst I have in later years become more aware of the fallibility of the police, nonetheless, the old notion of the all-knowing, all-sceptical omnipresence, has never totally left me. I might well take a chance on an out-of-date tax disc, but I wouldn't with drinking and driving. Apart from the possible consequences of being done, I just can't relax thinking that I have to ride the motorcycle, I'd feel like an escaped convict, convinced that someone will recognize me. It remains a source of amazement for me how people who I would consider to be eminently sensible, people whose road tax is always in date, and whose seat belts are always fastened, will down several pints and drive cheerfully off into the night without a qualm. I used to think two pints were OK. I would, on occasion – when I hadn't managed to scrounge a lift from someone – down a quart and ride, though I knew it affected me. But after reading so many horror stories about how low can be too high for the breathalyzer, I cut it to one, and very seldom ride even on that.

That night in Annie's bar I had one very weak half with a substantial meal of seafood and french fries, which I reckoned was OK. Talking of french fries, the fact that Americans call chips 'french fries,' and crisps 'chips,' and don't understand us if we use chips in the English sense, demonstrates that their influence on our language is greater than our's on their's. Which I guess is all down to the superiority of Hollywood over Pinewood, *hmmmmm*.

We took in one more bar, another timbered place down by a river. Buildings made of timber are not so unusual in America. In fact, outside of the cities, and in them to a lesser extent, buildings are made of little else. I like this. There's something extremely pleasant about being surrounded by timber, you feel closer to your roots, more in tune with the environment. It may sound fanciful or fashionably enlightened, but I believe there are absolute standards that are subconsciously, if not consciously recognized, by all but the most insensitive of the human race. The artificial environment of shining steel, nylon and plastic, which, in the fifties, was projected for the future, has not, blessedly, materialized, moreover, the trend certainly among the more sensitive part of society is for a return to heavy wooden tables rather than formica ones; and though almost all car interiors are, of economic necessity, plastic, people still salivate at the sight and smell of leather seats and wooden dash-boards. If the predictions of the futuristic magazines of my childhood had been realized, we'd all be crackling around in aluminium foil suits by now, living in insulated cities protected by giant domes to regulate our temperature and humidity to single percentage points of optimum comfort; but we're not, thank God. The rain still falls on the streets of London and New York, the roads still crack in the frost, and cars still slither about in the winter snow, whilst their occupants still roast in the summer heat. Bloody marvellous really.

A few years ago, when the worst gales to hit England in living memory brought millions of trees crashing down across our green and windswept land, the Royal Society for the Prevention Of Accidents' newspaper, *Care On The Road*, carried a headline:'Down with the Killer Trees.' The accompanying editorial applauded the effect of the hurricane which had been to fell a number of large trees growing at the side of the road, where their leaves in damp autumnal conditions had provided a hazardous surface for motorists who lost control on the bends shaded from the drying influence of the sun. The endeavour to make a scapegoat out of the trees for just being there, rather than the negligent motorists who should have realized that a shaded road in damp conditions overhung by moulting trees, would pose such a threat, irked me, and I wrote a letter on the subject to the paper, which to the editor's credit, was printed. Motorists and motorcyclists, who petulantly demand that the motoring environment be sculptured to accommodate their race track mentalities, deserve no more sympathy than smokers who demand public money be spent devising medical solutions to the detrimental effects of their indulgences so that they can persist with them in safety. Some people just expect too much from life.

To return to the subject of artificiality, it is one of the anomalies of mankind, that whilst we strive to dominate our environment, we become nervous when we feel ourselves detached from it. There has to be a sense of belonging, of involvement with the earth on which we depend. When I was at school, nylon shirts became very popular. I knew that there were some shirts in my wardrobe that I liked, and some that I loathed, but it was a long time before I caught on to which were which, and why it was. I suppose I was a little slow on the uptake. It is a reflection of the revolt against artificial things, and a desire for comfort first, that has practically squeezed the nylon shirt into well-deserved extinction. When I joined the merchant navy in 1971, the nautical outfitters where I bought my various uniforms, actually sold me several one-hundred per cent nylon shirts for use in the tropics. I was, in consequence, forever hitching the shoulders of these loathsome garments upwards between thumb and forefinger in the manner of a sweaty tennis player crouching to receive his opponent's service. I cursed the manufacturers of those shirts. If a department of culture and sanity existed, those manufacturers would be sentenced to months of imprisonment in Bangladesh, with ninety-eight per cent humidity as a minimum, all dressed in nylon shirts with heavy epaulettes to keep the gruesome material in contact with their cringing flesh. They should, in short, be exposed to the misery which I endured to sustain their ill-earned profits. On a scale of comparative immorality, I put the manufacturer of nylon shirts, together with their vendors, somewhere ahead of hard-drug dealers in terms of the inhumanity and selfishness which they propagated. As so often, I find myself asking of the perverse, 'How can you do it?'

The sixties were, as everyone knows, an age of great change, where everything had to be new to be good. Newness was synonymous with virtue, old was read as wrong, irrational, superstitious and irrelevant. The salvation of the world lay in science, in innovation, and it produced the most appalling load of tinsely, trashy, transient garbage, the world in all probability, has ever seen; but nothing, nothing whatever could compare for wretched sadistically inspired nastiness with the nylon shirt.

There were no nylon shirts in the second bar. Everything around me was wood, the floor, the stools, the bar itself. I was too tired to join the conversation, besides which it didn't seem to lend itself to the easy involvement of a stranger. That is not to say that anybody was being unfriendly, but the dialogue did not possess that tangible accessibility which enables fresh passengers to climb aboard. Rather than consisting of any kind of discussion involving expressions of thought, speculation and the exchange of meaningful information, it comprised little more than simple, though emphatically expressed, greetings and expostulations, which ran together like the windows of a fast moving train through which one could not view the passengers. Americans are very good at this, particularly when drinking. When an Englishman has nothing to say, he is more likely to say nothing, but not the American. He will fill the space with something for the sheer sake of it as if, rather like nature abhorring a vacuum, Americans abhor silence. They will bring drama to gratuitous conversation through a wealth of words allied to the volume of their delivery that convinces the casual observer that he is witness to some profound and dramatic discourse about momentous happenings when, in reality, after stripping away all the: Hey!–Shit!–What!–Man!–No shit!–The hell you say!–I dig that!–*Ryyyyat!*–Shit man!–You're shittin' me! and Shit!, again, you are left with little more than what might be more succinctly condensed to: 'Shit.' Like most generalizations, there will be countless exceptions to this one – Clint Eastwood's taciturn characters providing cases in point – but if you think it's completely unfounded just watch the Jerry Springer Show. Then again what about Chris Evans and TFI?

I was drinking Coke, the original, with sugar included. I couldn't bring myself to order the diet variety, though that is what I normally go for, as I like it just as much as the regular stuff. I was struggling to stay afloat now – difficult when you're tired – and making no contribution to the conversation. Why was everyone so big, I didn't seem to have been introduced to anyone under six-feet tall; most were significantly taller. Surely not all Americans can be this tall? What about Woody Allen, Al Pacino, Dustin Hoffman. Dustin Hoffman is only five foot three; that is a full two inches shorter than me. Dustin Hoffman was not in the bar that night – just my luck. That night I was surrounded by giants, nothing but giants. It was hard focusing on their eyes they seemed so bloody far up near the ceiling. Several times I checked to make sure they weren't standing on the rail around the base of the bar. At the same time I checked I really was wearing my new boots, the ones with the thick commando-type soles that cost me twenty six pounds in an army and navy surplus store. I bought them because I knew they would make me taller – and they did. When I put them on I felt instantly much taller, an inch makes a hell of a difference. What had happened now? Was the floor sloping? Was I the victim of localized subsidence? I was sure I wasn't this short yesterday. Apart from being so tall, these people all seemed wide awake. How could they be so awake when I felt so half asleep?

Some people, bikers especially, take a delight in going for long periods without sleep, as if some kind of machismo attaches to cultivated insomnia. As if the pleasure is directly proportional to the duration of sleeplessness; 'we partied till six in the morning man, then we had breakfast and then we partied for the rest of the day and the next night too.' How can they do it? Bastards!

My experience of most of these joyous revellers is that they stuff powder up their noses and sit around like grizzled hags at the perimeter of a coffin, maintaining a morbid vigil with beer cans for rosaries clasped in their hands, listening to abrasive rock until their metabolisms call in the receiver and they're evicted from their own consciousness. I detest this pathetic competition, partly because it's detestable and partly because in a peculiar kind of way, I envy the people who are capable of it. I'm the same with drunks and alcoholics; the attitude is a mixture of envy, sympathy and irritation.

It may seem a strange thing to feel envy for a sodden wretch hunched in a doorway with a can of Special Brew at nine of a winter's morning, but in a way I do. I envy anyone who is capable of doing something which I am not. It is an envy born of incredulity. How can these winos get up in the morning and start pouring booze into their faces? Don't they get headaches? Don't they get sick? And if they do then how, in the name of all unnaturalness, can they go on inflicting more punishment on themselves by absorbing more of the cause of their wretchedness while they're still feeling wretched? If I get myself into a state with alcohol at night, the last thing in the world I want to see the next day, is more of the stuff. Perhaps that night, if a sufficient recovery has been made, or the next day, but never, never, the following morning. How can they do it? I can't do it, how can they do it?

I lived for four years in Bethnal Green, close to Whitechapel High Street, which must boast one of England's most celebrated colonies of human derelicts. Some mornings as I would ride into work, I would see these scabrous carcasses of the living dead, hung over the curbside safety barriers with their ubiquitous cans, like drying fish on a ship's rail. I always looked at them, I still do, I want to grab them by the lapels, bash them up against a wall, and scream at them; 'Why are you doing this, how can you be doing this, how can you take this? Don't you get cold, don't you get sick? Doesn't your head hurt? How can your decrepit looking body survive this kind of abuse when mine, in much better condition, cannot?' If I drank what they drank, I would have to lie down, preferably in a bed with a bucket next to it. To stand here smoking and drinking and spitting amidst the human flotsam of this foul gutter, and then to do it the next day, and the next? My sense of normality demands answers. Why are you doing something which you can't possibly be enjoying? If I miss my morning shower I'm in misery, the sense of scumminess to me is almost unendurable. How can these people lie out in the open getting filthier and sweatier, and not revolt against their condition? These are not questions I want answered, I don't want to hear rational explanations of how it is that winos and junkies can live the way they do. I don't want to understand them. I want to smash their heads into brick walls until their skulls crack and shout, 'How? How? How?' very loudly. I don't suppose I'd get an answer even then, but at least they might have the decency to drop dead.

That night in the wooden bar nobody was dealing in this kind of excess. If anyone was behaving really excessively, it was me, for still being awake after over forty hours. It was time to go.

The ride back to Chip's house was a nightmare. Fine rain was falling, making it impossible to see through the screen of the motorcycle. Why do Americans fit such high screens to their bikes? Germans are tall, but they don't; I can see over the screen of a

BMW no problem. No one could have seen over the top of the screen I was peering through, Americans aren't that much taller, so what's the answer? Another bloody mystery to aggravate me. The only way that I could see where I was going was to hang out to one side of the screen like a motorist with a shattered but intact windshield, driving with his head out of the window. The darkness of the country road, combined with the rain, rendered it practically impossible for me to see anything, even without the screen in my field of vision. I felt that at any moment I might run across the road, or off it, into some uncomfortable and uncompromising object. I felt totally divorced from my environment, not only did I find it hard to tell which way the road was turning, I hardly knew where it lay in the vertical dimension. I supposed it to be beneath my wheels, but I felt unsure. I was like a traveller in a dream, I felt I might flip over and travel horizontally without warning should my tenuous sense of perspective desert me altogether. My only point of reference in this world of vagueness was the red glow of Chip's rear light, which I followed with the kind of trust demonstrated by the Wise Men in their pursuit of the star. At one point I lost it altogether, and disappeared up a fork in the road marked by a 'No Entry' sign. I wasn't enjoying this. I stopped fifty yards on from where I could hear an engine to my left, over which a voice was shouting through the trees. I backed up, rejoined the main road, and by a series of life's lesser miracles, successfully completed the journey to Chip's without mishap. Kicking down the sidestand, I climbed off the motorcycle with a sense of relief which I suspected was comparable to that experienced by fighter pilots disembarking at the end of their perilous missions.

Curiously, despite having been up for almost two whole days, I did not, when I dumped my exhausted carcass on a bed, feel like going to sleep. I didn't feel like doing anything else either, but I did not experience that luxurious relief that should attend the subsidence of the head onto the pillow after so long an absence. What I did feel was anxious, I didn't think I was going to sleep and worse still, I wasn't happy with the bike. It wasn't a single thing that I could put my finger on, but the experience did not compare to the brief one I had enjoyed aboard the bike in England that I had considered buying. Incredibly, I wanted my old Shovelhead back, this one wasn't for me – I'd made a terrible mistake.

THE JOURNEY BEGINS

I felt much better the next day. I'd had the benefit of a night's sleep without the debilitating prelude of alcohol to promote it artificially. The sun was shining; it was dry and clear. I was going to tear that screen off the Harley and head out across America for as far as it went, all the way through to the Pacific Ocean. America! It hardly seemed possible, but there were literally no obstacles left to overcome. A continent was at my disposal, all the splendours of National Geographic were out there for the viewing. I felt like a movie buff let loose in the Hollywood archives, a child with a tenner in a sweet shop. Chip handed me a roll of tools to remove the screen which I donated to him, for though he didn't look like a screen man I reckoned he could find a home for it as he's a bike mechanic, and it was a modest thank you for setting up the deal with the bike. He in turn gave me the tools which was a serious bonus to add to the superb Harley-Davidson throw-over bags which had come free with the bike, and which I was to see later in an authorized Harley-Davidson dealership in England marked up at £300.

Before I set off we went round to see Mike, a mate of Chip's who was working on an old Harley-Davidson motorcycle in his garage. I was struck by the amount of space these rural Americans enjoy. Chip's place was a large detached wooden house, standing at least forty yards from his nearest neighbour, a small estate almost, comprising an acre of land about which cats and dogs promenaded with a stately nonchalance, like nobles at the court of the Sun king. All this for about thirty pounds a week – less than half the rent of a modest London bedsit at that time. A more striking contrast with the claustrophobic intensity of New York would be hard to imagine. Mike's place was pretty much the same, with a broad coarsely gravelled drive which I negotiated with some trepidation on the unfamiliar machine, which at that time, sat a little too high at the saddle for my abbreviated legs. We sat around on a selection of boxes and assorted junk for half an hour whilst Mike reassembled the primary transmission of his motorcycle within the pleasantly timbered order of the huge garage, through which sunlight shone via tall barn doors. Mike's girlfriend Louise appeared shortly with a tray of coffee and beers for workers and onlookers alike. Meanwhile, a whiskery mutt thrust his nose into the chaincase to inspect the mechanical progress with a comical intensity of interest that his relaxed benefactor refrained from deterring – the admonishments commonly engendered by such unhelpful animal curiosity, almost conspicuous by their absence. I liked the atmosphere here, resting on an old automobile seat, gazing in my mind's eye beyond the open double doors, across the prairies, deserts and mountains that lay before me like a movie that was due to start later that afternoon, and in which I had, by good fortune, been selected by fate to star. I envied these men their comfortable homes with their Harleys and dogs and girlfriends, but the itchy restlessness which had been growing in me since I unbolted the screen from the motorcycle earlier that morning, was taking over, and I was eager to be off.

We stopped by at another house first, where Chip's brother Frank and a small crowd of friends were spending the afternoon. With the aid of a felt highlighter pen, they marked the simplest route from there to Los Angeles, following the Interstate south and then west across the continent, a distance of approximately 2800 miles from where I was. Curiously, as it seemed to me, they doubted whether I understood the scale of the journey I was undertaking. 'Do you realize how far it is to LA?' Of course I did. I knew it was the best part of 3000 miles, everyone knows American is about the same width as the North Atlantic Ocean – about 3000 miles – there is no mystery about that. Why should someone who comes from a comparatively small country, not be able to comprehend the scope of a large one? Perhaps Americans think that we believe New York to LA to be rather like the trip from London to Glasgow, only on the other side of the road. Why cannot they understand that we can understand, though I do find it difficult to understand why they cannot understand our understanding.

On explaining that I had friends on the West Coast, the bizarre suggestion was made, that I ride half way and have them fly out and meet me! There are times, usually in arguments, when somebody floats a notion that is so ludicrous, so improbable, that one is perplexed by the variety of valid counterpoints which simultaneously present themselves. One is left to suffocate in the paralysis of indecisive bewilderment, like a rabbit, caught in a car's headlamp beam, which suffers for its immobility, when any action would be preferable to none. I stalled for a moment, poleaxed by the preposterous possibility that had been suggested, whilst I formulated a response that did not presume the insanity of the advice's vendor. 'Strewth,' I thought, these people on the West Coast are friends, not subservient vassals with nothing better to do than fly thousands of miles to make a rendevous at some middle ground court which I might like to establish in the midst of the great divide. Who am I, Canute?

It may have been the same voice that later expostulated, as part of a brief discussion on Northern Ireland, 'Why don't you just get out?' What a sage! How come no British Prime Minister has ever thought of that one? 'First thing I'll do when I get home is write and share this pearl of wisdom with them,' I thought; better still, I'll send a postcard while I'm over here, it'll be like $E=MC^2$ all over again, the political equivalent of the Einsteinian watershed. Hey, the simplest ideas are always the best.

It was late in the afternoon when I stepped down from the veranda with the folded map, thrust like some wax sealed letter from the King, into the inside pocket of my jacket. I checked all my essentials, zipped, buttoned, and buckled various compartments into which they had been secreted, shook the relevant paws, and climbed aboard. I was at the final countdown for the off. Riding a modern motorcycle across America might not seem like such an ambitious thing to do, compared to more daring escapades, and in terms of risk, it certainly isn't. But for me, this particular adventure had held a near obsessive fascination for twenty years, since the days of my late teens when first I'd seen the movie *Easy Rider*. The symbol of freedom in the concept of that film totally captured my imagination, where, for two decades, it had remained, suspended at some indeterminate point beyond me like a carrot on a stick, a stick growing at a pace matching my own progress, tantalizing me with its perennial elusiveness. Finally the dream had been cornered, the mechanics of its control engineered. I had the large motorcycle I wanted. It always had to be a Harley-Davidson, because those were the bikes that were used in the film, because they're American, and because I love them, there was never, for me, any other choice. I had the Harley, I had a pocket full of money, plus a wad of credit cards to bale me out of trouble, I had a map, and all of America to go roaming in. No mouth watering yacht, no private jet, no manifestation of wealth or hedonistic indulgence could match the unparalleled excitement presented by the provisions and circumstances with which I now found myself equipped. The bike, with bedroll and tent strapped to the pillion seat represented the quintessential essence of freedom, better than flying or sailing, in that you can savour the variety of humanity in its varied environment close up. An illusion of freedom may be achieved by flying a light aircraft, but there is about that, a remoteness that robs the experience of the intimacy and potential of a terrestrial journey. The pilot can boast movement in a third dimension and argue that he is not constrained by the course of roads, but he has his constraints nonetheless, and the reality is, that they are more restrictive than those which apply to the biker. The plane has to land at airports, permission to land must be sought, the pilot cannot stop at the friendly looking diner or pause by the roadside to photograph a tree, explore a cave, or just sit on the grass listening to the sounds of the country. The pilot is the observer of a movie over which he has limited control, and which he views from a distance, such that the finer details are indistinguishable. The biker is in the projection room, stopping the spools at will, freezing the frame, reversing the show, climbing in amongst the action. The pilot can see, albeit from a great distance, but the motorcyclist can smell, he can hear, he can feel every inflexion of the environment into which he is woven. There are striking parallels with flying, sailing even, because like the pilot or small boat sailor, the motorcyclist changes direction by leaning his craft, not by a control stick or by means of a wheel or tiller, not by the use of any mechanical agent or intermediary, but with his body, simply, directly, instinctively. When people ask what it is that is so special about motorcycling, then the answer must include the factors of speed, of power, of acceleration – but these elements are common to cars. The rider enjoys them as the human temperament appreciates the strength and potential of muscles, but they do not constitute the soul. The soul of motorcycling depends for its existence on the solo nature of the machine, the narrowness is important given the congestion defeating attributes which that brevity confers, lending the rider a sense of innate superiority. There is a practicality about a solo motorcycle which is beyond question, but it is the steering mode that really separates it from other forms of transport. It's almost as simple as that. The wind in the face is very important to me, and wind blowing through the hair is better still – though not universally permitted these days – but that can be achieved in an open topped car, whilst even those who wear full face helmets claim to experience an exhilarating freedom from riding motorcycles, despite their heads being encased in these dreadful goldfish bowls. Through the bodily leaning of the machine though, a relationship between rider and machine is fostered by which a unique bio-mechanical entity is created, whereby the rider may assume the exercise of power that in reality, is confined to the engine which he temporarily controls. Such illusions may serve to explain the extraordinary physical confidence exhibited by some diminutive bikers after they have dismounted to address some violent situation of which they subsequently become victims, for alas the confidence is grounded in illusion and they are not the Minotaurs they thought themselves. Nonetheless, with a clear sense of perspective, the relationship may be enjoyed with far less hazard than is commonly attributed to it.

I sat on the bike, listening to the soft *rumpty-rump* of the staggered exhaust note, as the rubber-mounted engine oscillated happily in its cushioned frame. A theatrical pinching of the nose between the eyes followed, squinting melodramatically at the distant horizon, as if able to focus on my goal. I thought of flinging my watch melodramatically into the dust as Peter Fonda had done, but it seemed a waste. I would either have had to go back to pick it up, or buy another, besides, I like to know what the time is. I fished the sidestand out of the shallow crease it had dug with my left heel, noting the satisfying thud as it locked into its stowage position against the clutch housing – I was unhooked. All lines were gone fore and aft, chocks away, and NO HELMET! I pulled in the clutch and notched first gear, the bike jolting slightly as the transmission, like a tug of war team, took the strain. I turned a smug smile on the send-off committee lurking on the veranda, several hands rose in salute, my grin mirrored in their envious faces. The fat back tyre burrowed for traction in the loose surface, gripped, and propelled me down the road with a confident resolve as I clicked through the gears and the huge engine settled into an easy loping stride. Twenty years after I sat glued to my favourite movie in cinema history, I too went looking for America.

LOOKING FOR AMERICA

I camped the first night on an authorized camp site, devoid of tents before I erected mine, though a tail of residual smoke from a small campfire bore witness to a limited patronage which I associated with a lone caravan parked fifty yards from where I'd staked my claim. The campfire had been built within the confines of what looked like an old truck wheel rim, its rolling days over, this fresh function had extended its life of human usefulness and struck me as both novel and sensible. Had I suspected the existence of such provisions I would have taken the means to make a meal as I love sitting around campfires cooking food in the open, something which British campsites, without exception in my experience, do not permit. Perhaps such a compromise with the designated fire sites of limited scope might be adopted back home, if only as exceptional facilities on a few pitches for the minority of pyromaniacs, like me, who like to rekindle (pun intended) the experience of scouting days. In my view, camping is not really camping without a fire. Just as a tent provides us with the satisfaction of being able to recreate the pleasant features of our artificial habitation on a modest and compact scale, so the fire takes the experience an essential stage further. A fire provides a sense of completeness to a camping scene, the denial of which seems almost like a denial of a basic human right; almost as basic as the right to travel around the countryside, to swim in rivers or to float out to sea in a makeshift craft. I can't believe that in the days of Robin Hood there were any rules about the making of fires. In those days travellers stopped at a forest clearing and lit a fire – simple as that. They certainly always did it in the Westerns, usually by some convenient stream to provide water for coffee. Just as I have long wished to be asked the question in New York, 'Got a light Mac?' so I can respond, 'No, but I've got a dark brown overcoat,' so have I fantasized about a campfire scene which is disturbed by an unheralded visitor. There I am, stretched out with my head resting on my saddle that is propped against the base of a tree, a subdued fire relieving the pitch darkness as an old fashioned iron coffee pot steams quietly at its edge. My horse whinnies suddenly as a twig cracks nearby beyond a boulder. Placing my harmonica aside, I carefully liberate my Winchester from beneath its Mexican blanket covering and cock the firing mechanism as a lone figure rides slowly out of the night assuring me of his benign intentions by lifting both hands high, nothing between his fingers but his horse's reins. It is then that I utter the immortal words 'Coffee stranger?'

Never, but never, in any Western, is a cowboy snoozing by his fire, disturbed by some busybody poking his nose in on the scene and complaining about fires. Indian arrows hissing through the night, the odd owl hooting, a coyote howling, or a bounty hunter with a distinctive looking rifle all come with the territory, but never do we find the hero disturbed by the intrusion of a 'job's worth' with the line '*Oi*, you can't light fires here you know.' The scriptwriters wouldn't have it any more than they'd have a horse crapping when John Wayne is sitting on it.

Sometimes I think Hollywood scriptwriters should run countries, then life would be the way it is in the movies. As things are, it seems you just can't have the best of all worlds. No matter where you are, who you are, or when you are, every privilege and advantage of circumstance carries its responsibilities and restrictions. This American compromise on fires in simple improvised fireplaces seemed to me a splendid idea, possibly reflecting a closer relationship with the land that this fundamentally rural country enjoys.

So, fireless myself, for want of the necessary materials, I stretched out on my tent to test the lie of the land before following the simple construction technique demonstrated to me earlier that day by Chip, who had loaned me the equipment. I was far enough from the road to dodge disturbance from the scant traffic passing by at this late hour, leaving my ears empty to savour the sounds of the country, punctuated by the crisp snaps as the fibreglass poles locked out with a satisfying military precision – like firearms, primed, loaded, and cocked for action. There's a wonderful smugness in a tent. It's the contraption's potential for transformation from a sausage shaped burden, into a concise and adequate home, in which one can lay out possessions, rather as stage hands create an atmosphere by assembling scenery on an empty stage. It's the sense of self-sufficiency that appeals, the impossible compactness of the apparatus, the economy of money and materials which provide the nomadic independence which tent and motorcycle collectively represent. I extinguished the bike's headlamp, whose influence had illuminated my preparations, and crawled into the green army sleeping bag. My first night alone in the new world. Zipping up the bag, I turned onto my side, from which position, through the diaphanous weave of the cotton wall, I could identify the vague outline of the motorcycle's front wheel; 'good night Harley-Davidson, good night America.'

DISTILLED WATER

It was warmer today, as I headed south into Missouri. A fair breeze, induced chiefly by my passage through the air, pressed me back into the padded comfort of the well-upholstered Corbin custom seat bearing the sticker on its base, 'Made proudly in America.' I must, I thought, look after this machine, I've a long way to go and I do not want it to let me down, it was as near perfect at this point and closer to new than any machine I had ever owned, with only nine thousand miles registered on the clock, a claim supported by the pristine condition of its parts. There would be an orderly satisfaction to be drawn from pandering to its every requirement. I decided to start by topping up the battery, and parked up at a gas station in a small town.

It is said that Britain and America are two nations divided by a common language; a clever little line which reflects a degree of truth. An example of this divide presented itself in my encounter with the man in the gas station. He was a large, heavy-set fellow, comfortably substantial, rather than grossly obese, with hairy, sunburned forearms and paws that would have looked at home on a medium-sized Grizzly. The sort of man whose self-evident contentment induced envy in the impatient and aspirational. A thick even stubble covered the regular features of a face that might have conveyed intelligence were it not infected with a vacuous malaise. He slumped in a wooden chair whose arms supported his own as he focused all energy on grappling with my question.

'Do you have any distilled water?' I went for 'do you have' rather than the more English 'have you got' and mistakenly thought I was safe.

The man clearly did not know what distilled water was. Thinking that perhaps I had not pronounced the words carefully enough, I repeated my request with an attempt at the kind of enunciation which my secondary school elocution teacher would have considered a sarcastic parody of perfection. I failed in my objective; blank incomprehension met my request. When such a simple demand is received with this kind of confusion one gains an insight into the frustration of primary school teachers who cannot communicate to their pupils the preliminary elements of arithmetic. I felt myself to be in the position of a tutor faced with a stubborn student who cannot grasp the self-evident reality that one plus one equals two. There is only so far that you can reason with an uneducated mind before its inexperience blocks all endeavours for want of familiar references and similes by which one can translate the simple truth. I suppose many teachers must have suffered in this way, and I sympathize with them. I recall a particularly mild and patient mathematics teacher at nautical school, where most of the students were in their early twenties and should have had enough building bricks cemented into the foundation of their knowledge on which to raise the necessary walls of learning. This teacher was striving to communicate a feature of algebra to a West Country pupil named, appropriately, Wurzle. Wurzle, to his credit, was not a man to say he understood something when he did not, which in the case in question was the situation.

'I fail to understand how you get that,' he declared emphatically to the overwrought tutor.

'I fail to understand,' replied the latter, 'how it is that you fail to understand.' The class laughed at this logical impasse and Wurzle was abandoned to his desert of incomprehension, from which, I understand, it took him some years to emerge, he failed his exam because, as the line from the Moody Blues' track states, 'He was without understanding.' It was all rather sad in a way but I was still envious of Wurzle as he was hung like a donkey and very successful with women.

The man in the gas station didn't seem too quick on the uptake, failing to respond with any hint of enlightenment at all.

'What kind of water is that?' he asked.

'Distilled water,' I persisted, you know (though he clearly didn't), water that is just water, water that doesn't have anything in it; H_2O!' Strewth this was hard work, and fruitless too. Leaving him as perplexed as I was, by his perplexity which I can assure you was totally perplexing, I headed for the other gas station in town. There could not, I reasoned, be two establishments in the same town, both staffed by total morons. Despite these optimistic self assurances, I'd developed the pessimistic suspicion that rather than having discovered a moron I was actually unearthing a critical difference between our colonial cousins and ourselves, in language if not in motor maintenance procedure. Nonetheless, I decided to proceed with a repetition of my request in anticipation of the perverse pleasure I would derive from encountering an identical reaction. There is a pleasure in this self-inflicted anguish, which derives from framing the circumstances and digging the foundations to support the inevitable disappointment.

I have a friend who provides a good example in this connection. She is one of those people who proceed through life studiously protecting themselves from knowledge of things in which they have decided they do not have an interest, or which they think are beneath them. I recognize the attitude because I take a certain pride myself in having no knowledge of professional football and fruit machines. My friend does occasionally, albeit very hesitantly, drive a car, though not very far since she is limited by two factors. She cannot drive somewhere she hasn't been before, and neither can she operate a petrol pump. If I construct a scenario that requires her to exercise both of these extraordinary talents, then it is with the certainty that my suggestion will be rejected on the basis of some specious argument obscuring a sad reality, the absurdity of which is excruciatingly aggravating. It's rather like sticking one's tongue in a loose tooth that aches when moved.

It was in this, 'ready to be annoyed,' mood, that I entered the second gas station, where another fat, stubble-faced man in a baseball hat slouched behind a till munching peanuts.

'Hi,' I said.

'Howdy,' he replied. So far so good.

'You got any distilled water?' I made the question sound as casual as possible. Silence. Come on, I thought, either you have or you haven't, no need to look so confused, out with it man, yes or no? Slowly he leaned forward in his chair, the floorboards creaked, his faced creased with exasperatingly predictable incomprehension. Keeping his eyes fixed on me he reached sideways to turn down the radio, a conversation of this complexity was going to require maximum concentration.

'Do you have any distilled water?' I asked again, with a clarity that would have done justice to a BBC newsreader. The face beneath the hat remained blank, had I really spoken? Had some invisible word-scrambling screen been interposed between us? Was this man deaf? Had the other man from the first gas station, a brother maybe, rung him to warn of my approach?

'Hey Hank, this little Limey's gonna ask for distilled water, make like you don't know what he's talking about, he could be writing a book, we could end up fillin' a whole page.'

The blankness on the face before me was the kind of blankness that can be read as, I don't understand what you are saying and I don't want to ask you to repeat it because I'll feel like a deaf halfwit. I knew this was what he was thinking, but I didn't want to help him out because I was enjoying being wound up.

'No?' I ventured by way of helpful enquiry. He understood that.

'I, *ah*, didn't quite catch what you said,' he said. I was tempted to point out that I was speaking the Queen's English, but reflecting upon the colonial interpretation of the word 'Queen,' decided against its use. I tried repeating my question at a condescendingly turgid pace which bordered on the sarcastic. I failed.

'We got some mineral water,' he ventured hopefully. Mineral water, mineral water, what the bloody hell do I want that for, minerals are the last thing I want in the water. What I want is water without minerals, *aqua distillae*. Should I try Latin or French? Two parts of hydrogen, one of oxygen, H_2O! Jesus, didn't this guy ever do chemistry at school. Distilled water, like anything that is distilled, is water in its pure form, it's the thing without other things, by itself, solo, on its tod, nothing dissolved in solution, no bubbles, bath salts or rubber ducks, just plain water. 'It's a good job I'm not trying to buy oil,' I thought, he'd probably insist I have some with iron filings in it. I could, in the light of this experience, anticipate the incredulity that would greet my request for pure unadulterated oil.

'What, oil by itself sir, sure you wouldn't like a little steel swarf or this one here with rock salt additive, and then there's the latest with Arizonan sandstone granules, it's very popular.'

Such was the state of internal turbulence that I'd generated during this blighted encounter, that I forgot exactly what the answer was to the question. But what Americans top their batteries up with will, I suppose, have to join that other classic enigma, 'What does a Scotsman wear under his kilt?' I shall leave both to the efforts of more persistent enquirers than I to determine. For the present I purchased a can of Coke, drank the contents, filled the vacant space with tap water, and poured it, clumsily, over my battery, on the assumption that some of it was going down the small holes that led to the plates.

I have since heard from a number of sources, that buying distilled water is a waste of time, since the furring up of batteries due to the use of tap water, is of such a slow rate that the battery will have died from natural causes long before it succumbs to congestion due to impurities; an interesting theory which I must explore.

JESSE JAMES' CAVE

I continued riding throughout the remainder of the morning, feeling slightly piqued, my curiosity progressively excited by a series of huge hoardings encouraging me to visit the Meramec Caverns, one-time hideout of Jesse James. The size and number of these billboards constituted a visual pollution that came close to deterring my patronage as a gesture of disapproval. Curiosity however, overcame aesthetic morality, and I turned off the freeway at the sign indicating the entrance.

A large rock face bordered one side of the parking lot, in the corner of which stood a brown statue of the famous outlaw and his colleagues, peering anxiously into the distance, presumably looking out for officers of the law, who, interestingly, are less conspicuously honoured in American culture than their opponents. It is, upon reflection, much the same in this country, as in most. It is a feature of human curiosity, that our interest is provoked more by those who breach the law than by those who enforce it. There is a strange contradiction in our behaviour, that whilst we generally respect the need for law, we harbour a fascination for those who flout it, particularly those who do so blatantly, and especially when they're long dead, so that we do not confuse our patronage of their shrines with our approval of contemporary misconduct. Mindful of the existence of the scum who steal motorcycles, for whom there is no glory, I passed the heavy shackle lock through the forks of the Harley before passing out of the warm sunshine into the cool stony confines of the cave's interior. The natural foyer of the cave complex, was perhaps a hundred and fifty feet in length, and half as wide, with a ticket booth in one corner. Here I handed over five dollars for a guided tour of the famous hideout, and joined a dozen tourists lurking in the dimmer light at the entrance to the inner chambers and waited for the guide to appear. I was grateful for the warm padding of the motorcycle jacket I'd kept on, as the air in the damp interior of the subterranean grotto was on the chilly side of pleasantly cool. A petite teenage girl, who I took for a New Yorker, was less sensibly attired. Her flimsy T shirt and micro denim shorts were probably not listed in the caver's guide amongst eminently suitable clothing. I imagined she was regretting her outfit, but my sympathy was diminished by a selfish enthusiasm for her provocative taste, which relieved the lifelessness of the aged rock which surrounded her.

The tour guide was appalling. I have never envied tour guides their job, repetition is the father of boredom, but given that one is employed to talk to the public, some effort to do so in a manner that can be understood, may surely be expected. This character's accent and pace of delivery was such, that I'd have been surprised to learn that he knew what he was saying himself. I don't mind a regional accent, I like regional accents, they add colour and variety to life, and retard humanity's progress toward bland uniformity. But there are limits beyond which the indulgence of local dialect becomes gratuitous and irritating in any circumstance, and unprofessional where clarity is a prerequisite of employment. The linguistic travesty tumbling at Niagaran pace out of this character's mouth was past a joke, it made a British Rail tannoy announcement sound like Joan Bakewell at a national enunciation contest. I picked out a few key words like, 'cave', 'Jesse James', and 'outlaw', and then one whole line of commendable clarity that must have been practised diligently.

'Are there any questions?'

At this, a wag from the Manhattan brigade spoke up.

'Yes, could we have an English translation.' I like this about Americans, the way they speak up and complain when occasion demands it. The English are far more reticent in this respect and it makes for too much complacency, particularly in the service industry. I think English people do respect those who stand up and make a fuss, but by and large, particularly among the middle classes, there is a reluctance to behave this way ourselves. Perhaps it's the German blood in Americans, and there's a lot of that. Yes Germans are louder than us, you only have to go to a beer keller to realize that. Then there's the Italian blood. Italians are renowned for their excitable temperaments, all shrieks and gesticulations, which is where New Yorkers get their voluble theatrical style from. Remember Dustin Hoffman in Midnight Cowboy when the motorist hoots at him as he's crossing the road. A sneer or a gesture or a single expletive wasn't good enough. No, he stops right in front of the automobile and slaps his hands on the bonnet.

'Hey I'm *warking* here jerk, I'm *warking* here!' Bloody marvellous! We may be changing, I was sitting in a jam off the Marylebone Road in London a while back when a motorist hooted at a couple threading their way between jammed cars. There was nowhere the driver could go, except perhaps a foot closer to the bumper of the car in front, but she had a green light and she was going to hoot. The male component of the pedestrian duo whom she had startled by her hooting, stopped, raised one leg high in the air, and kicked the bonnet of the car with enough energy to send the whole rig bouncing on its suspension, while the hoity-toity tart behind the wheel sprang up and down like a nodding dog on a parcel shelf. I was tempted to shout '*Ole*,' but being English I restrained myself.

It was a step in the right direction, but we're still a long way behind Americans as the New Yorker's sarcasm illustrated. Something else in his comment aroused my interest; he wanted an English translation. This linguistic legacy of the British Empire is a very healthy thing. The Union Jack may not fly over as much of the globe as once it did, but what we have left behind is the most important thing of all, and damned convenient it is for us. Apart from the obvious convenience and simplicity for us, the supremacy of the English language has another significantly positive side to it. It enrages the French.

So jealous are the French of the overwhelming success of English as the international language, that their government introduced legislation to prevent the employment of English words in French advertising and schools. The French think that their language is the most beautiful in the world, and they may well be right, but a perennial blight affects their vaunted culture which they cannot evade; they are not and never will be – British. What would have happened had the French dominated North America scarcely bears thinking about, all the Westerns would have been in French. And can you imagine Clint Eastwood thrusting his Magnum up some punk's nose and threatening him with *'fait mon jour.'* It's unthinkable in fact. The punk would probably have broken out laughing, and Dirty Harry would have had to have hidden behind his hat – which wouldn't have been easy as it would have been a beret – and the glass of Beaujolais he'd have ordered at the local cafe wouldn't have had quite the ring of 'whisky' about it. No, I think the world has turned out for the best with everyone gravitating toward the English version of things.

It was in the midst of these reflections that I realized I was leaning for support upon the lower portions of a stalactite. They're the ones that grow downward from the ceiling, I believe. I noticed at this time a sign bearing the warning that persons causing damage to the caves were liable to fines of up to a thousand dollars. I took my weight off the structure and promptly slid several feet down a greasy stone slope into the pert buttocks of the New York nymph in the shorts. 'Damn slippery in here,' I remarked to the unamused teenager. The vocal wag in her group shot me a look of uncertain disapproval and I ambled over to where the guide was attempting, in his outrageous accent, to explain something.

We were led through a number of chambers culminating in a special one boasting a unique curtain of stalactites formed in the shape of organ pipes some eighty feet in height and half as wide. The time taken for natural forces to fashion these marvels throws the duration of mankind into a belittling perspective. In the case of these glistening gems, construction time to date has topped two hundred million years – nearly three times what it has taken the Colorado river to carve the Grand Canyon, and that's no spring chicken. Of course we do tend to assume that these geology boffins know what they're talking about when they quote these mind bending figures. One imagines their calculations are correct, but we do take a lot on faith. These organ-pipe stalactites did look the business, but for all I knew they could have been knocked up in plaster of Paris to celebrate the inauguration of Ronald Reagan a few years earlier. I suppose the odds are against that, though a patriotic dimension was lent to the tour's finale by the projection on to the stone of a cinematic facsimile of the American flag to the musical accompaniment of 'God Bless America.' It was all rather emotional.

There seemed to me something almost sacrilegious about the notion of a band of outlaws hiding out in this geological sepulchre, counting their spoils and cleaning their guns amidst the treasure of millennia. Just as well there was never a gun fight in the chamber with the organ in it. The fines for damage would have been horrendous.

Back in the outer cave, my group was urged to take a seat for a photograph, which was all rather embarrassing, the intention of course was then to induce us to buy a copy at some inflated price, an endeavour which, at least among my group, found no takers.

I nosed around the exhibits for a while, reading a collection of newspaper cuttings which captured my imagination. It seems in the fifties some old gaffer had appeared on the scene, claiming to be the famous Jesse James. He was in his nineties which accorded with historical facts and he did by all accounts seem to know a great deal about the famous outlaw and his activities, much of which was apparently not public knowledge. The papers of the day, judging by the cuttings I read, seemed to have taken the old man's claims seriously, and right up to the time of his death no one positively disproved his credentials. I found the story a fascinating and believable one. Of course Jesse James was supposed to have been murdered back in the nineteenth century by traitorous outlaws of his acquaintance, but the notion that such a fabrication could have been a ploy to get the lawmen off the outlaw's back sounds credible enough, certainly stranger and more devious plots have been engineered under the covert operations umbrellas of many governments. Without television in the last century, and an absence of good quality photographs of the miscreant, Jesse James' face would not have enjoyed the household familiarity that today would have made his disappearance a near impossibility. A corpse was buried in a grave with Jesse James' name over it which, according to the twentieth century claimant described in the newspaper cuttings, was a scam. I'm fond of stories like this, I like to think that the sly old bastard was who he claimed to be, the novelty of it is just too attractive to dismiss.

I like this sense of proximity that America enjoys with its most celebrated period of history. The 'Wild West' really wasn't all that long ago, and given a few outstanding examples of human longevity to bridge the gap between the centuries, a tangibility about those days survives. It's a tangibility that Arthur's Knights of the Round Table, for all their romance, do not possess. The picture of the white haired old man shuffling into his local sheriff's office and giving himself up as the outlaw Jesse James, is physically possible. If, however, some clot in green tights popped up at Nottingham nick, and declared himself to be Robin Hood, he'd be out on his ear for wasting police time.

I poked around in the souvenir shop for a while and bought what I always buy – postcards. I love sending postcards, the more absurd the comments on the back of them, the better. The important thing is to avoid the subject of immediate concern, not a word about the weather or what you're doing, that's the trick. Better to describe something that you might just as well have seen at home: a slug crawling across the bathroom floor of your motel, the sugar dissolving in a coffee cup, the fine points of boiling an egg, which is of course one of the hardest things in the culinary world to get perfect.

Outside in the sunlight I found myself partly hemmed in by a group of a half-dozen Harleys. The owners were seated around on the low wall wearing bandannas and cutoffs, looking cool and fondling the tame women that accompanied them as if they were extras in some appalling biker movie. I'm not used to parking my bike and finding it surrounded by other Harleys when I return to it. In England it would have been unusual on anything other than a Harley run and certainly would warrant a comment, a nod, a smile, some kind of acknowledgement of mutual taste. I might as well have been parked amidst cars about which the drivers were picnicking, oblivious to my presence, the difference being that in these characters I sensed an indifference that was more cultivated than natural; they were only one step away from hostile, I didn't like them but I couldn't match their silent poise.

'What's this a Harley club meet?' I remarked cheerfully. The response was subdued, mute in fact. I looked directly at the two characters closest to me but they affected not to have realized I had spoken, I may as well have been talking in another language. In my experience, most so-called 'outlaw' club members demonstrate this kind of ludicrous 'I'm too cool to talk to you,' bullshit, at least in England, and it aggravates me intensely. After what seemed a long pause since I spoke, one of the straighter looking riders took a step toward me.

'Excuse me?' He asked.

'I was just wondering,' I repeated, 'if there was a Harley Club meet around here somewhere.' With repetition the throw-away remark had acquired the character of a serious question that was not intended.

'No, no I don't believe so,' replied the other without a trace of humour. 'Oh right' I responded, feeling slightly ridiculous at this stage, 'I just, *err*, I just wondered.'

The discussion had ended and I extricated my machine from the pack with some difficulty and no co-operation. The ground being as uneven as it was, I came close to dropping the heavy machine as I wheeled it back and forth to negotiate the surrounding bikes, whose owners' indifference was really beginning to needle me. I would have liked to have sat astride the bike and paddled it competently about with my feet but an FXR is not the lowest of Harleys and without being able to get both feet flat on the ground such a method was out of the question. The thought of dropping the machine in front of this crowd just didn't bear contemplating.

With regard to my solitary comment, I suppose, on reflection, with Harleys being so common in America, this posey crew were genuinely bemused by my question, rather as a group of people in a car park would be puzzled if asked is this a car club? My bike was also not as 'Harleyesque' as a proper Harley rider's bike, looking more like it had been owned by a rider led more by objective than romantic criteria, and so to these dudes I was not quite one of the 'in' crowd. Nonetheless I couldn't help feeling that a little more geniality might have been exercised without disturbing their cool too much.

I started the engine and bumped over the grass back on to the path that led to the road, leaving the elite clique to stare snake-eyed into the afternoon sun.

THE LAKE OF THE OZARKS

Riding west I passed a series of advertising hoardings encouraging me to visit 'The Lake of the Ozarks.' Most were decorated with pictures of improbable looking dinosaurs wearing expressions which suggested the creatures were a little too pleased with themselves for my liking. I gained the impression from the frequency of these signs that the Ozarks were pretty 'big cheeses' in this neck of the woods, and had a greater than natural enthusiasm for being visited. Perhaps one was supposed to pay them some kind of levy before proceeding to the next state? The insistence of the signs reminded me of the written warnings in untenanted parking areas, 'Have you paid?' accompanied by threats of fines that would be levied on the owners of vehicles not displaying the necessary evidence. 'Have you visited the lake of the Ozarks?' asked the sign. I hadn't, and I couldn't if I was to make some reasonable progress, I'd used up my available free time in the Meramec Caverns and wanted to cover a good deal more distance before nightfall but I was haunted by the fear of one who has failed to pay his dues and is treading on 'unearned' earth.

It had been two days since I'd had a beer, a gap that represented a dangerously close approach to teetotalism. I'd determined from the outset that I couldn't go getting tanked up in the evenings or I'd never get out of bed in the mornings in time to cover the necessary distances. Six thousand miles in a month wasn't going to earn me a place in the *Guinness Book of Records*, but it didn't give me much margin for loitering either. The general store I'd parked outside had a refrigerator full of beer, mostly in six-packs which was more than I wanted. I fished a brace of Budweisers out of the plastic yokes connecting them to their colleagues, and plonked them in front of the plump girl at the checkout who stared at them for a second before speaking.

'I can't sell you those sir.'

'You can't sell me these?'

'No sir, I can't.' An immediate explanation did not seem to be forthcoming, but I reckoned if I stuck around long enough I might be able to break her code of silence. A direct question promised the best hope of expediting matters, so I gave it a try.

'What exactly is the point of having these beers here if you can't

60

sell them?' I asked.

'I can only sell beers in six-packs sir, I can't sell less than a six-pack.' What is this I thought, the pro-alcohol lobby of America. There seems to be in this country of innumerable pressure groups, an equal and opposite number of axe grinding opponents who provide a system of cultural counter weights to maintain some kind of socio-political equilibrium. I don't doubt it's a very healthy arrangement for a stable society, a mechanism for the cultivation of which, I was now witnessing. The puritanical prohibitionist lobby certainly needs some neutralizing agent to check the influence of its energetic zealots, but this enforced purchasing of minimum quantities was a little over the top. I didn't want to drink six cans any more than I wanted the aggravation of carrying them on my bike.

'It's state law,' the girl insisted by way of explanation, loosening up a little now. State law my arse, I thought, store policy more like it. I replaced the cans in the refrigerator and took out a quart bottle of Coors.

'Can I buy this by itself or do I have to buy a crate,' I asked, a mite sarcastically. Taking the modest two dollars for the goods, the sales girl moved ahead of me with a paper bag into which she thrust the bottle.

'No need for that,' I protested.

'I have to put this in a bag sir, all bottles have to go in bags.'

'State law?' I enquired.

'State law' she confirmed. It's bad enough when people put things in bags unnecessarily, but when their superfluous efforts have the backing of the authorities, the excess amounts to mandatory vandalism against the environment. America has led the world in packaging and disposability extravagances to a degree that makes the mind boggle. Governments can do a lot by way of legislation to cut this appalling wastage, but the everyday shopper can obviate the need for legislation by simply refusing to accept all this garbage. People power, that's what's needed, so why don't the majority act in the manner of the small concerned minorities? Why is it that given the overwhelming environmental threats facing the world, even now only a tiny percentage of humanity will join pressure groups, subscribe to the efforts of the front line campaigners, or even make the modest gesture of moderation when purchasing from indifferent retailers? The reason is that the

61

overwhelming majority of the population, even in the affluent West just do not give a damn, or at best, given some degree of concern lurking latent in their dim interiors, never translate it into any kind of positive action; it is a source of colossal depression for the rest of us. I can understand apathy with regard to almost any issue except the environmental one. If a lifeboat is sinking, the number one priority is to bale furiously; polishing the compass glass just has to wait, even medical attention to the injured may have to take second place. What is the point of stopping a man bleeding while the boat sinks, when all that assistance provides is an opportunity for him to drown with blood in his veins?

I over-simplify my case, not to imply that all other charitable works should be abandoned until the ecological crisis is resolved, but to emphasize that everyone should pay more than lip service to the environmental realities upon which the fate of humanity hinges. The obsession of retailers with putting things in bags has to be one of the most irritating extravagances imaginable. The scale of my own irritation at extravagance is not determined by the scale of the extravagance but by the degree of its pointlessness. If a rich man drives a Rolls Royce then I will salute his taste and not begrudge him his indulgence; maybe he's wanted one all his life and loves it as I love my Harley-Davidson, fair enough. But does the un-thinking shopper who never takes a bag to a shop and accumulates a thousand plastic carriers at home get pleasure from his indulgence? I don't think so. It is completely pointless extravagance that stems from thoughtlessness and while the Rolls owner's action may be attributed to selfishness, it is far less offensive to me because I can forgive, understand and empathize with selfishness in the name of self-indulgence, but zombie-like thoughtlessness – nope, that's just stupid.

Grudgingly clutching my bottle of beer in its heavy brown paper bag, for which I resolved to generate a secondary purpose, I let myself out of the store, whereupon I was accosted by a tall gangling character in Bermuda shorts. He stepped toward me from the door of his car as if he'd been waiting to intercept me, like some pavement canvasser.

'Have you been to the Lake of the Ozarks?' he asked.

'No, no I haven't,' I confessed guiltily, thinking perhaps I should have been, perhaps there's a state law which requires all visitors to these parts to make a pilgrimage to the Lake of the Ozarks to pay some kind of homage to its occupants. The stranger eyed me suspiciously as I admitted my omission, leaving me with the kind of feeling I got when I hadn't done my homework. Behind the inquisitor, his brood of infants pressed their faces against the side window of the automobile, their distorted features obscured in part by the presence of a large sticker bearing the legend: 'We've been to the Lake of the Ozarks.'

'It's been raining there all day,' continued the stranger, taking up the slack that had developed in the limp rope of our stilted conversation. That, I reflected, is probably why there's a lake there. Nature always gives itself away like that. I've never been fooled by those blue sky postcards from the north-west corner of England, something put those lakes there and it wasn't the Tourist Board.

'I've been ok,' I continued; 'no rain on me.' Trusting that the curse of the omnipresent Ozarks would not pursue me in the guise of some monstrous cloudburst, I threw a leg over the saddle of the motorcycle and trundled off across the parking lot, leaving the lake man staring after me like some suspicious detective who, dissatisfied with the answers to his questions, retains a substantial doubt about the honesty of the suspect he has just released.

The incident left me in an odd mood. I could not really understand why I should be expected to visit every feature to which my attention was directed, but I feared that in having shunned the Ozarks I might have committed some appalling *faux pas*, the penalty for which would be visited upon me at a later date. Early travellers mixing among primitive tribes and civilizations were forever running into this kind of trouble. Usually through total ignorance, some innocent word or gesture, some failure to respond to a host's initiative in a manner deemed appropriate by custom, would draw down upon the malefactor's head, the most dreadful consequences. In our more enlightened age, where the virtues and wisdoms of 'backward' civilisations are more sympathetically considered than once they were, it is easy to overdo one's enthusiasm for obscure cultures to the detriment of one's own. The notion that our own materialistic society is morally inferior to those of peoples whose simplicity and poverty are often objects of pity, is more often the product of fashionable affectation than sincere belief. There is a temptation to believe that what is unfamiliar, remote, and enigmatic, must necessarily be charged with a mystical sublimity, the subtlety of which is lost on our barbarous Western palates. The Trappist monk who spent seventeen years contemplating a stone wall from a chair for example, is ascribed a sagacity that transcends comprehension. As anyone with the slightest understanding of the polarizing power of ascetic dedication can tell you, this is a mechanism for divesting the mind of extraneous distractions and focusing it on significant profundities; to suggest otherwise is to court the caustic rebuke of philosophers. My own feeling is that anyone who sits in front of a wall for seventeen years is a bit of a tosser, but you have to be careful who you express that view to.

All this, however, flies somewhat wide of the issue to which my thoughts were, by the legendary Ozarks, directed, which was the unreasonableness of insular civilizations in assuming the universal familiarity of their bizarre etiquette. If a witchdoctor or guru worth his bones, is as wise as his position proclaims, then why can he not appreciate that the commission of indiscretions for which countless adventurous innocents have been barbarically punished, are no more than the unintentional blunders of the uninitiated. Why should a man, for wandering into the graveyard of an Indian tribe, be staked out in the desert sun with eyelids pinned back, if he obviously meant no harm? Western civilization may be guilty too, but we can be over-enthusiastic in apologizing for others through guilt-ridden self-deprecation.

There is a fascination with the Native American stemming from his roots in the land and his environmentally dovetailed identity which I have always found attractive. Of course we are right to respect the Indian's culture and right to question our own, but the Indian should have had the scope of imagination to realize that those who blundered into his ancestors' graveyards in the movies I saw, did not necessarily do so maliciously. Then again, given the treatment with which the white man dealt with the indigenous population in general, I guess they had every right to slaughter every one they met on the basis that if they hadn't done them any harm yet, they soon would.

I crawled into bed to drift into disturbed sleep where I dreamed of giant prehistoric creatures stuffing bottles into crackling brown paper bags, over which they peered critically at me with a smug reptilian disdain. There was as much premonition as recollection about this dream, as the following day I was to meet the biggest man in the world.

THE ENORMOUS MAN

I spotted him in a roadside diner in Kansas as I was tucking into hash browns and eggs. How I love hash browns and eggs after an hour's ride first thing in the morning! My jaws were just closing on a delicious mouthful of golden potato drenched in yellow egg yolk, when a shadow was cast across my breakfast by his astonishing bulk. I don't like eating in darkness. It's important for me to see what I'm consuming in order to ensure that all the occupants of my plate are devoured in equal proportions. I am not one to foist my culinary bigotry on others, but when I see people leaving all the white of their eggs, or all of their potato until last, I yearn for the reintroduction of stocks, ducking stools, thumb screws, racks, and all the paraphernalia of medieval correction. This may sound like reactionary intolerance, but I am convinced there is no other kind of language these people understand. I always ensure that every part of a meal is consumed at an equal rate so that no gluts of one factor or another remain to be consumed unaccompanied at the end. I just cannot understand how it is that some people can tolerate the asymmetrical evil of disproportionate consumption. Neither could I, or can I, understand how anyone can be as fat as the latest arrival in the cafe.

I had thought my employer, Big Dave, known also as 'Bigters' and sometimes 'Slim,' to be the fattest man in the world until Fat Frank bounced on to the scene and defied nature by being even fatter. Neither of these two bloated carcasses, however, could hold a whale blubber candle to the seam-splitting enormity now tilting the floor away from me, so that I had to push a folded napkin under the outer edge of my plate to halt the slippery migration of eggs in the direction of the beast. Perhaps, I pondered, this was his ploy for indefinite expansion. Whatever establishment he entered, the floor would tilt toward him, decanting its treasures downhill toward the walking amoeba who would sift between edible and non edible bounty, hungrily consuming the former. The cunningness of the ploy was matched only by its simplicity which warranted my reluctant admiration. There was no doubt that the tactic succeeded, as the consequent bulk was mind warping. There are times when the dimensions of some familiar object lie so far beyond the norm, that recognition is delayed. In the case of the man mountain squelching through the door, my initial belief was that I was looking at two men, both large, engaged in some kind of turgid combat which involved one holding the other in a headlock, thus obscuring his face from view, whilst, below head level the impression of a singular form was sustained by both combatants sharing a common pair of gargantuan trousers. This possibility was introduced to me by the recollection of the Crampton twins to whom my erstwhile friend MAZ was frequently referring. 'You know the Crampton twins,' he would say, 'I'm sure you've met.' I was quite sure I hadn't, a belief that was vindicated when he showed me a photograph of the twins.

'There's only one person in this photograph,' I declared.

'Of course,' replied MAZ, 'he is the Crampton twins.' The rationale underpinning this enigma lay in the size of 'the twins' who were, or rather was, so large that he could not possibly be one person, hence the 'twins' designation. I was impressed by this theory, despite its fallibility in the face of scrutiny. Certainly the irksome pedantics of officialdom would have rejected the concept as unacceptable. I doubted, for example, if a social security clerk would have accepted the notion that the large person standing before them required double benefit on the grounds that he must be two. Then again would such a beast be piqued if asked to pay double fare on a bus? Furthermore, should such a person, if learning to ride a motorcycle, be prosecuted for carrying a pillion passenger whilst still a novice? Certainly if double social security payment was being claimed, one could hardly protest at the injustice of such a charge. The encapsulating moral of this dilemma is best represented by the old maxim that 'you can't have your cake and eat it,' which for a person in this voluminous condition would surely represent the cruellest of ironies.

To return to the process by which the source of these speculations had achieved such proportions, we may gain some insight by considering American cattle. American cattle are fed steroids in order to increase their body weight, and Americans, by virtue of eating their meat, grow larger as a result, so it is believed. The character in question looked as if he'd short-circuited the system by conscientiously following a diet of steroid concentrate, helped down with bucketfuls of yak's butter topped off with lard sauce. No doubt when thirsty he swallowed pints of golden syrup, warmed so as to reduce its viscosity and expedite absorption. At a realistic estimate I would put his weight at somewhere between thirty-five and forty stone. Certainly the two big men in the queue for the food counter looked as if they would have fitted comfortably into his gargantuan frame with room left for a medium-sized German shepherd. The extremity of the man's condition reminded me of a line from the Rick Wakeman album, *Journey to the Centre of the Earth,*

'Dumb with astonishment bordering on stupefaction, we fled the forest.' In my case I fled the cafe, mounted my motorcycle, and headed further west across Kansas away from one mountain, and toward some others.

KANSAS

Kansas is not the most scenic of states. The flat marshy land I rode across as I approached Wichita reminded me of the soul-sapping wastes of my native Essex, between Dagenham and the Dartford Tunnel – as bad an advertisement as will be found for the county anywhere, and on the strength of which it should not be judged, though it frequently is. One noteworthy difference between this unspectacular stretch, peppered as it is with such forgettable outposts as Gravesend, Grays, and Tilbury, and the place in which I now found myself, is that Wichita has had a successful song written about it. I found myself humming Glen Campbell's *Wichita Linesman* involuntarily as the signposts provided a leisurely countdown to my arrival in the town which I'd decided was to host me tonight.

Whatever the mundane realities of a place, the perception of it by the inexperienced is indelibly embroidered by the fanciful immortalization of its name in song. Americans seem to write songs about everywhere of significance in their country, though whether it is the exciting aspects of places that provoke the musical muse or their mundane quality that demands artistic embellishment, no doubt varies from place to place and song to song. The fact remains that the good, the bad, and the boring all get a mention, whilst we British boast far fewer well known examples of this same kind of immortalization, despite having enjoyed the benefit of many more centuries during which to compose. Perhaps it's in the place names, Americans seem to have bagged most of the exiting sounding titles. San Francisco, Ohio, Los Angeles, San Antonio, even Wichita for that matter. It has an excitingly occult flavour to it that suggests some mystical quality. Compare it to Chelmsford, Scunthorpe, or Pratt's Bottom – now there's a name. Many people from the South of England will have heard of Pratt's Bottom, some must even endure the embarrassment of living there (and those who do commonly refer to it as Priors Botham), but who has ever heard a song written about it? I left my heart in Pratt's Bottom? Pratt's Bottom, Pratt's Bottom, so good they named it twice? I don't think so somehow.

As I drew closer to Witchita, the evening air grew stickier, providing a source of discomfort which had me raising my rump off the seat to encourage a little air into the nether quarters. A motorcycle is a bad vehicle to travel on when you're all clammy, it's the sitting down in one position that does it, particularly if it's cold and damp and you're wearing plastic over-trousers. Discomfort under these conditions can reach critical proportions. I'm particularly sensitive about stickiness when aboard a motorcycle, and would, were it possible, go to extraordinary lengths to ease my unhappiness. By way of comparison, I have heard that fisherman from the South Pacific have been known to have suffered such acute pain from the sting of the lethal stone fish upon which they have unwittingly trodden, that they have cut off their own toes rather than endure it.

I have never been tempted to adopt such radical measures over my problem with stickiness, in fact it would be a job to know quite how and where to perform the necessary surgery. What I have done, however, is to shout 'yuck' very loudly, which marks a significant step on the road to amputation. Those of longer limb may not understand this, but the shorter your legs are, the more severely the condition affects you especially when wearing over-trousers. Over-trousers inhibit the separation of the legs and effectively reduce the useable length of leg. When both feet can be planted firmly on the ground, leaving a gap between the saddle and the underside of the thigh, things are tolerable. When one has to stretch to reach the ground, pulling the plastic over-trousers taut against the skin, the stress, danger, the terror of embarrassment if the bike tips over, and the excruciating discomfort combine to convince the rider that it's really not worth being alive.

I was very glad to reach Wichita as the stickiness was really beginning to get to me, so much so that in the last few miles, the *Wichita Linesman* had been superseded in the silent orchestra of my mind by the cheerfully suicidal theme tune from *MASH*. I was looking forward to a shower and a decent meal and blessedly the opportunities for both were numerous.

Approaching the town through the outskirts, the traveller is presented with a bewildering array of advertising hoardings, inducing the visitor to sample one of a hundred restaurants, stores or motels. I had heard that restrictions on the size and number of these boards had been introduced in the interests of controlling visual pollution, and if that is so they need enforcing a little more vigorously around Wichita. The proliferation of billboards on the outskirts of this town imparted a tacky quality of impermanence to the place which robbed it of any dignity it might otherwise have had – on the other hand there was no trouble finding a restaurant. I couldn't help thinking though, that if all concerned agreed to ditch the big signs, then they could all save money and the variation in their respective fortunes could be determined more by merit than bluster, a naive observation no doubt, but there has to be some limit to the extent to which ad men control our skylines and commercialism rules our lives.

This competition to see who can erect the grossest hoarding is rather like the contest that reached such bizarre limits some years back in Britain were garages where offering ever greater multiples of Green Shield stamps to encourage custom. Of course the whole stamp sham was nothing more than legalized protection which the average shopper was unable to see. What really was the difference between a Green Shield man offering to sell you loads of bits of ludicrous sticky green paper for you to bother your customers with, so that you didn't lose trade to your neighbour who was doing the same thing, and offering to refrain from throwing a brick through your window, so you didn't lose trade to your neighbour who wasn't having bricks thrown through his? The money for the stamps, the book and the presents didn't come from the goodness of the Green Shield's boss's heart, it didn't come out of the thin air and, as has always been the way, it did not grow on trees. The retailer paid the Green Shield bosses and to sustain his profit margins he passed his costs on to his customers whose only real advantage lay in the amusement of sticking lots of little stamps in books, given that they had nothing better do to with their time. The only mob that really made anything out if it were the Green Shield parasites feeding off the retail trade and producing absolutely nothing whatsoever. Nonetheless I often ran into trouble when trying to explain this simple reasoning to apparently intelligent people who would look at me oddly when I described the realities of the scam.

'But I got a new toaster,' they might say.

'Who do you think paid for it?' I would ask, to which question they would expose me to the kind of suspicious scrutiny reserved for doorstep prophets.

When the game was tried in Australia, the Aussies told Mr Green Shield exactly where he could go and stick his bloody stamps, not so our own people who welcomed the spongers in with open arms for reasons which can only be guessed at. My father was so incensed by this blatant parasitism that he wrote to his MP about it, the only time he'd written to his MP in his life. The MP responded to my father's letter, explaining that the system was not so bad, as the option of redeeming the stamps for cash was being considered! Let us hope that our nation is no longer ruled by men capable of that kind of logic or contempt, or perhaps I should say, 'let us pray.'

I found a passable restaurant serving Mexican food, for which I have a great affection, and ordered a taco salad. It's pronounced *tarcho*; pronounce it the other way – as in rev counter – and brace yourself for a sly snigger or indulgent smile at best. There are some things of which, for the sake of street credibility, one should not be ignorant. For a man to be vague about changing babies nappies is no bad thing, but there is about Mexican food a certain gastric machismo that renders the uninitiated greener than grass. Not being able to pronounce taco is a bit like not being able to set the balls up on a pool table, it ain't very cool, nor for that matter was my taco salad, but it was great. It consisted of a bowl-shaped crispy cage, stuffed full of some kind of spicy mince intimately involved with beans and topped with a crunchy salad that provided a refreshing contrast to the sauce. Raising my head from the fiery trough to suck in air from time to time, I spotted the evolution of a theatrical scenario at a nearby table.

A young James Dean lookalike in a crisply ironed shirt and neatly cut hair, was trying to interest his bored girlfriend in something, exactly what, wasn't clear, himself possibly, but it was an uphill struggle. As he stroked her hair, whispered in her ear, attempted to draw her interest to something across the restaurant or out of the window, she maintained an air of consummate indifference so faultlessly consistent she might have been acting a part in an American movie. One sees girls like this in many movies, particularly ones of the early sixties or late fifties. Checked shirt, pony tail, blue jeans, she had the entire rig. Too pretty for the small town they live in, growing up with ambitious aspirations that can't be satisfied by the local environment; dreaming of faraway places like New York or LA, places as remote to many small-town American teenagers as they would seem to their British counterparts from Ilkley or Lower Wallop, or for that matter, Pratt's Bottom. The kind of girls that spend hours flicking through magazines wishing they were movie stars, toying with fantasies of girlish romance and materialism. This particular dreamer didn't seem too impressed with the company she was with – and no more so with myself, which was hard to understand. There was I thinking I cut a rather dashing figure with my gleaming motorcycle parked outside the window: suntanned, clad in heroically faded army strides, brown boots scuffed by a thousand gear shifts, taco stained map of America spread out before me on the table next to the bug splattered shades. Yes, taking it all round, this young belle really ought to have seen me as the natural alternative to the lad with his long quiff and short horizon who was presumably picking up the tab for her meal that night. She really should have been busy fantasizing about parking her pert denim clad buttocks on the pillion of the Harley and being transported out of Wichita, out of the state of Kansas, over the Rocky Mountains and all the way to the Pacific Ocean to go splashing in the sun-drenched surf. I maintained a steady, though discreet surveillance of her throughout the meal, seeking some evidence of her mental meanderings. For twenty minutes I studied her cultivated indifference for some betrayal of interest, hoping she wasn't irritated by my attention, hoping she didn't pop a bubblegum and spit 'Quit gawking creep!'

She didn't glance my way once.

Kansas is a tiresomely, flat, windswept state, stretching some five hundred miles across the middle of America. Loosely known as the Mid West, it forms a barrier to the traveller, not in the tangible sense that the Rockies form a genuine barrier, but by virtue of its soul-sapping tediousness. There is, by way of encouragement to the transcontinental traveller, a sign at some point, advertising the 'Middle of America,' all downhill from here I thought, which is not actually quite true.

Being high and flat, the wind blows with a tireless consistency that squints the eyes and creases the face, encouraging comparisons between the Kansas landscape and the open ocean. Both impose upon the traveller a quizzical, horizon-searching expression which lends itself to the belief that the scrutiny is inspired by a mission of epic significance.

I have always felt Kansas to be a state through which people are forever passing, or in which folk reside reluctantly whilst saving the cash or summoning the courage to go some place else. In the Westerns, the woman from this part of the USA is always looking out for her man who has gone, staring after his departing dust trail or waiting for its reappearance to herald his arrival. This is the woman who stands on the porch, apron a-billow, one hand shielding the sun from her eyes, as, behind her, a screen door slams in the dry wind. Like at sea, everyone is looking for something to grow out of the expanse, a ship, a lifeboat, an island, the sea is a place of transience, so is Kansas, well at least it was for me.

I had to stop now and then though, if only to eat, and my immediate concern at this time was breakfast. Motels, unlike our bed and breakfast places, don't serve breakfast, so I tended to ride for an hour or two in the morning before hunting down some nosebag. It was good to work up an appetite this way and made the stop all the more welcome. This morning was special, I'd spotted just the place to eat, an establishment which compelled investigation. I pulled up on the rough parking lot outside and cut the engine. As a low moaning wind blew the dust from my line of sight, the weathered legend on the cracked board swinging squeakily in the remorseless air snapped into focus, confirming the impression gained as I'd ridden by a moment earlier, yes this was some kind of diner.

'Harold's Place – Hot Beer, Poor Service.' I smiled at the sign and kicked down the sidestand, any man with a sense of humour like that, deserved to be patronized. Turning the door handle, I pushed, but to no avail; a second sign caught my eye, 'Closed.'

A mile down the road I came across another restaurant, this one was set a good fifty yards back from the road, reflecting the fact that space is not at a premium here in rural Kansas. But, with no other buildings or trees in sight, there was no danger of missing it, it stood alone on the open prairie like a man-made oasis of food in a culinary desert. No self-deprecatory wit operated here to attract custom or deter the humourless. The name sounded encouraging, given my empty stomach gurgling like a bear's in spring. 'The Grizzly Restaurant.'

I left the road and rolled across the rugged ground, levelled but not paved, to park by a corral style fence bordering the veranda of the eatery: a long, low, brown-timbered barn of a place, decorated over the door with a huge pair of buffalo horns. Two girls seated on a bench with a small child outside in the veranda's shade, greeted me.

'Hi, how ya doing?' Americans use 'how ya doing' the way Londoners use 'all right,' even if they're not.

My old friend 'The Bubble' once claimed to be 'all right' when in fact he was suffering from an acute case of scabies, a very un-alright condition for a chap, plus anyone unfortunate enough to be sharing his towel. I did not know at that time that scabies is one of the most contagious and unpleasant skin disorders known, but having since learnt that, I can now understand the spontaneous migration from where The Bubble stood at the bar of a local pub, where he made the candid response to the question:

'All right Bubbles?'

'Well, I've got scabies actually.'

The girls on the bench didn't look as if they had scabies, representing the face of healthy rural America as they did. They were from Oregon, a beautiful hilly state to the north of California, and it seemed a strange thing to me that they should leave such a place to come here to live in this windy prairie. They agreed, in fact they were planning to return to Oregon quite soon. I didn't have time to take in Oregon on this trip, though I would like to have done. I would clearly miss out on far more things than I would experience, but one thing I was not going to miss was breakfast.

I liked the Grizzly Restaurant instinctively, it had uncovered floorboards and red chequered tablecloths. I WANTED to eat there. And even though the hash browns were a little greasy, the overall experience was terrific. Food for me is not just about re-fuelling my body, it is a culturally stimulating adventure every time I sit down with the eating irons in my hands. I know there are a lot of people that don't think that way, and eat only from necessity, and I know it takes all types to make a world, but I cannot help treating with the utmost distrust, those who do not rate eating at, or at least near, the top of the list of life's physical pleasures.

'More coffee?' asked the waitress, who appeared to be running the place. Most American restaurants serve coffee indefinitely at no extra charge beyond that of the first cup. It's a fine idea that I would like to see catch on in Britain. I sat drinking the coffee slowly, drinking more than I wanted really, just to savour the pleasure of being there, letting my breakfast settle and scribbling out a couple of postcards that I'd picked up over by the counter. Beyond the windows the two girls on the veranda with the small child between them were still talking, swinging their legs in the sunshine while scanning the highway, where the passage of the occasional truck would draw their heads in unison, like the retarded passage of a ball in a slow-motion tennis match. There was a friendly unaffected warmth about the typically American hospitality of the Grizzly Restaurant that extended to its environs which, like the decor, belonged to an earlier age. It was an impression that was sustained by the gas pumps, a brace of vintage items, tall and simple looking, with big mechanical clockface gauges set in circular housings separated from the main bodies and lending them a more human identity than that enjoyed by their squat robotic successors.

The two girls, smiling still on their veranda perch, watched as I carefully filled the tank to the top while the old fashioned needle spun round the dial, the solitary vane of a gasoline windmill. As the owner hove into sight it occurred to me that this probably wasn't a self service station though no fuel cut offs or amplified voices from behind security screens obstructed my efforts as I helped myself. A weathered old timer in dungarees cast an appreciative eye over the motorcycle as he waited for his money with the patience of a man whose life proceeds at a pace determined in another era. I breathed on the dark glasses I'd removed from my face and polished their lenses with the tail of my cotton shirt whilst waiting for my change which approached me by way of a ragged chicane as the old man's legs hinged and buckled unevenly as he made his way across the lumpy track of the virgin forecourt. Back aboard the bike I set about generating my own dust storm through which, in the mirror, I identified the farewell waves of the Oregon girls

75

whose infant charge clung to their skirts, shielding his face from the low cloud of airborne debris streaming from my fat back tyre. Once on the even asphalt, the bucking of the bike ceased abruptly; I opened the throttle, shifted gears, and headed west into the steady prairie wind.

Running with this consistent half gale blowing on one side is a bit like how I imagine wind surfing to be. I found myself leaning the bike continually into the wind in order to hold a straight line. Although an almost unconscious action, this effort has a tiring effect on the traveller after a while, despite the air being very warm, which is, all said and done, a damn sight better than it being very cold as the stress of being wind dried like a piece of dehydrating fish is not so terrible as long as you're not cold. The sense of exhaustion, of roughing it, of battling the elements is provided under these conditions without the acute misery that prevails in the rain and cold. The dryness poses an alternative threat however, which has still to be taken seriously. Skin protection is a must, either you cover up, grease up, or dry up. I was a little late adopting either precaution, so that by the time I had recognized the necessity of protection, my lips had dried to crisps in the unequal contest with the elements. As I ran my tongue over them, feeling the brittle edges of dead skin, I thought at first there was a fly carcass in my mouth, however, after furious spitting provided no relief I took a look in the mirror and learned the truth. How could I be so careless? I'd asked myself the same question a week earlier when I'd left two poppadoms under the grill. In one minute they were reduced to bubbling black ashes, it was all very disappointing. My mouth wasn't in much better shape, not having had much to say to myself for a while, my lips had been stood at ease, now as I moved them masochistically about, I began to feel like an Egyptian mummy that the moths had got to.

DODGE CITY

By early afternoon I was too hot despite the breeze, and I decided to sit out the worst excesses of the sun in a small town whose name sounded mighty familiar – Dodge City.

I don't know what distinguishes cities from towns in America. In England the credentials are more or less ecclesiastical, with the presence of a cathedral usually conferring the title of 'city' on a place. I don't think Dodge has a cathedral, but it boasts a history that has made its name synonymous with the drama of the Wild West. I cruised along Wyatt Earp Boulevard and parked up opposite a reconstruction of the old main street. The original burnt down in a fire which is a bloody shame as I would have got a great feeling from knowing I was standing on the same floor in the same bar as those old gunfighters. Back home, I lived a few hundred yards from the 'Blind Beggar' pub where the Krays had killed rival gangster George Cornell. I didn't go in there very often but I liked the idea of living with a bit of history around me, and we had quite a lot in Bethnal Green. Jack the Ripper had conducted his nefarious deeds only half a mile up the road in Whitechapel where the 'Elephant Man' lived in the London Hospital. Half a mile beyond that is the Tower of London which has played host to more than its fair share of hapless fellows, Milton Keynes it is not, and neither is Dodge. Pity about the main street burning down though.

As I pulled into the parking lot I noticed a BMW motorcycle, one of the modern, water-cooled ones with four cylinders in a line like an aluminium ice cream wafer or brick, from which comparison the model earned its nickname, 'the flying brick.' The machine was heavily loaded with camping gear, including a towering tank bag like some multi tiered wedding cake over which the pilot could barely see. The rider was from Croydon, another God-forsaken satellite on the outskirts of London, not as remote or dreadful as Milton Keynes, but possessing nonetheless a peculiar kind of horror for me as a despatch rider. When I became a courier, Croydon joined the list words and phrases which, throughout my life, have struck chords of terror. The earliest of those words that I can recall, was 'Sunday School.' 'Is that boy going to Sunday School?' After dinner on a Sunday, when I wanted to go out and make bonfires in the garden with my father, the terrifying instruction would be received, and I would have to be scrubbed clean, hair brushed flat, clean shorts pulled on and polished shoes laced in time for an hour of bible reading in a musty parquet floored hall, surrounded by pictures of Jesus amidst flocks of sheep. I didn't resent the indoctrination, I was an instinctive believer, it was the knee scrubbing and nail clipping that I resented, like a show poodle that wanted only to go and roll in the earth. When I was a little older, the word 'homework' superseded 'Sunday school,' then in the mid sixties it became 'haircut' and in my seafaring days 'boat drill,' and, as a navigator, the expression, 'where are we Mr Mutch?' In more recent times the verbal provocation of nerve tingling apprehension, administered usually by a spiky haired girl of confused sexuality called Dawn or sometimes, 'Dawn the Dyke' was 'Croydon,' followed by the word Mutch – my name. 'Croydon. Mutch.' Dawn would spring this on me whenever I had over-indulged my enthusiasm for verbally abusing the sisterhood of strangeness and their male equivalents. Frustrated with my politically incorrect diatribes of colourful vulgarity, Dawn would leap to her feet with malicious intent, stride toward me with retribution etched into her podgy young face like a German SS officer giving a conscript his marching orders for the Russian front. 'Croydon. Mutch,' she would slaver triumphantly, savouring the word as if it was 'Stalingrad.' Croydon is a long way from the city by Central London despatch riding standards, but not long enough to really make you a substantial amount of money on its own, unless there were a number of jobs to go with it, or a return to bring you back, thus earning both ways. As a solitary one way job, it was all rather a waste and a dismal one at that, the journey comprising a protracted series of high streets that dictated slow progress for the twelve miles or so that separate the southern suburb from the rich picking-laden City.

The man on the BMW had come from Croydon, and presumably by now is back there again, and good luck to him. I suspected, even at a distance, that he was not American. Most touring American motorcyclists ride either Harleys or Honda Gold Wings (Japanese Harley-Davidson Electra Glide imitations, boasting fairings equipped with hi-fi, luggage compartments and drinks dispensers, they are even more massive than the bulkiest Harley-Davidson). This man from Croydon was riding a different kind of machine altogether, one that dictated a crouched racing posture ill-suited to a journey of such length; furthermore he was wearing a full-face, heavily padded crash helmet, within which his small face nestled like a shrew amidst a substantial nest of foam compressed by a powerful G clamp. A full-face helmet is a huge cumbersome affair that weighs almost as much as the head it surrounds, and, as the name suggests, completely encircles the jaw, leaving a slot three of four inches wide to peer out of, like some medieval knight. I utterly detest them. The prevalence of full face helmet use in Britain (I estimate ninety per cent of riders use them), is one of those things that reinforces my conviction that I am very different from other people. The frighteningly restrictive, claustrophobic discomfort of these devices is so appalling, that it's a source of bewilderment to me why anyone would tolerate wearing one for the shortest of excursions, let alone adopt one for regular use. It might sound bigoted to chastise others for the adoption of practices that don't harm anyone else, but it's not that simple. On the one hand there's a kind of socio-political bullying developing from initially passive peer pressure, and on the other, there is the disturbing sense of isolation that stems from finding oneself part of a mysteriously dwindling minority amidst a majority apparently driven by the most perverse of forces. I hate crash helmets, and have fought for a repeal of the law compelling their use for years. Leaving aside, however, all the moral arguments pertinent to the issue, the equally, if not more interesting question remains: how can people's behaviour be so easily manipulated by that of the herd? Looking back through history, numerous examples of behaviour may be found, that seem so at odds with present practice or standards as to invite speculation about whether the human race has undergone physiological as well as social evolution. I am not drawing comparisons with Stone Age man but with our forebears of a couple of centuries back, when, so we are told, people just did not wash. This negligence was not confined to the lower orders of peasants who lacked the convenience of facilities, no, even the poncing nobles and courtiers who flounced around the effetely populated environs of Louis XIV's court, avoided bath-time like the plague, despite the ironic relationship between the neglect and its consequence. Now everyone knows that when you're all hot and sticky you feel uncomfortable, you have a bath or a shower and you feel a hundred per cent better. You don't need a fashion pundit to persuade you that this is so. The conditions and remedies are universal; absolute, are they not? How is it then that these revolting pansies and parasites flouncing around the Sun King's palace, resorted to nothing more thorough than a dowsing of perfume and a dusting of powder to alleviate the vulgar stench of their putrid bodies? What was worse still, in those days clothing tended to involve a lot of high necked collars which must surely have imposed the most purgatorial discomfort on the wretched stinkers within. The Masai of the African plains, I have heard, do not wash, but then they wear only the scantiest of clothes, so their problem cannot be comparable. Consider by contrast, the ludicrous ruffs and frills of the Elizabethans, which might have been designed by sadistic tailors to aggravate the tortured hides of the rancid sixteenth-century aquaphobes.

The question must be asked, were the people happy in that condition? Was their indifference sustained by ignorance of something better? It is hard to imagine that no one ever bathed, and so assuming that they did, albeit occasionally, then surely the experience would prevent the ignorance from being sustained? Or were they simply being led by fashion in the face of the natural choices which comfort alone might otherwise dictate? We do not have to return to earlier centuries to identify examples of this masochism. Consider the winkle-picker shoes of the Teddy Boy era, nylon shirts, skin tight jeans or, for that matter, almost all women's shoes. The length of self deception to which people will go in defence of their 'chosen' attire is, to the rational observer, even more aggravating than the offending indulgence. It's the same with motorcycles. I knew a chap called Kirk who bought a Harley-

Davidson that had been custom built for a man of six-foot five, Kirk was, and still is, five-foot five. The bike had a stretched frame fitted with a short straight handlebar, whilst the foot controls were fitted about as far forward as they could be placed without fouling the front wheel. A mile behind the front of the bike, perched a meanly padded seat whose unyielding qualities enjoyed no compensation by way of the frame from which all traces of suspension had been removed. Bouncing down the road with his hands and feet practically in contact like some airborne toe-touching gymnast, this oddly-hinged character would proceed, a horizontally disposed human 'V' rattling toward his orthopaedic doom whilst denying the reality of the purgatory, as a victim of the Inquisition might have affected his stoic indifference to the racks and thumb screws of his ecclesiastical tormentors. 'It's surprising,' he would say. 'You may not believe me, but it's actually quite comfortable.' And do you know, Kirk was right, we didn't believe him, though he maintained his fatuous pretence until spinal discomfort persuaded him to visit a doctor who explained to the diminutive masochist that his back was broken. X-rays proved that one of his vertebrae had actually cracked under the unnatural stress. In response to this disturbing news, Kirk changed his bars and his seat, thus providing an alleviation of misery that was completed by the efforts of some unwitting Samaritan who stole the appalling contraption. Never did so loathsome an act deliver so benign a consequence.

I was diverted into these reflections by the consideration of the full-face crash helmet whose wholesale voluntary adoption constitutes an enigma which belongs in the same volume of mystery as sweat encrusted ruffs, stretch jeans and rigid motorcycles, with the additional absurdity that, on all but the beefiest and broadest of riders they look absurd to boot. A large bear shaped character might not be too unbalanced by the dimensions of these contraptions, but small narrow shouldered wimps tend to assume the appearance of fragile insects that might snap apart at the joints given a sharp shove in the back. In fact, such a possibility is not so far from the truth since, as heavy helmets have been implicated in cases of death due to spinal fracture, which is a serious consideration in its own right. This fatal possibility aside, how, how, how can anyone of stable mind, in possession of their mental faculties, voluntarily expose themselves to the wretchedness that these helmets impose during hot weather? I recall once seeing a film called *The Hill* with Sean

Connery, in which wayward soldiers serving time within their own army's penal system, were forced to run up and down a steep manufactured sand dune. One wretch singled out for particularly harsh treatment was forced to complete this purgatorial exercise whilst wearing a gas mask. The film, taken ostensibly from within the mask to provide the victim's tortured perspective of the cruel world to which he had fallen victim, provided a graphic illustration of the claustrophobic horror of this gruelling experience. The man from Croydon however was not an errant soldier, POW, or other unfortunate who had fallen prisoner to some cruel authority. No, he was voluntarily wearing a full face crash helmet in ninety degree heat, in a state that didn't even have a compulsory helmet law!? What do you do with these people? I had ridden all the way across the state bareheaded, and I was still too hot. At least the Londoner, unlike my old friend Kirk, was honest enough to admit that he was uncomfortable in his padded cranial cell, but convention nonetheless held a tight grip on his behaviour, even when removed from the environment where such perversity is considered normal. There is a good deal of brain-washing that emanates from the so called 'safety' lobby, which promotes the virtues of full-face lids, but I suspect that fashion has a lot to do with it. My old friend Shortie used to wear quite a tasteful open faced helmet, fitted with a pleasantly classic leather lining; then one dark day, up he popped with a device out of which his small face peeked like some wretched laboratory monkey, clamped into one of those sadistic contraptions that features in the harrowing recruitment posters distributed by the Anti Vivisection League.

'What?' I demanded to know, 'are you doing in that?' adding that he looked absolutely ridiculous. His muffled response reflected a perversely diseased logic that I found profoundly depressing.

'Well who'll recognize me anyway?' he argued.

'Stick one of these on your head and you're Mr Anonymous, one of the crowd.' This casual statement spoke volumes about the human race in general, and Shortie in particular. People may applaud the concept of individualism, they may applaud individuals, they may envy individuals; to be charged with not being much of an individual is clearly an insult. We laugh at the endemic conformity of the Japanese, just as we make jokes about the German's legendary obedience of orders. Within limits, non conformity is good, it demonstrates self-confidence, and the exercise of intellect. Artists, progressive thinkers, and martyrs, are invariably nonconformist. A whole religious faction even adopted the collective title of the 'Nonconformists' and proudly flew the flag of its revolutionary doctrine in the face of savage reactionary persecution. Nonconformists, like evolutionary mutants, are the catalysts of human progress who either dictate new courses or are destroyed. Meanwhile the vast population remain, as they have always been, hidden in the anonymous safety of the ranks, glad that others take a pace forward to volunteer but, simultaneously, suspicious and fearful of them.

Jack Nicholson made a similar point in the classic film *Easy Rider* about the majority response to the demonstration of freedom. Then, as today, the image of freedom was manifestly demonstrated in the powerful imagery of the motorcycle, bedroll strapped to the handlebars, scorching unfettered across the giant American landscape. Sitting around the campfire with Dennis Hopper and Peter Fonda, getting quietly stoned, Nicholson explained to his benefactors, from whom he'd hitched a lift, why it was that the 'rednecks' feared them.

'People may say they value freedom,' he drawled, as only Jack Nicholson can.

'People may write about freedom, sing about freedom, even fight for freedom; but when they see a truly free person, it scares them.'

It would be overstating things to claim that people are scared of riders in open-faced helmets, or that by wearing one, the rider automatically aspires to a 'free' status that is the envy of the full-face followers. Rather, the wearers of these massive fibreglass cages invariably pity what they perceive as the reckless neglect of those who reject their more comprehensive protection in favour of briefer models, or none at all. The Englishman on the BMW looked rather like a refugee whose clothes are ill suited to the environment in which he now finds himself. Given our present situation, with high temperatures and low speed limits, sitting back helmetless on a Harley, with the wind whistling through my hair seemed a sight more appropriate than hunching up over a hundred and thirty mile an hour machine wearing a full-face helmet that left the rider looking about as laid back as *The Man in the Iron Mask*.

I offered to help the Croydon refugee cool off with an iced tea in the local Kentucky emporium that lay within sight of where we met. The existence of iced tea explained the extraordinary question I'd been asked earlier when ordering the drink. 'Do you want it hot?' I had thought at the time that it was a damn silly question, a bit like asking if you want your ice frozen. Do I want it hot? Of course I want it hot, how do you think I want it, lukewarm? I had not given voice to these sentiments, but I was intrigued, at least until I discovered iced tea which, surprisingly, is not at all bad. Iced tea, at least in the Kentucky, comes in a cardboard carton jingling with ice, there's no milk, it wouldn't be right.

Apart from the two of us, the Kentucky was crowded with teenage schoolgirls dressed in uniforms that put me in mind of cheerleaders, all short pleated skirts and bobby socks; the sight of which cheered me up enormously. I don't suppose it was always like this coming into Dodge City. The classic image involves some desperado riding in to town on a horse which he hitches to the timber rail by some curious knot which, simple though it seems and rapid though it be to tie, nonetheless never comes undone until the owner is ready to leave. You watch carefully the next time you see a Western, the cowboy will throw his reins carelessly over the rail and walk into the saloon with not so much as a backward glance to check that he really got that knot right. And the horse will just stand there – amazing!

The teenagers were a lot easier on the eye than a band of grim faced gun-toters off an Eagles' album sleeve. I suppose they made more of an impression on me than ordinarily they would have done, because in the last four days I'd seen very few females, which is unusual visual abstinence for someone who spends most of his working day riding around the heart of the Big Smoke getting receptionists to sign bits of paper in exchange for the envelopes and packages which I give them. My camera, which I'd placed on the table in front of me, went off automatically at this point – many people will not believe this, but it is the improbable but actual truth. I suppose I must have knocked the delayed action lever accidentally. Whilst the click of the shutter did embarrass me slightly at the time, I looked forward with relish to the result. Imagine my disappointment several weeks later, when I discovered that I had recorded nothing more felicitous than a carton of Colonel Saunders' french fries decorated with the familiar smug face of the silver-haired old bastard. Not so much as a single cotton pleat.

I spent half an hour chatting to the Londoner before parting company and wandering over to Boot Hill cemetery at the end of the reconstructed main street. I'm an incurable tourist and I wanted to see this. I'd draw the line at watching a staged gunfight, but I wanted to go to the spot – that's important – being where others had been. I'd been to Galilee and Gethsemane and now I was at Boot Hill, or rather, I wasn't. The spot I was looking at, the gravestones, or rather 'grave timbers', were, like the buildings on Main Street, reconstructed. The original Boot Hill cemetery was a little way off in another part of town. I'd photographed the graves by the time I realized this, however, and didn't doubt that the wording thereon bore faithful witness to the original. Humour or justice featured more in the text of these frontier epitaphs than the customary lines of respectful emotion .

'Jack Wagner killed Ed Masterton, April 9, 1878; killed by Bat Masterton, April 9, 1878; he argued with the wrong man's brother.' And another, 'Edward Hurly shot Jan 17, 1873 – he drank too much and loved unwisely.' None of this 'rest in peace' stuff, and quite right too. Who the hell wants to spend eternity resting? The whole point of being reborn into eternal life is having, just that, new life and new inexhaustible energy. Rest in peace! what a bore; just imagine the conversation

'Hello John what you been up to?' .

'Having a little rest mate.'

'Oh right, me too, got anything planned for the next eon then? '

'Oh just lying around resting.'

'What then?'

'Well I dunno really, bit of this, bit of that.'

'What like, a bit of a rest and then a bit of a longer rest.'

'Yeah that sort of thing, want to join me?'

'Don't mind if I do John, very comfy spot you got here eh – give us a shout in a millennium or two will yer.'

Oh fascinating, bloody marvellous eh! Be better off dead.

The old jail house on site was the original item, a small, barely eight-foot square timber construction that didn't look like it could keep in anyone armed with more than a nail file. I stood in the doorway and photographed myself using the time delay on the camera, hoping no-one noticed. Blessedly, the place wasn't crowded, and I extricated myself from the well worn cubicle of incarceration without being spotted committing an act of great corniness.

On the edge of the graveyard a museum had been built, housing an exhibition of artifacts. Among the features was a slide show describing the local history, from which I learnt a few things. Firstly, Dodge City was essentially a cattleman's town. One thinks of cowboys as characters with hats and guns who were forever fighting Indians as if they, the cowboys, were a rival race. At least that was the simple impression which I harboured throughout my early youth. I never really thought of the word, 'cow-boy' as meaning someone who works with cattle; cowboys were just cowboys as in cowboys and Indians, the only other major players on that stage of conflict being the US cavalry, who we all used to cheer at Saturday morning pictures as loudly as we booed the Indians. A terrible thing really when one thinks about it, it represented seriously immoral indoctrination on the part of the movie makers. I remember being quite surprised the first time someone told me that actually the Indians got rather a bad deal. There was no doubt in my mind which side I identified with – cowboys were definitely where it was at. I didn't want to kill anybody but I fancied riding across the country with a bedroll and a harmonica, making campfires, sleeping under the stars, saying 'Coffee stranger.' I never really thought about them doing a job. I suppose I'd have got a pretty nasty shock if I'd gone out there looking for work in the nineteenth century and found that more was expected of me than shooting a revolver in the air, as I *yee-haad* into town to prop up a bar and watch the *cancan* girls. The awful reality of course was that all this 'ropin' ridin' brandin' that Frankie Lane used to sing about on *Rawhide* was pretty serious stuff; twelve to eighteen hours in the saddle would soon have put me right off that idea. I found it hard enough coming to grips with the fact that a ship's officer has to do more than swan about in a natty uniform leaning on taffrails under the tropical moonlight chatting up beautiful female passengers. The fact that all occupations, in fact life in general, is loaded with little or large disappointments, suggests something fundamental about the human attitude of optimism. The enthusiasm of youth no doubt has much to do with the comparatively few experiences of disappointment which, in later life, accumulate in the deposit account of one's mortal log to fuel that morbid pessimism which drives some to drink, whilst propelling a desperate contingent to suicide, leaving a third category of morose and vindictive characters to share their discouragement with the world by committing it to paper. Some, motivated by the melodic muse, commit their unhappiness to music, and are thus able to share their distress with those, who, through circumstance, find themselves the unwilling victims of those dreary melodies. Of all human gifts, the capacity for facilitating the enjoyment of unhappiness, through the propagation of some saleable merchandise, is as certain a path to wealth as any I have encountered, and explains why Leonard Cohen, though perhaps not the epitome of cheery ebullience, will nonetheless always be able to afford that better class of misery with which the materially fortunate console themselves.

I would often hum some Cohen when awoken at an ungodly hour to tramp along the snow-covered deck of a merchant ship preparing to dock in some blasted nook of our storm-swept world. There is a suicidal jollity about its morbidity that makes human theatre out of dreary desolation. Just as it is crucial to be hated, if not loved, in order to evade the desperation of mediocrity; so too, one must consciously lick the wretchedness of circumstance in order to savour its bitter quality, and thus escape the drudgery of indifference.

The American slaves were experts at this, with their mournful reflections on how 'far, far from home' they were when 'way down upon the Swanny River,' wherever that may be. It is an ability that survived their emancipation to evolve into the blues, which 'woke up one morning' just like the good lord knew it would. Let us applaud the miserable, for they do not vex our spirits with raucous joy.

The American Indians were not a race with a lot to laugh about after the white man got stuck into them in a serious way, undercutting the foundations of their civilization, at least in the case of the Plains Indians, by destroying the buffalo herds on which they depended. I knew this before I saw the video in the Dodge City museum, but what I didn't realize, was that the whole genocidal ploy was carried out in just four years. In four years over a million buffalo had been slaughtered, their hides shipped back East while the carcasses rotted in the sun or fed the jubilant carrion who doubtless grew fat on this abundance, while the indians starved. Such reduced circumstances produced a more malleable population to herd into reservations, leaving the land free for the white man to plant his crops and graze his cattle. Thus went the dialogue of the guilt-ridden video to which I was the solitary witness.

Climbing out of the gloom of the dimly lit cinema, I wandered around the rooms inspecting the exhibits which were much as one might expect the content of a Western museum to be. Guns, traps, ploughs, saddles, tomahawks and tepees, Indian head-dresses and ten-gallon hats, old sepia photographs of men with moustaches in waistcoats, and some reconstructed rooms occupied by reconstructed people. One such notable, dressed in a crinoline and seated amidst the accoutrements of her bedchamber-workshop – which provided the environment for that most ancient of professions – has survived into history under the enigmatic title of 'Squirrel Toothed Annie.' This notable *femme fatalle*, retained by way of an alternative to her transient male company, a squirrel, restrained by means of a lead which the stuffed whore, if you'll excuse the expression, held in her hand. Where the 'toothed' element of her nickname originated was not clear to me, but I am sure there was a reason as good as the husband which a woman of such distinction must eventually have attracted, for, according to the available information, most whores married before they were out of their early twenties; which is nice to know.

On a different theme, another model, that of a silver-haired old man, sat apparently playing a mouth organ, whilst oscillating gently in a rocking chair. The hair on the dummy's head was, I noted, particularly well made, while the harmonica emanated a plaintiff wail that complemented the environment without fuelling the corny appetites to which one might expect such a place to pamper. I walked around to the other side of the room in which this character continued reciprocating, taking in the set, with its silver snuff boxes, brass oil lamps, feather quills and menagerie of antiquated paraphernalia. The harmonica playing ceased and I was about to applaud the musical mannikin when blow me down, it spoke, 'Howdy'. Even then it took me a moment to recognize the error of my presumption.

The musical old timer deserved better, for two reasons. The harmonica music was good, and the player was real. Considering how closely I'd studied the 'dummy,' I was at first embarrassed by this unexpected revelation. I paused to talk to the harmonica player who, it transpired, was a master of disguise. Pulling out a pack of photographs, he talked me through them. 'Sometimes I'm the grave digger' he told me, thrusting a picture of himself with a spade into my hand; 'and here I am as the pharmacist,' a picture of the same man with a mortar and pestle. Despite the slightly cranky qualities one instinctively diagnoses in a character of such irregular occupation, I sensed that this fellow was no fool. Furthermore, his ancient and contented appearance belied an ambitious appetite for travel, in particular to Europe, for which excursion he was collecting addresses. I was given his, in return for which my own was requested. This was a tricky one as, when I had left England, it was under the shadow of impending court proceedings for my eviction on the grounds of being an illegal tenant. I gave him my employer's address as an alternative, and was surprised when, several months later, I received a Christmas card from Dodge City.

After perusing the rest of the museum, I took a stroll down the main street, following the wake of a stetson-topped buckle-booted fellow who, it transpired, was a visitor rather than an exhibit. All the shops were, I'm sure, faithful reconstructions of the originals, as was the saloon, which, like the jail, was smaller than the movies would lead one to believe. What has to be considered I suppose, is that it is difficult to convincingly record a movie in a space which would scarcely accommodate the personnel and apparatus of the film crew. A similar misconception has for years been purveyed by the producers of Coronation Street, who assert that the average living room of a terraced working man's home in the North of England, is the size one would associate with a residence in the affluent suburbia of the Surrey stockbroker belt. American middle class sitcom living rooms meanwhile, would appear to be capable of accommodating space shuttles while still leaving room to swing an adult snow leopard held by the extreme end of its tail.

The saloon in Dodge was of more modest, and I don't doubt, realistic proportions, a realism that extended beyond the dimensions, to the materials, wood being the prevailing commodity used for walls and floor, which creaked pleasantly beneath my heavy boots. I consciously enjoyed the sound of my footfall on the bare planking which served to reinforce the comforting illusion that I was a pretty heavy dude. Fortunately, the old folks masquerading as the original proprietors of this celebrated emporium were not of wardrobe proportions, and failed to disturb my egotistical self-appraisal. In fact, the old couple in the pharmacy looked as ancient as to tempt speculation that they might indeed have been the original incumbents of the incinerated street, of which this was a replica.

'This is exactly like the pharmacy that was here when I was a boy,' the elderly pharmacist assured me. I believed him.

THE QUESTION OF THE BUFFALO BURGER

The last shop on the street was a restaurant, and it was open for business, dispensing food whose, 'sell by' date was positively twentieth century. I noted, that among other things, the restaurant served buffalo burgers. Now, as someone who worries about the moral and environmental implications of what I eat, I had to think twice about this. To give myself more time for consideration, I went outside into the roasting afternoon sun, where an original engine from the Santa Fe railway stood reflecting heat like a big mobile radiator. I had been told by the old boy in the pharmacy, that a herd of buffalo was kept nearby, from which I inferred that there was no danger of the animals becoming extinct. Given that we are living in a more environmentally aware, albeit more destructive age, than the nineteenth century, I reckoned that whoever was responsible for the herd could work out that if all the buffalo were eaten, then there wouldn't be any more left to make money from in future. Since I understood that the animals were not the victims of intensive farming, that ruled out our objections on the humanitarian side, at least as it related to most of the animal's life, so really I was left asking myself the question, 'Have you become a vegetarian yet?' I had only a moderate appetite and was motivated more by curiosity than genuine need, after all it's not every day that you get the chance to tuck into a buffalo burger.

Increasingly these days I suffer moral qualms about eating meat. For one thing, it's very uneconomic to produce. There are staggering figures relating to how much land is needed to raise crops to feed cattle, when we could as easily eat those crops ourselves. That aside, the slaughtering of animals does seem, in spite of all the regulations to limit suffering, a damn nasty business. I saw sheep slaughtered in a New Zealand abattoir once, and the sight has remained with me as one of my most vivid recollections. I was a cadet at the time, on a ship berthed in the small South Island town of Bluff, where we were loading lamb for Japan. The Japanese, incidentally, eat very little meat, and most of the lamb we took there was minced up with flavourings to make what passed for fish paste. The raw material for this paste were milling about in a large holding pen oblivious to the fate which awaited them at the top of a ramp, up which they were encouraged to run by the aptly named 'Judas sheep,' whose example was followed by the hundreds of ill informed beasts. The Judas sheep, having made its run, is led off to safety to repeat the manoeuvre for the 'benefit,' of others who arrive later. Out of the sight, thankfully, of the sheep in the barn, just beyond the top of the ramps, lurk the killers. They work in pairs, one performing the deadly deed, whilst the other handles a simple preliminary. Both looked like characters from a nightmare; either Maoris or Samoans, these hugely-muscled, ghoulish apparitions, with brutish features set in expressions of total indifference, hungrily awaited their helpless victims. So outrageous was the appearance of the ones I saw that day, that I speculated on the possibility of a Hammer Film's talent scout rejecting both on the grounds of being unrealistically over the top. The success of suspending disbelief must depend to some extent on the plausibility of an appearance being genuine; these jokers looked like they'd gone to sleep in the make up room and fallen prey to the overzealous efforts of the special effects crew. The actual killer was the worst; a huge shambling figure, his face hung in folds through which reddened eyes peered balefully with the zombie-esque despair of one who kills because he must. This was the archetypal brute, whose encounter on a dark night in an alleyway, would not be welcomed; a brightly lit supermarket on a Saturday afternoon, for that matter, would be bad enough. Here, mooning over his theatre of gore, huge blade in hand, rubberized apron glistening blood like a matador's cape, he was indubitably in his element, gazing toward the ramp as Satan might, with hungry malice, await the howling souls which, fallen from grace, tumble into his roasting chamber of incomparable horror – a right tasty geezer.

One consolation the sheep enjoyed stemmed from the brevity of their discomfort as distinct from the protracted misery of Milton's hapless hordes. From the instant each creature arrived at the platform beyond the ramp, only a few seconds elapsed before its lifeless carcass rolled down a sloping rail on a hook to which one of its hind legs had been shackled by the slaughterman's assistant, prior to the rapidly executed throat laceration concluding with the severance of the spinal cord. It's a gruesome business to watch, as the twisting forms roll past, disgorging blood at a rate Sam Peckinpah at his most excitable extreme has failed to match. We were told that this method was as humane as any, and more so than some, since the duration of anxiety was minimal, given of course that the slaughterman did not walk amongst his victims peering intently into their faces with a bowl of mint sauce held to his salivating mouth. Such a prelude would, I am convinced, have promoted cardiac arrest, which is not only painful by all accounts but adversely affects the flavour of the meat.

Leaving aside for now, the moral indignation which these tastelessly frivolous comments might inspire, is not the pious rumination on the comparative misery to which we subject animals for the pleasure of our carnivorous appetites, just so much sentimental hypocrisy? Given that is, that we've bodged the moral workpiece by rejecting vegetarianism?

I'm inclined to the belief that our concern at the feelings of our dumb charges, reflects positively upon the spiritual status of the nation. I'm a great believer in the concept of a grand design, and I believe that animals exist partly to facilitate the working of that design by providing man with an opportunity to exercise the virtue of compassion. Those despairing of the existence, in this world, of any supreme being, frequently point to the tragedy, cruelty, and indifference of its people, in defence of their belief that no such intelligent creator can possibly exist. A world devoid of wrongdoing, in which all appetites were painlessly satiated without injurious side effects, would however, be a world without challenge, within which the spiritual evolution of the human race, about which I believe the purpose of life revolves, would be impossible.

The concern which society exhibits, by demanding humane slaughtering methods, represents a favourable reflection upon the humanity of the race that requires them. Departures from legal procedure by the people directly responsible for carrying out those procedures do not necessarily detract from that state of humanity unless those departures are public knowledge, and that public fails to respond with efforts to rectify the situation. The good or evil of people may be measured more accurately by the manner in which they respond to actions conducted on their behalf than by those actions themselves. The vociferous campaigns against the Vietnam war may well be judged to have said more about the American people than did the napalm that was dropped in their name. The people of the world, certainly in what we call the 'free' world, are wont to look back on the culture of previous centuries in a critical manner for its barbarous inferiority – a reflection that, in part at least, we are in my view justified in so doing.

One measure of the progress of spiritual evolution in a corporate sense, is the law. The law reflects the collective consciousness of the society that makes it. In this sense, the laws that control the slaughter of animals, demonstrate the compassion of the country that frames them. In the West, we are eager to chastise ourselves for hypocrisy when expressing repugnance at the punitive excesses of Islamic fundamentalists, whilst ignoring, for example, the parlous state of our own prisons. Similarly we are reminded of the White man's genocidal endeavours against the American Indians when condemning some of the more shocking traditions of those people. It is implicitly alleged by the more philosophic historians, that an intellectual superiority attaches to those who practise such enlightened self-effacement. In as much as such self-criticism is a healthy antidote to self-righteousness, it is a good thing, but to stifle expressions of retrospective outrage inspired by the cruel excesses of spiritually primitive societies, for fear of appearing hypocritical, is to exhibit a reticence that serves no purpose. If the Incas sacrificed humans then they were well out of order and no mistake, and we we should not be shy of saying so.

I believe our society is enjoying a degree of moral evolution, albeit with innumerable hiccups. Our concern over factory farming methods and the steady drift toward vegetarianism is evidence of that. Those who point to man's naturally omnivorous appetite as an adequate defence for its indulgence, deny the traditional concept that spiritual evolution is achieved through the denial of natural appetites. Most things are relative of course, and the measure of an act's morality must be made with reference to the circumstances of its perpetrator.

The vegetarian who finds meat physically repulsive, and never eats it, may of course be spiritually inferior to the man who loves it, but foregoes the pleasure three days a week in order to at least minimize the scale of the offence he feels himself to be committing.

Christ made this point abundantly clear when he contrasted the generosity of the poor woman flinging her two mites into the temple coffers, with the apparent largesse of the rich men unloading a small part of their wealth, the loss of which in no way prejudiced the enjoyment of the routine luxuries they enjoyed.

How much of what we might deem civilized behaviour, is the result of individual goodness, and how much the product of social engineering through regulation and peer pressure? That is the question that needs to be addressed in order to quantify an individual's spirituality.

A man protesting at the cruelty of bear baiting in the eighteenth century may warrant more applause for the exercise of his humanitarian instincts than a late twentieth-century man protesting at fox hunting, if only because what was then accepted as normal is now increasingly perceived as intolerable. The peer pressure has been reversed, so the personal courage which the protest demands, is less. It would of course be wrong to ascribe to the twentieth-century man an inferior spiritual status to his historical counterpart on the grounds that his dissidence demanded less moral courage. All that we can infer from a comparison of the acts is that one provides more evidence of moral courage than the other, which is not to say that one party necessarily possesses more moral courage than the other.

The hero whose heroism is identified and applauded as a result of fortuitous circumstance, may be no braver than the noble fellow whose anonymity is preserved by the unexceptional nature of his circumstances. For the conduct of such intimately subjective assessment, we must rely upon a power of much greater perception than our own, but for the measurement of a society's moral development, an examination of its law and punishment provides us with, if not an infallible gauge, at least a useful insight. It may be contended, for example, that the Iranian's restoration of Islamic fundamentalist penalties, such as the severance of hands for theft, marks their society's moral inferiority (compared to our own), as extreme behaviour of this kind represents the legitimacy which that society ascribes to the indulgence of revenge, a privilege which our own Bible clearly confines to God alone. When such savage revenge enjoys the authority of law, which supersedes the exercise of compassion, or the virtue of moderation, then the law, and those who administer and approve it, must surely be subject to criticism of moral inadequacy. Then again, if the Moslem believes this to be the will of God, who is he to argue? The decision has passed from his hands and he is simply the instrument of execution rather than the true judge.

In the West, with the exception of the USA, we have progressively rejected capital punishment, just as we have introduced welfare benefits to protect the less fortunate or successful members of society, as well as regulations to limit the distress of animals in our charge.

The collective indifference of the Spanish to the suffering which, in the name of sport, they inflict upon bulls, is an indictment of their reprehensible insensitivity. They, when accused by the British of cruelty, are inclined to retaliate by citing the frequency of child battering that takes place in this country, an offence which is apparently far less common in their own. The important distinction here, is that child abuse is against the law in Britain, whilst bullfighting is legal in Spain. Both savage indulgences reflect the moral imperfections of members of the respective populations, but the prohibition of child abuse in Britain exempts the legislature and therefore the collective conscience of the population from accusations of moral torpor. The Spanish authorities, however, cannot absolve themselves of the responsibility for bullfighting, since this macabre spectacle is endorsed by dint of a morally remiss authority which sustains a neglectful *laissez faire*.

Now all of these judgements depend to a great extent upon the recognition of fundamental or absolute truths about right and wrong. Most people would recognize evil in the encouragement of another's suffering. As definitions go, I suggest that is about as close to the universal perception as one can get; certainly as an example of evil it would qualify in most people's estimation.

To determine whether the bullfighter, or the bullfight spectator, is truly evil, it is necessary to discover whether pleasure depends upon the actual suffering or from associated amusements which are not necessarily dependant upon that suffering, however inevitable the suffering may be. It would require some subtle observation on the part of a judge to determine the psyche of a given subject . The degree of evil or culpability is more a function of motivation for, than consequence of, a given action.

British law certainly incorporates that belief in its sentencing policy, which takes more account of the perpetrator's intention than the consequences of his act. Thus it is that a drunken driver, despite the emotively vociferous demands of certain lobbies, is treated less harshly than the deliberate murderer, and rightly so. The drunken driver may be negligent, careless and most certainly optimistic or overconfident, but he does not proceed with the intention of causing harm; malice and evil are not features that dictate his behaviour. It could perhaps also be argued that the thief who, caught in the act of robbery, kills the man who confronts him, did not intend such a conclusion, and, more relevantly to our identification of evil, derived no pleasure from the act. The law tends to deal more harshly with those whose behaviour demonstrates clear evidence of premeditation, since such preparation bears witness to an evil resolve rather than an emotional aberration or tragic quirk of fate.

To return to the case of the blood-sportsman, in quantifying the degree of offensiveness of his act, it is necessary to isolate the precise source of his pleasure. If the pleasure for the fox hunter is in the chase, the contest of wits, of stamina, of resolve, or pure spectacle, to which the gruesome conclusion is incidental, then it may be argued that evil motivation is absent. Of course, the absence of evil is of little consolation to the fox, as it affects his fate no more than a drunken driver's victim is affected by the lack of evil motivation on the part of that driver. What is affected, however, is the regard in which we hold the perpetrators of these acts, and hence the penalties or lack of them, which their conduct earns them. In determining whether or not to outlaw the hunting of foxes in the traditional manner, the suffering of the animals is a prime consideration from a humanitarian viewpoint. But the motivation for taking such a legal initiative may draw from a well of spiritual ambition to advance the cause of human development. Conversely, in as much as our negligence in curbing the indulgence of evil is concerned, such negligence constitutes an indictment of our collective responsibility for promoting the spiritual evolution of society.

Where an evil pleasure in causing suffering is identified, the agents of that evil clearly deserve the opprobrium of which blood-sportsmen are popular targets. Since few advocates of the hunt would admit to an evil delight in the pursuit of their activity, the determination of the existence of evil must draw upon the art of intuitive speculation. To pursue the huntsman further, it may be argued that to sustain indifference to suffering, even if no conscious delight is drawn from it, is itself evidence of evil. Consider the wretched situation of the concentration camp inmate during the Second World War. Inured by repeated observations of torture, his response to the suffering of a fellow tortured prisoner is, let us say for argument's sake, one of indifference. Is he evil? I think not. The sadistic torturer on the other hand, who derives pleasure from his victim's pain, is clearly evil.

So where does this leave us? Is the fox hunter who enjoys the chase, but draws no pleasure from the fox's distress, evil? By our simple definition he is not, but can indifference to suffering amount to evil? The indifference of the concentration camp victim (the one witnessing but not being tortured), may be excused by the desperation of his circumstances, but where the indifference in question is exhibited by the perpetrator of the act, to the consequences of which he is indifferent, then his responsibility is surely manifest.

One hears of criminals, a minority of exceptional and unusually diabolical criminals, who are considered to have no conscience, people who quite simply do not possess the ability to feel guilt or remorse; the kind of person who can for example beat up a defenceless cripple and steal his money without a qualm. Whether that apparent incapability to feel remorse exists seems doubtful, since such an incapacity would, by the standards of the Christian faith at least, negate that person's reason for existence. It would not be fair to introduce into the world somebody who had no capacity for comprehending his own wrongdoing, any more than it would be fair to field a legless man in a running race. If justice is to be served, then the raw materials must be present from which to manufacture the finished item. If running a four minute mile is the objective, then the candidate must be equipped with legs to develop for the purpose. If spiritual perfection is the objective, then the candidate must have the capacity to feel sorrow, sympathy, pity, regret and remorse – the whole gamut of human emotion – in the absence of which he is not fully human, since this abstract potential is an ingredient of the soul. If justice is alive in the world, then even the most hardened of criminals must have the capacity, if not the inclination, to exercise these virtues.

How then to classify the degrees of evil reflected by different acts? The person who, in the course of a burglary, employs gratuitous violence, would, by the earlier definition, be considered evil. The person who, in the same circumstances, employs a level of violence that is the minimum necessary to effect the burglary, would rightly be deemed to be exhibiting at least a lesser degree of evil. By the prevailing standards of society, however, evil would still be attributed to his behaviour. The distinction of course must be made with reference to the motivation of the criminal. If the suffering the victim endured in the course of trying to protect his property is a matter of no consequence to the villain, then that villain may be judged to be guilty of a lesser degree of evil than the felon who derives pleasure from the violence he employs in the course of his efforts. This may seem like nit-picking, but the distinction is relevant to an analysis of evil and the consideration of 'guilt by indifference.' To put it bluntly, the thug who draws pleasure from causing as much misery as possible, must be judged more harshly than the thug who doesn't care for the fate of his victim, who he perceives only as an obstacle to his criminal endeavours. Both would be considered evil, but a difference in degree can be identified. Similarly, the fox hunter who loves the kill, and revels in its protraction, must be more evil than the huntsman who is indifferent to the fox's pain, which he views indifferently as the inevitable concomitant of the exercise of hunting.

If we accept that it is possible to be guilty of evil by indifference, then a charge may be laid at the door of the Western world for its neglect of the underdeveloped countries, where famine and disease are rife. One might pose the question; is the man who looks at the picture of a starving child on an appeal poster evil, if, despite his observation, he makes no contribution to the appeal fund? Most people would think that too harsh a condemnation, certainly there would be other factors to consider, such as laziness. A distinction could then be drawn between the man who intended to do something about the situation, by posting a cheque when he got home, for example, and the man who couldn't care less. Which is as much as to say that there is virtue in intention, even though it does not resolve itself in action. In other words, there is validity in the old maxim, 'It's the thought that counts.'

Not wishing to lose sight of the animal rights argument, it is frequently claimed that if each of us had to slaughter the animals we eat, we would all be vegetarians. I don't doubt this is true, so, are we any better than the slaughtermen whose unpleasant employment we sustain by our carnivorous appetites? That, I suggest, depends upon which slaughterman we are talking about. If we are talking about the slaughterman who enjoys the pain and fear he inflicts, then the answer is more likely to be yes than no, if we are comparing ourselves to the slaughterman who is indifferent to his victim's feelings then it is less likely to be yes, and if we are comparing ourselves to the fellow who hates the job and regrets the distress it entails, then the answer is much less likely to be yes. In the third case, the degree of evil exhibited by the vendor of death, becomes almost indistinguishable from our own responsibility for the animal's fate. In fact, judged against the earlier prerequisites for evil, he may upon examination emerge innocent of both malicious pleasure and guilt by indifference.

There is a parallel here with the reluctantly conscripted soldier. Donovan once wrote a song in which he endeavoured to lay the blame for military conflict upon the shoulders of the common soldier, simply because he conforms to prevailing expectations by joining up when so requested. The nasal bard implied that not only war but military forces were essentially wrong, which really opens a subject somewhat broader than the examination of pure evil so we'll leave that.

In endeavouring to absolve oneself from guilt over eating meat, whilst condemning those who revel in blood sports, the attempt to sustain a clear moral distinction can become harder the deeper one explores the subject. It is generally recognized, or at least accepted, that killing for pleasure is wrong. Very few animals kill for pleasure, and those that seem to, tend to be viewed with a caustic disdain which is sometimes used to justify their persecution by those, who in all probability, are searching hard for an excuse to enjoy themselves at another creature's expense, the case of the fox hunter again leaps to mind as the classic example. But what of the notion that killing for food is acceptable, but hunting for pleasure is not? If meat was essential to the human diet that claim might be sustainable, but what if it is not? A huge proportion of the human race call the lie to the claim that an omnivorous diet is essential, by surviving on a vegetarian one. What if meat isn't essential then, how can we justify eating it? Are we not merely eating it for pleasure, thus rendering us as culpable as the huntsman, of the charges we eagerly cast in his direction? Not quite, I hope, but I'm not sure. Returning to our definition of pure evil, the huntsman who enjoys the suffering, still comes out on top, or bottom, whichever way you look at it, but the difference between the huntsman who is simply indifferent to the suffering he causes, and the meat eater who displays a similar indifference, must be harder to determine.

Many a kind-hearted old lady sitting down to a steak and kidney pie, with a cat on her lap, would probably not take kindly to comparison with a blustering huntsman *hallooing* over the hillsides with a pack of hounds. She would probably respond to the suggestion that she was no better than he, with the protest that she could not contemplate such violent indulgence. The charge of hypocrisy is a tempting one to direct at the cat-stroking geriatric, and the only real defence against it, depends upon the nebulous notion that some moral virtue attaches to sensitivity. If that sensitivity resolves itself in a determination to reject meat eating, then the virtue is obvious, but if the sensitivity simply exists as an abstract entity which finds no tangible form in gastric policy, then does it retain its virtuous component? My hope is that it does, if all that it represents is a start, a step in the right direction on the path of spiritual evolution.

The basis of most religious theory relating to the purpose of life, is that it provides opportunities to develop through exercise, the spiritual aspirations around which the object of life revolves. In tune with this concept, is the perception of the world as a test-bed in which the spiritual potential of human engines can be evaluated. If there were no physical world, no pain or cold, or misery, hunger or disease, no lusts and temptations, then how could intellects and souls be developed? Could the processes of intellectual and spiritual evolution transpire in an intangible medium of non-physical suspension? If a host of souls were created with the same potential for good and evil as normal human beings, could they evolve spiritual identities and moral qualities in the absence of a material context? Would a bunch of pontificating ethereal entities progress toward spiritual perfection? It would be easy to sit around thinking good thoughts and academically rejecting all manner of cruel indulgence or selfish lusts, when those experiences lay outside the scope of one's ability to physically enjoy them. The realities of the world, with all its physical temptations and potential, provides the soul with a medium in which to explore and develop its own potential.

One hears of dragsters which 'will' produce colossal horsepower and are geared for some astronomic speed, but no one really knows how they will perform until they are tested on the track. If performance could be reliably predetermined by the construction engineers, or physicists, then the boffins could put their heads together and announce the winners without the need to burn fuel and rubber, whilst the absent spectators could be informed of the results without the inconvenience of leaving home. Life, thank God, is not like that. On mundane as well as sublime levels, it requires the stimulus of multifarious influences to determine a meaningful course. No one would trust a motorcycle that had never been ridden, and no one would trust a man who had never been born, or a God for that matter, is this not after all, why God sent his son into the world?

To return to the woman with the cat and the steak and kidney pie, we must ask ourselves, is her revulsion at the huntsman's indulgence, nothing more than hypocritical sentimentality? Or does the sensitivity from which her revulsion springs, reflect a degree of spirituality that, even in the absence of some tangible moral resolve, such as the adoption of vegetarianism, is nonetheless good? Or, like the decision of the soul in a jar, is it meaningless? With intelligent life forms, thought precedes action. The Bible warns against sin of the mind: thinking bad thoughts which are bad in themselves, even if they do not precipitate bad actions. If we accept this, then by inference, good thoughts are good in themselves, even if they do not resolve themselves in good actions. Perhaps then, the woman with the cat is a better person for thinking that hunting for pleasure is wrong, even though she still eats the steak and kidney pie?

It may seem that I am undoing my theory that the 'souls-in-jars' approach to spiritual attainment is inadequate without a physical context, to which my response must be that such isolation constitutes an inferior medium for spiritual exercise, though not an irrelevant one. Spiritual development can take place in the 'classroom,' but it requires the experience of the outside world to test it. The cat woman's sensitivity must earn her some points even in the absence of a critical introspection which might uncover a degree of hypocrisy. I say 'even,' when perhaps I should say 'because of.' If the woman's natural goodness tells her that gratuitous cruelty, as exhibited by some huntsman, is wrong, but her limited intellect inhibits her mind from the introspection which might disturb her unconscious complacency, then should she be criticized for foolish sentimentality, hypocrisy, or mental inadequacy? Certainly the third, possibly the second, but the first is, I suggest, a virtue rather than a vice. In short, soft-hearted people are better than hard-hearted people.

The measurement of evil must take account of the perpetrator's awareness of it, as well as their capacity for awareness, their perceptive potential if you like, or intellect. Let us suppose that the old lady is rather dim, and has never thought about the suffering associated with the slaughtering of the animals she eats; it would be unfair to ascribe to her a degree of evil which she clearly does not deserve. Evil by indifference would also be an unfair charge, given that she doesn't see the killing and is not directly exposed to the unpleasantness in the face of which indifference would be reprehensible. Perhaps a lesser charge of evil by stupidity could be levelled, but there is an argument that ignorance and thoughtlessness, which are often closely associated with the stupid, provide a defence against the charge of evil, since there is an absence of conscious malice.

The joy of stupidity and the burden of the intelligent, thoughtful and perceptive, sustain the justice of evaluating evil in terms of the capability of the evildoer to perceive the true nature of his actions. In that sense, life is a handicap game, in which the lower one's handicap the greater score one is expected to attain. Handicaps can take the form not only of varying degrees of intellectual prowess, but of environmental circumstances. A man raised in a rural hunting community, to believe that there is nothing wrong with hunting for fun, will require a greater moral effort to resist the temptation to indulge that evil, than will the man raised in a sensitive environment where such practices as ritual hunting, are viewed as barbarisms of a less civilized age. It cannot be a coincidence that most hunt supporters come from rural backgrounds, and most protesters from urban ones. No doubt the huntsmen view their town-dwelling antagonists as airy-fairy radicals who don't understand the country, and should mind their own business. What they would be unhappy to admit, one hopes, is that they had, by upbringing, been brutalized by evil practises which they regard as part of a normal way of life. Their background therefore provides them with a degree of protection from the full blast of moral indictment, as does the cultural heritage of the 'hands off' Islamic fundamentalist. That is not to say that their indulgences are not evil, or at least wrong, but that the quantifiable evil which they demonstrate in committing them enjoys a measure of circumstantial mitigation. To be fairer and in case one should wish to cloud the issue by introducing pest control arguments, it might be better to substitute hare coursing for fox hunting, since the hare is caught and then released from a sack to be pursued by hounds.

An intelligent, perceptive man who had been raised in a hunting community but who was aware nonetheless, that his enjoyment in inflicting pain was evil, could not really submit his upbringing as a defence for his wrongdoing, since his defence is destroyed by the intellect which facilitates the introspection whereby the evil is illuminated.

Kris Kristofferson hinted at this kind of wretched dilemma when he penned the poignant lyrics, 'never knowing if believing is a blessing or a curse,' the less poetic converse of which is even more concisely encapsulated by the fondly repeated assertion, 'ignorance is bliss.'

All of these thoughts passed through my mind as I sat on the bleached timbers of the sidewalk stirring my boots in the Kansas dust. It was while contemplating the prospect of a buffalo burger, my curious appetite competing with moral reservation, that a bell tinkled quaintly. It tinkled a second time as I pushed open the glass panelled door, and stepped into the cool air of the restaurant. Surveying the refreshing milk shake and Ma Orvilles' enticing Home Baked Cookies, I pulled a crumpled five-dollar bill from the sweat-stained breast pocket of my shirt. The sales girl in the blue cotton print dress smiled inquiringly at me, unconscious of the introspective preamble to the spoken order that my lips now framed, 'Buffalo burger please.'

BEYOND THE BURGER

Sharing the restaurant with me were a brace of swine in cowboy outfits. I don't mean that these people just LOOKED like pigs, I mean they WERE pigs, monstrous bloated porkers, squelching out of their fancy embroidered shirts like over-filled sausages, silently stuffing their incessantly moving mouths without conversation, mute caterpillars remorselessly chomping through the leaves to which they clung with glutinous tenacity. I can take people dressed up as cowboys if they are engaged in herding cattle, or at least riding horses, but I find this infantile role-playing by adults a little hard to swallow. The boar and sow duo, who, judging by their complexions, cleanliness, effete powderyness and Ford pick-up; came as close to equestrian hardship as a London stockbroker, cut a comic if ludicrous picture. Heads bent over their troughs, boot-lace ties swinging in their french fries, they sustained a speechless commitment to their feast, indifferent to the scrutiny to which I was subjecting them.

The boar wore spectacles, contraptions which always seem at odds with the cowboy identity. Who, after all, ever saw a cowboy wearing spectacles? Did Clint Eastwood ever wear spectacles? Did John Wayne or Kirk Douglas ever wear spectacles? Of course they didn't. The frightened clerk in the telegraph office wore spectacles, the wretched teller in the bank with his hands in the air and a gun at his back, wore them, and the owner of the general store was allowed them too, but NOT the cowboy. They just didn't go with the hat and the bandanna, and not even John Denver could change that. A cowboy, disturbed from his slumber at the base of a tree by some ill intentioned rogue, might scrabble for his gun – but how would he have looked, fumbling amongst the leaf mould for his spectacles? In the Wild West, you either had good eyesight or you didn't go. If you were a little on the myopic side of 20-20 then you squinted. Squinting was OK for your prairie cred, in fact, squinting was positively encouraged. Charles Bronson always squints, whilst Clint Eastwood indulges in the mannerism so much it dictates the whole pattern of his face, the contours of which have, over the years, aligned themselves with the demands of this threatening affectation, though one suspects that in his case the expression may have owed more to cheroot smoke than myopia. Either way, this squinting business can look pretty cool if you can carry it off. I put off wearing glasses for years so I could cultivate the Clint Eastwood look. I reckoned that by the time I was forced to hook on the lenses I had the features trained to a tee. All I needed to do was jack them up about a foot higher.

All this aside, there was no getting away from the fact, that if you packed a gun, glasses were a no-no. I guess you might just have got away with contact lenses, provided that is, that nobody saw you putting them in at sun up, or taking them out at night. Imagine it, as the harmonica notes drift with the campfire smoke across the star-speckled prairie skyline, what kind of anomaly would be represented by the sight of a cowboy silhouetted by the moonlight with a vanity mirror in one hand and eyelid hitched up like a girl's skirt; what would Wishbone, the stubble chinned cook from *Rawhide*, make of that? Staring with inquisitive disbelief from a perch in the tail of a chuck wagon, a gnarled gargoyle of the saucepans, his caustic response might easily be imagined. 'What in tarnation are yer doing boy?'

'Oh just taking out my contact lenses Wishbone; a man can't sleep in contact lenses.' Nope, I'm sorry, no glasses, no contact lenses, I'm just not having it!

The frauds in the restaurant, with their cameras on the table and their plump soft hands, and their spectacles, weren't fooling me, no sir. They did interest me, however, as archetypal specimens of an odd breed of ludicrous wannabees. I watched, fascinated as the sow bent over the table, fat migrating laterally to accommodate the movement, like snow churned outwards to the roadside by a mobile plough, as she hinged at the middle, a ponderous dowager of the dinner plate, to capture another mouthful of steaming burger in her gaping maw. Bowed in this quest, the expanse of stretched shirt striving against long odds to retain the integrity of its seams, suggested to me the absence of some familiar component. Without taking conscious thought, I had been searching, I realized , for the irregular inky stamp of the familiar trademark, 'DANISH'. The absence of the lettering clearly indicated that this commercial labelling was performed after, rather than before slaughter, indicating that the beast before me was still clearly being fattened for the kill.

All was now clear to me, and so, with the crystal vision of the spiritually enlightened, I was able to leave the restaurant in a superior mood of gnostic calm, my departure drawing no trace of interest from the swollen feeders who, like frenzied hyenas lost in the orgy of a hapless wildebeest carcass, paid me no heed.

I spent a half-hour wandering Main Street. The buildings, according to the characters employed about the place, represented a faithful reconstruction of the original line-up which had burned down in the fire many years ago. A great shame I thought, but that's one of the dangers of building from wood, its longevity is less assured.

Frankly, I get a bit fed up with these buildings that are forever burning down, particularly when you can't see how the deuce they can. I mean buildings that aren't made from wood. Buildings made almost entirely from stone, or brick, or steel and glass, magically turn into infernos when someone drops a lighted cigarette in a corner. When I think of the tiresome efforts I spent trying to coax life into a campfire back in my scouting days, half a dozen hungry patrol members standing around like ravenous Oliver Twists, cutlery sets, enamel plates, and empty cocoa mugs a-jangle with anticipation, whilst I crouched, blowing at some feeble ember, it makes me sick to think of these splendid municipal buildings sprouting flame into the sky like man-made volcanoes just because someone drops a dog-end in a corner. How do they do it? It has to be sabotage. I never believe this fag-end bullshit, or the 'frayed wire on a light fitting' theory. How can they know, how can anyone possibly know, when they're looking at a pile of ashes that used to be a five-story department store, that the fire started in a cupboard on the second floor, at the back of the women's lingerie department, where an electric heater shorted out against a shoe rack? Was there somebody inside the cupboard watching it go spark, and then calmly walking home as their site of employment went up in smoke, telling the puzzled fireman about it later when quizzed by the investigating officer? Or do they have an old gipsy swathed in scarves, bent over a crystal ball with a reverse gear to provide a retrospective potential. No, these Sherlock Holmes-like deductions have to be, to quote a Yiddish colloquialism, 'a load of old moody.' My guess is they've got a list of possible causes of fires in a book, like a string of recipes. When the newspaper reporter rings up to ask for an opinion on the source of the fire, they simply open the pages and pick one out, with the proviso that it wasn't the same one they used last time.

Despatch company controllers employ the same kind of deceit when impatient clients ring to ask why their packages haven't arrived. 'What shall we tell them this time?' the desperate apologists wonder. Flat tire? Broken clutch cable? Stopped by the police? No, we used that one on this client last time! Anything but the truth is the normal recourse. One company I worked for employed a girl called Caroline who was so dim that, when jokingly told to explain to the client that a lorry-load of caged monkeys had overturned on the A4, and the rider was helping the driver recapture them, she actually repeated the story verbatim to the sceptical caller. 'Oh yeah, no bullshit mister, straight up, a lorry load of monkeys, that's what he told us.' The expression on the boss's face as she relayed this transparent fantasy was something to behold as he covered his features with both hands while silently erasing another name from his shaky customer base.

'He's hung-up Les,' squawked Caroline, spitting her chewing gum into a bin.

'Course he's hung up Caroline,' groaned Les the boss, 'he thinks you're taking the piss out of him.'

'Well that's what you told me to say Les,' persisted Caroline with defensive petulance.

'It – was – a – joke, Caroline,' explained Les, labouring the words for emphasis. 'A – fuck – ing – joke!'

I class these frayed electricity cables in the same category of inspired speculation. If the truth be known, most fires are inspired by the imaginative initiatives of employees in the government job creation departments, who operate to cultivate employment for firemen, demolition contractors, and builders. When they're not actually engineering disasters, they're ringing round with hoax warnings to keep the boys on their toes, which explains why ninety-nine times out of a hundred, when you pass the scene of a supposed fire, dramatically surrounded by engines sprouting hoses all over the street like so much limp spaghetti, there isn't the slightest whiff of smoke in the air. It's all so disappointing, just when you expect to see a cheery blaze lighting up the night sky, surrounded by a band of opportunistic chestnut vendors, all you find is a blue posse of superfluous fire fighters standing around lamely, like bloodthirsty commandos whose enemy has fled. The only decent fires one ever sees, where chaps are really up ladders pumping thousands of gallons into indifferent infernos, as they should be, are the ones on the Nine O'clock News, which are all pieced together using touched up old war footage from the blitz. As I said, it's all moody.

Dodge City Main Street did, I believe, burn down. There doesn't seem to be much doubt about that, anymore than the probability of the fire having been caused by an oil lamp with a china reservoir being knocked over during a brawl and setting the curtains of the saloon ablaze. That kind of explanation I can believe, because it was ALWAYS happening in the Westerns, every time there was an indoor fracas in fact. Which prompts the question, why were people so slow to recognize the advantages of manufacturing these lamp bases from some material that didn't smash every time they hit the floor? There were, after all, such things as metal containers around in the nineteenth century. They had canned baked beans didn't they? Those delicate china paraffin vessels made perfect Molotov cocktails, and considering the preponderance of clumsy inebriated oafs stumbling around Dodge City in those days, it might have been prudent to have had a by-law dealing with the subject. Still, I suppose we shouldn't thirst for too much bureaucracy, a sentiment I am sure the rowdy desperadoes of Dodge would have echoed.

The pity of it all is that the original street burned down, awful bloody shame. Like most people I like things to be original, and it's irritating to discover, after staring at a spot on the ground for several minutes, convinced that beneath it lies Ed Masterton, 'who argued with the wrong man's brother,' that in reality, his headstone marks nothing more sophisticated than a community of woodlice.

Beyond Main Street was a large detached house which had, apparently, been the residence of a local dignitary, whose descendants bequeathed it to the historical trust under whose stewardship it was now open to the public. Inside, I discovered to my pleasure, a pretty teenage girl – a real one. Dressed in clothes of nineteenth-century style, she sat gently oscillating in the comfort of an upholstered rocking chair.

'Howdy,' came the laconic greeting as she eyed me with a steady confidence, unusual for a girl of her years. It made me wonder whether her apparent poise was the product of a surprisingly premature worldliness, or the innocent reflection of a pleasantly dim intellect. From the ensuing conversation I discovered that she lived in Dodge City, had lived there all of her life, and that this undemanding occupation represented her regular employment. I was led to the conclusion that the last part of my idle speculation was more probably the correct one. This was the kind of girl who could sit happily on a five-bar gate, a straw between her perfectly formed white teeth, staring dreamily at the floating clouds, mesmerized by the soporific hum of energetic insects, against which musical backdrop she is borne in on the gently undulating swells of an endless summer's afternoon.

The imagery engendered by her sensually smiling presence, returned me to that dreamy epoch of my adolescent school days when, armed with a quart of Bulmer's Woodpecker and a copy of Laurie Lee's 'Cider With Rosie,' I had reclined against the timbered walls of the potting shed on a pile of dusty hessian sacks, studying the distant forms of the sixth-form netball team springing athletically about the court in their pleated white skirts. Fearing a pathetic conclusion to these nostalgic reflections in such amiable company, I disentangled myself from the web of dangerous sentimentality into which I had unwittingly flown, by making my farewells, and stumbling outside into the harsh dry heat that prevailed on the latter side of high noon.

It seemed no cooler now than it had when I arrived in Dodge, but I had a few more jobs to consume some time before the sun sank to a less tortuous altitude. There were letters to post and a phone call to be made. The local post office helped me out with a fistful of dimes, which I fed into a coin operated box in the entrance lobby. The voice on the other end of the line sounded surprised, 'You're where? Dodge City – Kansas – USA! I thought you were in Bethnal Green!'

'That's a funny thing' I thought, I must have forgotten to tell Pepper I was planning to visit her. The last time I'd seen her she was waving goodbye through the back window of a taxi, as I stood outside my prefab in London's East End while my late neighbour's house swung through the air on the hook of a mobile crane. It was not the kind of act that bolstered a sense of residential security, and as I polished my shades in preparation for the demands of the afternoon sun, I pondered the possibility of the old hut still being where I had left it, filled with my worldly possessions that I'd entrusted to the doubtful stewardship of a friend, whose good intentions usually exceeded his ability to realize them.

I'd left London with an eviction order hanging, like the sword of

Damocles over my head, with no guarantee that my home would be where I had left it upon my return. As I pulled out of Gunsmoke Street on to Wyatt Earp Boulevard, Bethnal Green, London, England all seemed a long long way away. The redeeming, if transient, advantage, of being evicted from a house five thousand miles away, is that the sense of immediate distress is diminished by distance, rather as a telephoned threat is a little less alarming than one made by a man brandishing a fist in your face. Eviction, like death, is one of the world's grim realities which is best pressed firmly into the back of the mind, where it can jolly well stay until the relentless march of time conscripts it from the ranks of pestilence to wreak its cheerless havoc.

For the moment, I steered my mind toward happier considerations. Why should I worry anyway ? I'd seen Dodge City and was leaving it, alive, and it's not everyone that can say that. Bat Masterton certainly couldn't, and neither could his compadre beneath the turf, Cactus Pete.

As I rode west into the sinking sun, the late afternoon flies clustered between my fingers where they curled motionless on the fat rubber grips of the bars, their stunned cadavers drying rapidly in the austere bakery of the plain's natural grill. With each movement of clutch or throttle, I felt their dehydrated carcasses crunching like crisps within the gory mangle of my sunburnt digits.

Meanwhile, overhead, a great black claw of cloud stretched ominously across the sky. A threatening army of dark vaporous menace, racing along my flank with its damp legions of unwelcome precipitation. In an endeavour to outrun the threat, I increased my pace to sixty miles per hour then sixty-five. Wet heralds tickled my bald scalp, prompting the throttle hand with a defensive automation that pushed the speedometer needle to seventy and then seventy-five miles per hour whilst my weather eye maintained a nervous scrutiny of the moist claw whose progress I hoped to outstrip. With growing apprehension, I felt the contact of more water speckles; a fat drop exploded on the lens of my glasses, the headlight chrome was starred with water, whilst the cloud, moving in a north-westerly direction, was converging with my own vessel. What did the rules for the prevention of collision at sea dictate? Stand on for a vessel crossing from port to starboard, maintain course and speed. The problem here was that the other vessel was navigated by a force that hadn't read the rule book. There seemed little prospect of it giving way, maybe it wasn't even looking where it was going, maybe the bridge of this colossal airship was manned by an uncertificated officer, maybe it wasn't manned at all or, worse still, maybe it was manned by a Greek! A chilling thought indeed. I glanced upwards as another fat drop disintegrated upon the left lens of my specs. I retaliated by opening the throttle further; eighty miles per hour appeared on the dial. My old Shovelhead Harley wouldn't have liked this, my fillings would have been rattling loose by now, but the Evolution-engined beast beneath me seemed to be getting even smoother as I speeded up. Thank God I didn't have to wear a helmet, at this speed the strap would be practically decapitating me. Blessedly I out-ran the rain.

REALTERS

I was unusually glad to finish today's riding. I'd enjoyed it but the constant wind and higher speeds, coupled with the anxiety about rain had tired me and I was pleased to pull up outside my room at the motel, cut the engine and kick down the sidestand. Hitching the throw-over bags onto my shoulder, I felt every bit the cowboy at the end of a day riding the range as I pushed the key into the door and focused on the interior.

Dumping my exhausted carcass on the double bed, too tired to read, I switched on the television. The programme to which I was tuned was about a multi-millionaire who'd written a book explaining the secret of his success; my interest was aroused. The programme took the form of an open discussion in which several dozen of Mr Slick's disciples were arranged atop an outdoor podium, seated on chairs from which they would individually rise to provide their personal testimony to the effectiveness of their mentor's methods. How had these people made their fortunes, I wondered? Had they learnt the art of academic success and become accomplished professional people? Had they developed a skill for which there was a broad and urgent demand? Had they concocted some brilliant innovation that enhanced the efficiency of industrial processes? Were they, in short, employing their time in any manner likely to be of value to America or the human race in general? Of course not, they were doing what many of the parasites who make huge fortunes fast do, sucking the blood of men's toil by latching leech-like, onto the housing market, and creaming off the profits from insanely escalating inflation, to which, through their involvement, they provide an additional impetus.

Realtors is what these scum are called in the USA. What we in this country would call with equally euphemistic generosity, estate agents. If ever a more unnecessary breed of poisonous spongers inflicted itself upon society, then I have not heard of them. Drug dealers, by contrast, are a comparatively benign bunch, since their merchandise does not constitute one of life's necessities, but appeals simply to the overactive appetites and curiosities of the foolish or wayward. Everyone, however, needs a roof over their head, and to force people into lives of penury for the purpose of fattening the plump fungi who masquerade as worthy middlemen, is, to my mind, far worse than peddling drugs which no one really needs. The building societies have a lot to answer for too, as their escalating lending has pushed the whole situation, at least in Britain, out of the world of sanity and moderation.

These dealers in debt are, to the housing market, what a water selling cartel, charging exorbitant rates, represents to a parched desert traveller. It seems that America, in common with Great Britain, has yet to devise a compromise that recognizes and encourages healthy entrepreneurism, whilst discouraging the conniving of these fare-dodging, back-breaking freeloaders.

What appalled me about the realtors in the TV programme, was that rather then keeping their heads low and cultivating a discreet anonymity, as might heroin dealers, these wretches were standing up like keen school kids eager to impress the class with their knowledge, and blatantly admitting the offences against society, of which they were proudly guilty. Had the programme producer possessed a gram of sensitivity, the faces of the miscreants might have been obscured by black oblongs, whilst dim lighting and low volume, appropriate to the shame of their confessions, could have been employed. Not a bit of it. Each told his story with a guiltless ingenuity that assumed the sad naivety of a large proportion of the American public. As the grand puppeteer of deceit called upon each person in turn, up they would pop, polished mannequins of success, oozing clean-cut enthusiasm, to briefly explain how, after a number of successful property deals, they were able to give up their regular, often useful employment, and sit back raking in interest from profits and rents.

As one bright-eyed turd after another jumped up to tell their personal tale of happiness and degradation, a deepening sense of nauseous disbelief ballooned inside me like the gassy prelude to noxious flatulence. As the slime bucket reappeared to announce, with the plastic enthusiasm of a game show host, 'Yes folks, you too could become a millionaire,' I switched off the set, deriving slight satisfaction from my power to check the flood of poison, at least within the confines of my rented kingdom.

The whole sickly show was like a parody of the most facile profile that America ever projects of itself. The entire stomach-turning charade served to encourage the question, why is such garbage not rejected on the grounds of being too tasteless to broadcast? As a self-inflicted indictment of American society, I saw no worse example throughout the time that I was in the USA, than this embarrassing pantomime of moral bankruptcy.

Perhaps those who penned the anti-drug slogan, 'Just say no,' should turn their pens on the realters and urge us to,

'Just say die, scumbag.'

BUTTERMILK BLUES

I liked Colorado and was enjoying my morning's ride at a steady fifty-five miles per hour, the giant engine loping easily along at half its potential speed. Up ahead I spotted a general store and down changed, signalling well in advance and leaning the bike gently toward the well marked landing strip across which I weaved a little unnecessarily for the sheer joy of doing something other than heading in a straight line. I wanted to buy a few bits and pieces among which was numbered a carton of buttermilk. I'd never had it before, but the name appealed to me. Two attractive words with smooth, pleasing associations, combined in one name, can't be bad I thought. I was wrong. Before I had a chance to find out, however, my attention was diverted by a small drama unfolding outside in the parking lot.

A young couple were sitting in a compact Ford eating sandwiches. The driver's door was open, the driver's leg outside it, his foot resting on the ground as he chatted to the woman alongside him. As I paused, a few yards away with my carton of milk, I became aware that a note of anxiety had crept into the warming Colorado morning. A Chevrolet saloon with two elderly women aboard, one of them at the wheel, was backing slowly toward the car with the couple in it. There was something about the movement of the Chevy, in conjunction with the manner of its driver, which suggested that here was a vehicle that was not properly under control. The driver's blue rinsed head, barely protruding above the back of the seat, was held stiffly at an upward tilted angle, while the hands on the wheel gripped it with a desperate resolution, pulling the upper body close to the windscreen, the resulting posture suggesting a conspiracy of myopia with paralysis.

The signs were not good and as the Chevy was moving backwards with no apparent movement of the steering wheel, it seemed inevitable that in the course of time it would collide with the Ford. The driver of the threatened vehicle had clearly reached the same conclusion and had suspended eating to withdraw his leg, close the door, wind down the window and simultaneously sound his horn. Incredibly, the car kept coming. I shouted, but to no avail, deafness was clearly among the woman's encyclopaedia of

115

disorders. Surely she'll stop, surely she must hear that horn now, surely... *Cruuummmp*! The rear fender of the Chevrolet impacted the door of the Ford as the driver shot upright, standing on his seat and thrusting his head and torso through the sun roof as he flung the remains of a sandwich in the direction of the attacking vehicle. In the Chevy, the two old ladies rocked momentarily up and down like nodding dogs on a parcel shelf as contact was made. Then, in comical unison, their heads, as if operated by a common ratchet, turned slowly inboard and backward, the faces peering astern, one alongside the other, a siamese geriatric surveying the reason for this abrupt termination of its manoeuvre.

The Ford's driver had now jumped clean through his sun roof and was studying the penitent pensioner with an implicit rage that her gender and age frustrated him from exercising. His tongue however, was definitely within bounds.

'Lady did you not hear me hooting? I mean, 'I hooted,' he said as he squeezed an imaginary bullhorn.

'Sir I heard you,' rasped the old lady, 'I heard a horn and I looked to the left and then I looked to the right.' She gestured with a veiny hand first in one direction, and then the other, turning her head each way in turn for emphasis, retracing the acts of the pantomime as if seeking to convince herself that all possible precautions had been taken.

'I couldn't see anyone at all so I just kept going.'

This perplexed the young man for a moment, and he straightened up whilst digesting the idiocy of the remark before continuing.

'Call me old fashioned lady, but when I'm going backwards I have a habit of looking behind me.'

There was an unassailable logic in this but I lost the finer points of the argument, as I had my own problems to contend with in the form of the buttermilk. I really didn't wish to have my life complicated by being a witness to a minor, non-injury accident and had walked on a few yards to absent myself from the scene of the misery.

Now one hears occasionally about the mugging of tourists in America, and while my experience with the carton of buttermilk will not appear among any police statistics, it bloody well should have done, at least some charge under the product liability laws might have been brought. If ever a name belied an identity this was it. What kind of imagery does the name 'buttermilk' conjure up? Smooth, creamy, bland, milky even? All of these culinary preconceptions primed my palate with optimistic anticipation; how cruelly disappointed I was.

Making a generous opening in the corner of the carton, I tipped it backward so that the contents poured rather than gargled out of their container, striking the back of my throat like a snowy Niagara, and provoking a spasm of nausea more powerful than anything I'd suffered since I gulped a mouthful of chemicals that had been quietly restoring a badly-stained mug I'd picked up by mistake in the back of a bike shop. Had a concoction of the most piquant sauces blended with the bile of a terminal dyspeptic filled that carton, it could scarcely have revolted me more. The lease on my mouth enjoyed by the disgusting effluent was as brief as it was putrid and with a spontaneous contraction of muscle that prompted something between a shout and a vomit, I belched the poisonous scum over the bleached paving stones of the parking lot. After staring at the carton as if some explanation might be forthcoming from the benign cow decorating its waxed walls, I took a pace toward a nearby litter bin and dropped the gruesome pack inside. It hit the bottom with a fat *plop*, while I peered after it much as the victor in a mortal struggle might watch his enemy plummeting to certain death beyond the edge of a precipice. That cigarette packs carry health warnings when items like this do not, poses as serious an indictment of American health priorities as any that I came across between the Atlantic and Pacific Oceans.

COLORADO

On the road again in warm sunshine, I rode for two or three miles, spitting profusely as the dreadful taste slowly faded into the grim recesses of my injured memory.

I liked the look of Colorado. A sign by the roadside proudly proclaimed, 'COLORFUL COLORADO' and so it is. I was riding through flat dry territory, speckled with bushes and rocks, which, from the variety of colours, might have tumbled from a fountain of blended pigments brushed across the landscape with the sensitivity of a Van Gogh, they bear witness to a creative force of incomparable subtlety.

Fruit and vegetable stalls punctuated the roadside, the swollen lushness of the wares suggesting the operation of artificial irrigation in this dusty environment. Sad donkeys, some wearing straw hats, perforated to accommodate their ears, stood sulkily beneath trees while the dark-skinned fruit vendors lounged beneath their tattered canopies, eyeing the passing Harley as I rolled by at little more than a man's running pace, counting the revs. The housing in this region was, to the exclusion of all else, poor. Flaking paint characterized the tired timbers of these rural cabins whose dilapidated porches hosted the crude furniture on which sleepy Mexicans could be identified, slumbering beyond curtains of drying fig plants.

Screen doors swung in the light warm breeze and chickens pecked about the rustling rug of autumnal leaves, kicking up dust and strutting the weathered planking of sun-bleached verandas.

Though providing scant sign of affluence, these simple homes conveyed an earthy karma with their hanging plants, stone jars and corn cobs, scattered like features in a Harvest Festival painting from a bygone age. Not a satellite dish in sight, these were dwellings at peace with the environment, which they complemented as plants do a rockery. I was reminded of Steinbeck's *Cannery Row* and its slothful population of likeable winos, harmlessly unfolding their lives under the Californian sun with a little bounty of the vine to lubricate them through the trickier phases, and a little more still to fill in the gaps.

I stopped tonight at the town of Pueblo where I booked into a motel before taking a walk around the warm evening streets. It

118

seemed a safe enough place, the tidy grid of tree-lined pathways separating comfortable detached wooden houses with well kept gardens. An elderly man playing a hose over his well-tended lawn broke concentration to wish me a good evening, while a pretty dark-haired girl shouted from the open window of an Oldsmobile packed to the gills with revellers. She waved me toward her, but the battered car wallowed onwards, its tyres squealing slightly as the soft suspension sank on a tight corner, and then she was gone, a memory of white teeth wavy black hair and slim brown limbs. Probably for the best I thought as I strolled back to my motel.

It was a warm night, though it was more than heat that kept me awake. From outside my room came the ceaseless banter of what sounded like a drunken rabble. I couldn't make out quite what they were saying, though it sounded for the most part like a continuous chorus of jovial jibes characterized by volume rather than wit. After half an hour of this tiresome evensong, I climbed onto a chair to look out of the high narrow window facing the source of the din. All I could make out was a correspondingly narrow window in the building opposite, and through it, an impression of bars along which a hatted figure was walking. I'd spent a while deliberating upon which motel I should stay in this night and, as I now realized, had rather cleverly plumped for the one that backed on to the local jail – brilliant.

THE ROCKIES

I'd been riding toward the clouds for several hours, the long, low line of darkness slowly gaining form and substance as I rolled westward toward what I imagined was some seriously bad weather. It's a curious thing how the mind, once convinced of something, sometimes totally fails to explore any other possibility or interpretation – rather like a motorcycle caught in a tram line – until reality is forced upon it by unassailable evidence. The 'clouds' up ahead were acquiring a distinctly well-defined outline that aroused my suspicions to the point where I stopped, unfolded my map of the United States and drew a startling conclusion – I had arrived at the Rocky Mountains.

I hadn't expected the change from flatlands to mountains to be quite so abrupt. I'd assumed there would be an intermediary landscape of gently rolling hills that would gradually lead into the Rockies proper, but no. From a distance the massive dividing range that separates the West from the rest looks every bit as defined as the Great Wall of China.

The curving roads and dramatic scenery that I soon found myself amongst, provided a welcome contrast to the arrow-straight blacktop that I'd followed for what seemed like forever, across plains and prairies. Up ahead the bulk of an eighteen-wheel Peterson broke into view. Like the one in the movie *Convoy*, it was haulin' logs and making something of a meal of the effort. I doubted if the truck's speed was much above ten miles an hour, a speed which it achieved at the expense, I imagined, of a frighteningly high fuel consumption judging by the great clouds of black diesel smoke belching out of its polished exhaust stack. They're magnificent beasts these American trucks, with their huge bonnets, massive fenders, and horns like ship's whistles. European style units with their engines below the cab just don't cut it. They're like the Chinamen of the road haulage world – all weak chins and button noses. Just as the old steam trains with their boilers, funnels and huge flywheels, evoke far more sentiment than the featureless diesels which succeeded them, so too have the Big Macs and Petersons got it all over the Volvos and Dafs that populate European roads. Even the names don't sound right; Daf, I ask you?

As I drew alongside this one, a *Queen Mary*-sized blast issued from the polished hooters as an arm in a chequered sleeve protruded through the window. Quite a lot of American truckers ride bikes, and the camaraderie of the eighteen-wheelers is not unlike that enjoyed by those on two. All modern knights of the road in a sense, sharing a common identity characterized by ruggedness and the romance of travel. Masters of their own destiny, lone wolves hunting on the limits of society.

I was puzzled at first to find the truck travelling so slowly, as I hadn't even changed down from fifth gear on the Harley. but looking backwards and down, I realized at once why this highway supertanker was making such a meal of it. These wagons might be able to top some pretty impressive speeds when they're rolling on the flat, but get them on inclines like this and their gear boxes start earning their keep. The massively torquey Harley motor ate the slopes with the casual confidence of a smug cat demolishing a saucer of cream, its 1340cc engine lunching on inclines that would leave most machines panting for breath in a frenzy of cog swapping. If I haven't corrected my initial impressions before, it was long overdue; I liked this bike.

Seldom, if ever in my life, had I seen scenery quite like this. Despite the altitude there was plenty of green with dense pine forests clothing all but the peaks of the mountains that were separated by broad lush valleys and hooded by a sea-blue sky dotted with harmless white clouds. It was like something out of a picture book. I had to stop, I absolutely had to, and pulled over into a broad lay-by on the edge of an escarpment that commanded a view extending perhaps twenty miles across this idyllic land. Not long after I'd first seen *Easy Rider*, I read *Lord of the Rings* and recall still the profoundly stimulating image of that cover design. The foreground populated with the silhouettes of the adventurers staring out into an infinity of peaks, pines and sun dappled valleys, beyond which in the far distance hulked the ominous forms of mountains that spoke of giants, dragons, goblins and fearful danger – all ripping yarns and derring-do. I'd long dreamed of finding a land that looked like that book cover and invoked those sentiments, and if this wasn't it then it was one hell of a good imitation.

I sat on the forest floor of warm pine needles, my back against a tree – my moment to sit and stare. Before long the truck reappeared, groaning up the last yards of the ascent like a lethargic sumo wrestler, before shifting gears for its downhill run, the engine sighing with mechanical relief as responsibility was transferred to the anchors. I watched while the diesel dinosaur lumbered into the distance, brakes squealing as it declined to matchbox dimensions, the gout of thick smoke diminishing to a single hair of a brush stroke, pencil thin against the expansive backdrop into which it was progressively absorbed.

THE WEST

West of the Rockies the environment changed dramatically. Forest soon surrendered to scrub and then desert. I was sorry to leave the Rockies behind, the arid baroness of desert seemed a poor swap for the lush green, and I was soon missing the aromatic smell of pine needles. I was in the real West now, and a less familiar landscape stretched before me, bare and hostile with little prospect of sustenance suggested by the barren vista. I was now in the land of the movies, the flatness interrupted by colossal cliffs and fingers of rock that punctuated the landscape like the masts of sunken ships at low tide. The only animals I saw were dead, here a sheep, there a cow, one flat on its back, its legs stuck out stiffly in the comically tragic paralysis of *rigor mortis*. Had they wandered out into the desert by error and perished for want of water or died on transporters and been pitched overboard? There was no way of knowing, though their closeness to the road inclined me to the latter. 'Surely,' I thought, 'the whole desert could not be littered with bodies like this?'

I felt suddenly alone and the notion of running out of fuel suggested itself as a realistic possibility which prompted me to double back to a small town that I'd left ten miles behind. Here I topped up to the gills, and with renewed confidence, headed west again, aiming for a point on the map from which I learned that four states could simultaneously be viewed.

With time I came to the place marked as 'Four Points' at which the state borders of Arizona, Nevada, Colorado and Utah meet at a single spot. Naturally the site was a tourist attraction and traders lined the road approaching it, selling their goods from simple trestle tables over which crude roofs of plastic or straw had been contrived to protect the merchants from the baking Arizona sun. A crudely-made sign at the roadside was daubed with the slogan, 'FRIENDLY INJUNS AHEAD.'

These were the Navajo, a race of people foreign to my experience, they represented my first contact with American Indians of any tribe. First impressions were that they were much smaller than I thought they would be. I could see little resemblance between these short asiatic looking men of thin or dumpy physique, and the awesome braves who had whooped and scalped their way across the cinema screens of my formative years. It was hard to believe in looking at them, that the contest between the Red man and the White could have been anything but hopelessly one sided, as in fact it was – but not in the way that one might have imagined at a glance. A concrete arch, perhaps twenty feet in height put a name to these people, 'Welcome to the Navajo Nation' it read. It's all very well being welcomed to a nation, but I felt that the archway should really have been made of stone, certainly there was no shortage of it around there and yet there it was, a bloody great lump of cement painted a rather discordant shade of pink.

I avoided examining the wares of these traders too closely as I had no intention of buying anything. Space on a motorcycle is at a premium and the chances of getting home with any of this pottery intact was slim. It was nice stuff though, nothing tacky. No glazes to give a plasticky effect like a Victorian Toby Jug, and not too much detail as one might expect on a Chinese vase. Priceless they may be but they're overstated in my view – too fussy. Complex garden scenes packed with multitudes of improbable creatures claustrophobically co-existing with fat Mandarins may demonstrate the artist's skill, but seldom a plausible reality. The Navajo pottery bore witness to a simple people living close to the land. Clear elemental pigments of sky blue and earthy brown clothed the elegant contours of clay in whose delicacy an endearing vulnerability was reflected. There would be no chance of these vessels bouncing like synthetic modern equivalents. Drop them on the ground and they'd shatter into fragments; back to the earth like wild birds escaping cages. Attraction in fragility, elements borrowed from the earth, not stolen and disguised. Pity there was no mail order service.

I'm a little uncomfortable around desperately poor people; maybe it's the inheritance of the White man, a legacy of guilt. There's an issue – original sin – that's weird stuff. I believe Jesus Christ is the son of God, but I can identify with the faith of the American Indian, though I know little of it beyond an impression about their closeness to nature and their respect for animals. They may have killed them, but not for fun and not in unsustainable numbers; they were a people in balance with nature just as we are a people out of balance. They looked at me with my big shiny motorcycle, bulging saddle bags and fat wallet, but I don't know what they were thinking. Did they see a free spirit, some echo of their ancestors, or just a rich paleface with no damn room to stow anything that they might have sold me.

I stood on the spot where the four state borders met and took a couple of scenic pictures. I felt awkward and touristy, like I didn't belong. Stuffing the camera back inside a pannier, I pulled a buckled strap down hard to close the cover and glanced over my shoulder before pulling out of the parking area, not that there was any sound of traffic up here, just the wind, but I glanced anyway, partly out of habit, partly to see if the Navajo were watching me – they weren't.

GRAND CANYON

The dramatic quality of the Grand Canyon is generated not only by the Canyon itself, but by the startling nature with which it introduces itself to the visitor. A mountain, by contrast, will be seen first from a great distance, as a feature of apparently modest dimensions, gradually increasing in stature as one approaches, until its full magnificence becomes manifest. Thus the grandiose shock is diminished by visual acclimatization; just as a climber, by looking downwards at numerous stages of his ascent, must lose at least some of the drama of the view available from the summit.

The Grand Canyon is different. As one approaches along the road through the desert, there is no foretaste of the spectacular sight that awaits the visitor. The road climbs steadily upward to a considerable height, about a mile and a half above sea level at the highest point, depositing the traveller on a green plateau of stunted forest. This forest is part of the Grand Canyon National Park, through which a single-track road runs parallel to the edge of the Canyon, which lies, invisible, a few yards away, hidden by a screen of twisted juniper trees.

A sign indicating a viewing point attracted my attention, and I pulled into the secluded lay-by, where a tourist with a camera mounted on a tripod stood surveying the sight through his lens, like some minion at the shrine of a geological idol.

So spectacular is the sight of Grand Canyon (the initiated drop the 'the'), so out of this world, so exaggerated is the scale and dramatic the impact of its appearance, that I was tempted to think myself the victim of an elaborate con-trick. It looked like a theatrical stage backdrop, and I felt that if I could creep right up to the edge and lean out a little toward the other side, my hand would encounter a painted canvas which would undulate at my touch. I would have needed to have leaned a long way, however, the Canyon at this point was seventeen miles wide, and with a mile drop to the ground, my curiosity would have cost me dearly.

Comparing preconception with direct experience, the Canyon was far more complex a shape than I had imagined. Rather than a simple sheer-sided railway cutting on a grand scale, it boasts a multitude of peaks, promontories, sub-gullys and gorges, painted in a variety of shades underlaid by a prevailing reddish brown. At

126

points, tall columns of stone stand isolated, topped with precariously balanced boulders like inverted exclamation marks. It's no simple cutting, it's a titanic sculpture.

The existence of phenomena like Grand Canyon, serves to reinforce my confidence in the concept of God. Would a force with so grandiose a capacity as the Canyon reflects, not apply that same creative talent to engineer a spiritual master plan for a creature as subtle and complex as a human being? In past discussions with atheists about the possibility of there being a God, I was often frustrated by their line of argument without identifying the stumbling block that was obstructing rational debate. That stumbling block is simply the lack of common terms of reference. Without common terms of reference there can be no debate, just as two people speaking in different languages are going to find progress very difficult. For the atheist the stumbling block lies with his reluctance to abandon the constraints of the natural world and its physical laws and think laterally beyond them. Many believers in the supernatural find themselves derailed from their main train of thought through pinning their faith on trivia, for example by pointlessly defending the supernatural associations of ghost sightings or apparent miracles. The pragmatist will respond by offering rational and natural explanations for any phenomena and the real nub of the issue is lost in the detail.

A friend for whose logical capabilities I have considerable respect, tripped on this stumbling block when considering, albeit in his adolescence, the possibility of the Ten Commandments being carved in stone by lightning. Lightning, he claimed, can not cut into stone, an unassailable fact which, he insisted, refuted the biblical claims on the manner by which our most crucial tenets of law were imparted, thus undermining the notion that their origin was supernatural. Had he borne in mind the geometric maxim that, in seeking to vindicate a theorem, one must be wary of employing that very theorem, he might not have committed the error of rationality of which he was certainly guilty. If one, in the course of seeking to establish, for example, that the square on the hypotenuse is equal to the sum of the square of the other two sides, uses that very theorem, which it is very tempting to do, then the proof is invalidated, since it represents nothing more than presumption. It is as valid as a court that seeks to divine the identity of a murderer, beginning by deciding that the man standing in the dock is definitely the guilty party. Similarly, in claiming the physical impossibility of carving stone with lightning, my friend presupposed the impossibility of the supernatural forces whose existence he was endeavouring to disprove. As an instrument of logic, this is a no-no.

Thus it is that a debate between atheists and believers is destined to irresolute conclusion, since the believers' most potent arguments must appeal to the subjective appetite of a receptive mind. A mind whose scope outreaches the empirical sphere to which the atheist confines debate. To the believer, two molecules of hydrogen and one of oxygen only make water as long as God allows them to. He who makes the rules can change the rules, but the Godless mind often thinks only within the context of the rules. What kind of a God would it be, who, having made the rules, could not change or overwhelm them if he wished to?

Of course the meaning of the word supernatural is that which lies beyond the natural. My own dictionary defines the supernatural as 'due to or manifesting some agency above the forces of nature.' Is a God who is bound by the forces of nature a God? Of course not, by definition, as God by definition, is supernatural. To say that an apparently supernatural act cannot have happened because it defies natural laws is to presuppose that there can be no supernatural. Put another way, there is no superantural because the supernatural defies the laws of the natural. God can't have carved the ten commandments in stone with lightning as lightning does not cut into stone in the natural world.

My feeling about the Grand Canyon in this context, is that the very existence of such emotionally stimulating phenomena, indicates the operation of a force of incalculable sensitivity. That same force displays itself in all of life's subtle elements, providing clues leading to an inevitable conclusion. Whether the medium is a butterfly's wing, a waterfall, or in a more abstract sense, the pleasure of laughter, the lack of objective necessity for the existence of so many of the world's finer features collectively substantiate the conviction that a power of unfathomable creative refinement is at work. No effort of convoluted reasoning to provide a clinical rationale for the existence of these marvels can ever displace the indelible certainty of the believer, since faith is impervious to rational argument, much to the irritation of the pragmatic atheist.

Just as a juror, presented with a mass of 'irrefutable' evidence pointing to a defendant's guilt, may decide, on the basis of a trustworthy instinct, that he is innocent. So the believer's faith confounds the atheist's scepticism.

The juvenile sceptic will commonly ask of the believer, 'If there is a God why does he not show himself, why does not he reveal himself to us?' Such an expectation denies the notion that God demands faith – which is belief in something without proof. In the presence of proof there can be no faith as it is obviated by evidence. Evidence and the recognition of evidence is a mechanical facet of life, whereas faith is a spiritual one. If God wants us to attain spirituality, which I believe he does, then it is entirely rational that he should deny us empirical evidence in order to test our faith. Moreover, it is not only rational to do that – but essential.

Atheists will often dismiss spiritual considerations as lying beyond the bound of rational thought since they have no basis in knowledge, and, to the scientific mind, that which cannot be proven cannot be respected and is commonly derided. Derogatory labels like 'superstition' are typically attached to all spiritual beliefs, while science and its advocates enjoy the more attractive adjectives such as 'enlightened'. To the secular mind the material ascendancy of the enlightened nations over the superstitious cultures provides implicit evidence of superiority. The White doctor's penicillin out-performing the witch doctor's bowl of bones, for example, provides us with a simple metaphor for what is seen as modern, true and devoid of humbug. The derision of 'primitive' cultures by European conquerors may have been led by swordsmen with a Bible in their back pocket, but it was followed by educators with *The Origin of Species* in theirs.

I see the mechanism by which we are encouraged to arrive at a state of belief rather in the same way that I see the workings of a civil court action. Whereas a criminal court must provide clear and conclusive evidence to arrive at a conviction, a civil court embraces a more subjective methodology. In a civil court a plaintiff must make a case for what seems most reasonable or probable to a degree which is convincing, albeit empirically inconclusive. In short, circumstantial evidence is more likely to be accepted than in a criminal court where it is viewed more guardedly. The world is packed with circumstantial evidence of a creator, and though the atheist may cling to Darwinian theory as a complete explanation of everything, it clearly satisfies no spiritual aspiration whatsoever. The quest for the profound demands more than fortuitous coincidence and chemical coalescence to justify the subtleties of life on earth. Our demand for a fuller explanation, for a spiritual destiny, can never be satisfied by the notion that we are nothing more than the beneficiaries of an organic lottery. We cannot be satisfied by such superficial explanations for the simple reason that we are, potentially at least, spiritual entities and as such we are equipped to realize a spiritual state. We have the opportunity to dismiss all spirituality and satisfy ourselves with entirely secular perceptions of life, but in seeking satisfaction from such confidence we will inevitably fail since we are imbued from birth with a deep seated perception of our own spiritual destiny. To turn from such a destiny is to be in indefinite denial and to court frustration, misery and dissatisfaction for the simple reason that we will be able to identify no purpose in life whatsoever, for without a spiritual destiny there can be no purpose.

I once encountered a prominent advocate of atheism, a Professor Flu of Reading University, who was delivering a lecture to the Society for Individual Freedom, of which I am a member. The subject was education, which provided me with an opportunity to pose the question that the education system could not fulfil its broadest remit if it released young people into the world without providing them with the slightest notion of why they were born. I referred the audience to my impression that my own education in the sixties was dominated by atheist doctrine even though the state schools paid lip service to spiritual elements through a morning assembly and religious education in the curriculum.

I maintained further that if there was no God there could be no significant meaning to life as everything was impermanent. Our sun would one day burn out and life here cease. The history of man would be lost. In consequence there could, against this profoundly bleak outlook, be no significance in any endeavour. All values were relative all effort ultimately futile and the comparative merit of one man's efforts against another's of no more eternal importance than the relative qualities of vegetables. Professor Flu appeared greatly irritated by my suggestion and demanded to know whether I thought that there was no real difference between the significance of Mozart and a road sweeper. Indeed there is not, in fact there is every possibility that the road sweeper's spiritual achievement may be far greater than Mozart's since spirituality by definition, survives mortality, and so his ultimate significance may indeed be far greater.

In seeking to attach significance to transience the atheist is on a hiding to nothing. For what ultimate significance can there be in transience ? Without a God there can be no ultimate purpose in life beyond this life and if one recognizes that the sun will ultimately expire, then there can be no value in acquiring knowledge to pass on to future generations. The more optimistic scientists may hope that knowledge will ultimately equip our species to survive all the catastrophes of the universe, but in the absence of a spiritual dimension what would be the purpose? Certainly it would be no more profound than an indefinitely self propagating bed of mushrooms. There is in atheism a wretched self deprecation that recognizes in the line 'dust to dust' no more than the completion of an organic cycle. What a deeply inconsequential epithet that sober line provides and how tragic that great academics can so easily accept its limited interpretation. Dust to dust – no more than vegetables. The 'greatest' minds of all ages can identify the most complex mechanism of life and yet fail to recognize one scintilla of evidence for its purpose. What is it that the Bible says about the truth being hidden from the wisest and yet revealed to the simplest goat herd? Something like that. Meaningful truth is spontaneously acquired and comes from faith or is faith. Those who wish to deny God can look at any marvel of creation, be it a bird or a canyon, and satisfy themselves with a physical explanation. Anyone can look at a craftsman's work and turn to his tool box for an explanation of how it was fashioned; they may even do so without ever seeking the craftsman. The discovery of the tools may satisfy the secular mind just as Darwin's discoveries studies of Galapagos' finches has satisfied generations of academics. The truly adventurous mind, however, asks not only how, but why?

Just looking at Grand Canyon gets your mind thinking big, thinking significant, thinking spiritual. Besides the more sublime motivations, it is tempting to think that in anticipation of the efforts of the great architects, the Almighty, in fashioning the Grand Canyon, was throwing down an unassailable challenge to keep our mortal vanities in check. This may be a fanciful idea but there's an ecclesiastical air about the Canyon that inspires in visitors a respectful demeanour expressed in the hushed tones of folk who, like pilgrims, approach the lip of the great chasm. Those who sit pensively at the edge gazing into the depths, enjoy from newcomers the consideration afforded to the human precedents one encounters seated thoughtfully in the pews of city churches in quest of sanctuary from the bustle outside their walls. As in those churches, at the Canyon boisterous children are quickly reproved by parents who stand close together, speaking in theatrical whispers as though a service were in progress while, a mile below, the Colorado River sends plumes of vapour floating and curling upward like incense, compounding the religious tone with a dreamy mysticism that hypnotizes the motley congregation.

The overwhelming sense of awe which this spectacle dictates, draws for its mesmerizing potency, not only on its scale, but on its motionless serenity. Nothing seems to move in Grand Canyon, the distance from lip to bottom freezes even the movement of the water and that unnaturally static quality lends it a disturbingly powerful eeriness. A forest, by contrast, is alive with movement. A field of corn waves in sympathy with the breeze, even though the motion might be too slight to register, the subconscious notes it and a sense of normality is appeased. Grand Canyon is impervious to these trivial disturbances, sustaining a sagacious intransigence in the face of all futile endeavours to elicit from it the fluctuations of expression for which the passage of millennia are required.

The simple explanation for this condition lies in the nature of the material of which it is composed – rock. Rock symbolizes the essence of indefinite dependability. Christ advised us to build upon rock; his compliment to Peter was to synonymize him with rock, the 'rock of ages.' Our whole world, though dressed with water, trees, plants, earth or sand, is mostly made of rock, and man's greatest and most enduring monuments are fashioned from this potent fundamental. Grand Canyon is widely recognized as the most spectacular natural rock sculpture on earth. To the geologist it is an open instruction manual of graphic clarity on an incomparable scale. The Canyon is to the geologist what a Tardis would be to an historian. In a sense it is both; for in the book end of exposed strata, we can read the pages and chapters of a diary that opened at the dawn of time. It is the suggestion of wisdom, that attaches to a formation of such endurance, which generates the sense of awe by which means the most cynical visitor is overwhelmed.

In trying to assess the magic of Grand Canyon, my thoughts consistently returned to this aspect of motionlessness, for there is a contentment about the static state which tacitly subordinates those forms that must be forever weaving and scurrying about the world, to an inferior order. Conversely, the essence of movement derives from dissatisfaction, whether with location, condition, or circumstance, we seek to appease the appetite of endless ambition by the device of perpetual motion. The restless spirit forever roaming the world may, in the perception of others, enjoy a romantic identity which is the envy of the domestically committed, but the footloose, in candid moments, will frequently admit to hidden appetites for the permanence which their lust for variety compels them to reject.

Grand Canyon's permanence, enables it to assume an air of unrivalled superiority that deters any notion of serious competition, and from the unassailable podium its supremacy provides, the message it conveys to the scrambling minions that scuttle about its environs is abasing. The humiliating message is one of indifference, total indifference. In the time of the Grand Canyon's making, geological ages have overtaken one another, dinosaurs have surrendered to mammals, Ice Ages have come and gone, and, in the comparative seconds of recent history, human empires have risen and collapsed, during which time barely a wrinkle on the Canyon's face has altered one iota. The magnitude of the time scale so evocatively demonstrated in this place, hurls all the history and endeavour of man into a belittling perspective, deriding our greatest vanities with a charge of comical transience. One feels about the Canyon a certainty that its stony indifference will survive the most appalling indiscretions that the collective destructiveness of mankind can concoct, and upon that reassuring certainty rests the conviction, that in looking into Grand Canyon, one is looking into the face of eternity.

I camped on a site at the Canyon's southern end that night of my first viewing, having surrendered the reasonable fee for what I considered a great privilege. The mode of payment, in keeping with the spiritual quality of the area, was based on trust. A box was provided at the site entrance, into which one was invited to drop several dollars for the pleasure of camping on one of the best sites I have ever stayed at. Unlike most British sites, which are mostly open fields crammed with as many tents as the available space can accommodate, this one was subtly divided into natural plots of varying size approximately dictated by the dusty clearings within the aromatic forest of juniper trees.

The advised procedure was to establish a territorial claim by attaching the ticket, collected from an open holder near the entrance, to the marker stake which identified each area. I misunderstood the protocol and discovered, upon my return that a camper full of vigorous Germans had parked next to me. This caused me no inconvenience, however, and I set to with the bundle of timber I'd bought at the local store, to establish a barbecue, on which I grilled the steak and beef-tomatoes I'd bought earlier. The timber burned fiercely on the elevated barbecue stand, but for just long enough to cook the meal which I generously lubricated with a couple of cans of Budweiser.

I would have liked to have had a plate and eaten at a table, as I'm keen on a touch of formality at meal times. It's very difficult to enjoy a meal as much when you aren't seated at a table – particularly if it includes things that need chopping up. My old friend, Baron Jean Bart Voegel, disagrees. Paradoxically, he is something of a gourmet, and when not eating out in restaurants of commendable reputation, he prepares splendid concoctions at the flat in Leytonstone which he shares with my old school friend Ratso. Where the element of inconsistency appears, is at the point of consumption, for, having prepared some continental delight of impeccable good taste, invariably embellished by subtle sauces and accompanied by the recommended garnishes to provide a repast of consummate perfection, he then kneels on the floor, cravat and all, and, hunched over his plate, devours its contents like a jealous Doberman guarding a fondly chewed slipper. It is a truly dreadful sight to watch, and serves to support the theory that the aristocracy are prone to mental instability. The embarrassing revelations about our own Queen Mum's cousins spring to mind, whilst in quest of further historical corroboration, one may look to the sad case of King George III. It was he, who, having completed his daily motions, was wont to wipe his arse on the palace curtains, behind which he then hid until flushed out, so to speak, by some patient courtier. Let us not forget, however, that he also kept an orang-utan at court. Historians tells us that the ape had achieved a remarkable state of domestication and would join the King at dinner where he would be seated next to dignitaries whom the King knew were horrified by the experience. More remarkable still, the ape would smoke a clay pipe and regard his dinner guests with a confident scrutiny that some found unnerving. Of all the arguments advanced in favour of retaining the monarchy I can think of no sounder one than that from time to time the family throws up such wonderful characters as the mad King George.

Lacking the necessary crockery, I sandwiched my ten-ounce steak between two slices of bread, each approximately an inch thick – a sandwich colossus which I expanded further by including an entire beef-tomato, cut into four substantial slices. The result was a vast, soggy mess, which tasted, for all its indelicacy, quite reasonable. Less reasonable was my bed. Lacking a foam mattress or air bed, I had only my sleeping bag to cushion me from the stony forest floor. Juniper trees do not seem to provide the spongy luxury of a leaf-mould mattress which one associates with deciduous English woodland – at least not when they are growing in a semi-desert environment. I couldn't find a suitable hole for my hip, and so lay flat on my back, making faces from the shadows on the canvas, as cracking twigs betrayed the clumsy footsteps of the forest's nocturnal inhabitants.

What I should have done the next day was get up very early and watch the sun rise over the Canyon. I missed that, and so packed up my gear, waved to the Germans enthusiastically breakfasting in their camper, and rode down to the Canyon to inspect the ruins of an ancient Indian settlement.

Sited amongst the trees, a few hundred yards from the Canyon's edge, this place had been home to one of two tribes who inhabited the region; the Havasupai and the Walapi; one of whom lived at the top of the canyon, the other at the bottom. This much I gleaned from the information supplied at the tourist centre, a discreetly constructed building manufactured from local stone, in which was housed a collection of exhibits excavated from nearby ruins by means of which the story of the inhabitants had been reconstructed. Among them was a model of the ruined village, featuring cheerful characters with shiny black hair carting baskets of maize and corn about, whilst the women scraped deer hides, and children played with pet dogs. In the centre of the exhibit featured a young Indian woman, naked from the waist upward, holding a bowl of some kind of cereal which, for reasons best known to herself, she was pouring in a cascade between her splendidly formed breasts. The picture created by the optimistically imaginative artist, struck me as an idealized interpretation of the situation which had prevailed, but I was happy to indulge the fantasy of this idyllic community until my concentration was disturbed by a growing awareness that I was being critically surveyed by the leader of a school party, a stout, fusty woman in sensible shoes with austerely trimmed hair and thin tight lips. There was a tense criticism in her demeanour that I didn't care for. It agitated me in a manner, and to a degree, which might be experienced standing in the prospective path of an arrow held in an archer's bow. If you can imagine how discomfiting that would be, then you can as easily imagine how that humourless woman's harsh scrutiny disturbed the harmless musings to which my colourful imagination had given birth.

Outside in the crisp, fresh-smelling woods I discovered two girls, perhaps twenty years of age, as they stood quietly, staring intently into the trees. I approached as discreetly as one can in heavy boots on a gravel path, and asked then what they were looking at. They indicated a young deer a dozen yards away, standing apprehensively on its slender legs, whilst returning their scrutiny with a fetchingly Bambiesque innocence. The girls, it transpired, were from Sevenoaks in Kent; the deer, in the absence of any claim to the contrary, I took for a local. It was a wonderful moment.

In the main Information Centre at the other end of the Canyon, I joined a party of tourists for a free half-hour guided walk. We were shortly joined by a young woman of healthy, sturdy, and sensible aspect, clad in a khaki uniform, grounded in serious brown walking boots at one end and a broad- brimmed hat, much like the original scout hats, at the other. In one hand she held a small rucksack, into which she placed a number of stone samples, which bulged unevenly in the lower regions of their canvas home, a discomfort to which the wearer presented a stoic indifference. After introducing herself with an enthusiasm that would have been impossible to feign, she led us down a stony path to where a broad rock afforded a suitable vantage point from which the Canyon could be viewed. Here we were invited to arrange ourselves for the first of several brief lectures, delivered with evangelical fervour from a position of superior altitude, rather in the manner one imagines that Christ addressed the crowd during the Sermon on the Mount. I found myself a position not too close to the front of class, where I could lean my back against the trunk of a tree and view the majority of the group with comfort. There were some splendid stereotypes in evidence. A trio of lightly bronzed teenage girls, wearing shorts and trainers, chatted amongst themselves, apparently oblivious to an oily lothario, who'd shadowed their progress from the start with the persistence of a hunter-submarine in the wake of a convoy. I had him marked for an Italian what with his dainty shoes and slick zippered hip pouch, from which he extracted a limitless supply of French cigarettes like a smouldering magician.

The European contingent were primarily represented by Germans laden with expensive-looking camera equipment including, in one case, a video device with which the owner swept the horizon, demonstrating a meticulous efficiency which suggested the collection of intelligence for a pending military initiative. An elderly American gentlemen in bright yellow trousers swatted ineffectively at a brace of persistent flies, attracted no doubt by the near luminous quality of his pristine strides. Nearby, a bloated woman who I took for his wife, deposited her lard-arsed rump on an uneven rock, upon which she oscillated precariously for a moment before her fluid posterior moulded itself to the contours of her perch and, like a plump goose settled on her eggs, looked about herself through a pair of ludicrous plastic framed spectacles balanced on a burnt nose, white with cream. Together with her canary coloured spouse, they resembled a comedy duo about to commence their act. First off, however, was the Baden Powell acolyte with the bag of rocks. 'Howdy everybody,' she chirruped. 'My name is Sandy, and I am your guide for this morning's geology tour.' With her opening line, the German had swung his video camera around like some aroused Dalek swivelling its mono-eyed periscope on to its target and evaporating the guide's smile as she caught sight of the Aryan's grimaced features aiming the barrel of his camera directly between her eyes. Composing herself in the face of this Teutonic scrutiny, she continued talking above the faint hum of the video motor.

'How do we make a canyon?' The talk proceeded in the manner of a children's educational TV show with audience participation, as clues to the various essential criteria were served up with cheerful effervescence.

The fat woman with the burnt nose was first to the line, her flabby white arm held aloft with scholastic propriety.

'Yes?' invited the teacher, delighted by the enthusiasm of her class.

'A river,' croaked the human walrus, clearing her throat half way through the answer.

'And what river would that be?' continued the benign interrogator with sugary innocence.

'The Coloraadaarr,' drawled teacher's pet. The canary spouse who'd fiddled incessantly with his hearing aid throughout the exchanges, cast a look of reproof in the direction of his substantial partner, a caustic expression loaded with tacit criticism of his wife's limelight-hogging behaviour. The German, meanwhile, was surveying Mrs. Lard with disdain, his lens pointing into the tree tops to protect his viewing audience from distressing visions of a corpulent kind.

'The Colorado, that's right,' a beam of approval rewarded the eager participant, whose head nodded with defensive self-gratification in the direction of her critical cohort. The latter looked away in resignation, as a gangling insect alighted on one bony knee.

Teacher's bag was now opened, and a selection of rocks passed around to illustrate the content of the lecture. The German studied each with analytical scrutiny, whilst the Italian had to be nudged by the class swat, whose endeavours to pass him the exhibits, contended unequally with his unsubtle scrutiny of the closest teenager's nubile figure.

The lecture continued with dramatic contortions from Miss, as she described the titanic forces which had compressed and fashioned the various levels we could see. The names were familiar from my schoolday geography – metamorphic, sedimentary, igneous – but the enthusiastic delivery of the tutor, allied to the incomparable location, brought a refreshing vigour to the subject. Learning geology at Grand Canyon is like learning astronomy in a space ship, you're there. Teacher was crouching now, on her haunches, palms outspread, moving vertically downwards to demonstrate the pertinent influences as the Hun's camera whirred afresh to capture the didactic pantomime. The teenage girls meanwhile, had absented themselves from the group, leaving the Italian lothario to study the taut lines provoked in Teacher's pants by her strenuous exertions.

I scratched my back on the tree trunk and smirked knowingly into the indifferent abyss.

Thanking the guide for an exceptionally spirited delivery, I rode to a comparatively quiet lay-by where I left the bike. Walking a few yards to sit by the Canyon's edge, I made notes on my impressions and watched the climbing sun apply its deft touches to the coloured rocks, whose hues responded to its flattening angle as the molten oils on a canvas blend beneath the bristles of the artist's brush.

As I sat, shirt-less, leaning against a warm stone, I was visited by a sense of anxiety for the large dark birds that swooped and circled yards from my face beyond the Canyon's lip. Ordinarily, one feels no concern for birds, however high they fly, but for some reason, encountering these creatures at my own level, with such a drop beneath them, engendered an irrational empathy from which a curious concern developed.

'You mind you don't fall,' I called to a broad-winged fellow as he launched himself from a nearby ledge, dropping from sight and reappearing seconds later, borne aloft on the invisible hand of one of the benign thermals with which this place is generously endowed. Watching these accomplished aeronauts reminded me of the time, years earlier, when, on voyages into the Southern Ocean, which separates Australia from Antarctica, I had encountered that supreme master of the skies, the albatross.

The albatross inhabits a band of latitude, known as the Roaring Forties, where the winds required to sustain its considerable bulk, blow with the necessary strength and consistency. The velocity of these currents, which make life easy for the albatross, exert a contrary influence on the seafarers, whose less graceful craft ply these turbulent waters. Many times I have jammed myself against the wheelhouse doorframe of a merchant ship describing its ungainly plunging track through these tempestuous latitudes, pounding into the huge swells which racked her frame with painful shudders. The contrast of our laboured progress, unsympathetically battling against the elements alongside the albatross's instinctive manipulation of them, provided me with a source of wry amusement as I braced myself against the violent movement of our tortured craft. I can't say that I ever saw an albatross laugh, and sneering, I am sure, lies beneath the lofty principles of these airborne aristocrats whose fabled camaraderie with the seafarer depends upon the attractive legend that their bodies host the souls of drowned sailors. It's a compelling notion that provides at least a fanciful motive for the persistence with which they pursue the sea-borne trials of their surviving colleagues. What I have seen, however, is an albatross wink. It's the wink of the surfer overtaking the swimmer, the yacht overhauling the steamer, the urban cyclist outpacing the Maserati; it's the wink of good-humoured one-upmanship, where the level of superiority is inversely proportional to the effort invested in its achievement. There will be those who will doubt that I've been close enough to an albatross to see it wink, but it is a fact, I have. They fly so close to the bridge wings on which I've stood, that a tall man with a lengthy stick could reach out and touch one if the bird had the tolerance to permit it. A creature with a twelve-foot wingspan is an imposing sight at such proximity, and yet, with a feathered inclination riding on a mental whim, they can turn and be shrunk to specs, lost against the glittering expanse of their salty realm in the time it takes the ship to breast a dozen swells. As if to underscore the degree of their superiority, they'll turn a mile astern and head upwind in pursuit, without a trace of a wing beat, inexplicably harnessing a force that blows against their track, to propel them in a direction contrary to its own. I do not to this day understand how this feat is achieved. A powered aircraft flying into a wind will inevitably lose in headway over the ground, whatever part of its velocity is equal to that of the wind, no increments of power obtained from an enhanced engine can alter the fact that speed lost to a headwind is equal to the velocity of that wind. What the albatross achieves in apparently denying these irresistible forces, appears as something so close to magical as to persuade the observer he has fallen victim to an illusion. There must be an explanation, a rationale, of which no doubt, the albatross is cheerfully unconscious, for ignorance is bliss indeed when the fruits of knowledge are available without its encumbrance. Such is the essence of instinct of which the albatross enjoys a magnificent inheritance.

They're smug bastards these albatross, with their in-born knowledge of thermals and their perfectly designed bodies. Man may be the most versatile, intelligent, and adventurous creature on this earth, but wherever he goes he is reminded that he is a jack of all trades and master of none by the specialists who preside over every domain into which he pokes his meddlesome nose. Perhaps it is part of the grand design, that numerous reminders of our inadequacy are provided at every point of observation in order to lend perspective to our perception of ourselves, and so discourage vanity, perhaps, who knows? What I do know, is that no creature in my experience, makes such an impressive display of its innate superiority as the albatross.

I returned from my first voyage to the Southern Ocean, grateful for the privilege of observing this animal on its sky-borne throne, I felt that the contact had enriched my life, and been logged within the deposit account of experience that lends our existence some sense of achievement. More even than that, I perceived, or imagined, that my own status had been enhanced by the contact, perhaps a notion as fatuous as it is conceited, but, like a Moslem who has visited Mecca, I felt that my life had been embellished through meeting the albatross, by which means I had collected a token in the game of life. I believe that the purpose of our life revolves about the attainment of wisdom, and the pursuit of spirituality through the acquisition of truth and the development of a will of adequate strength to overcome the temptations which, if surrendered to, stunt our spiritual growth. To escape the confinement of mortal appetites, one must be able to imagine a state of superior sublimity that so far outreaches the highest physical aspirations of this world, as to render the epitome of human luxury pure wretchedness by comparison.

The problem of those who would urge us on a path of spiritual progression lies with the inability of the average mortal to visualize any state that could be more wonderful than the highest condition of physical perfection, wealth, and opportunity, which the material elite of this world so often appear to enjoy in such abundance. What could be better, to posture a crude example, than to be, in the case of the man, a six foot four Mr Universe look-a-like with infinite wealth, limitless female concubines, perfect health, and immense appetites for every physical and cultural pleasure available, given of course that you did not feel dissatisfied with that state? Given, furthermore, that you were ignorant of any higher state. If ignorance is bliss and contentment, of necessity, rests on that ignorance, then one might argue, why should one seek a higher state? The answer to this must rest with the assumption that ignorance is not bliss, and merely provides us with an illusion or half best.

I once read on a board outside a church, the slogan, 'Peace is not the absence of war, peace is the presence of God.' Essentially, this may be interpreted as both a warning against complacency and an inspiration to extrapolate one's endeavours to a higher plane. That such endeavours are essential to the achievement of ultimate peace of mind is obvious, since the ability to appreciate the physical pleasures of this life is confined to so brief a span. Mortality, in effect, is the catalyst of spiritual progress, since human aspiration cannot tolerate the finality that physical death suggests. Those who postulate that if there were no God then man would create one, assume that in the absence of a spiritual dimension and supernatural entity, man would retain the aspiration to survive his natural span. What seems more probable than that, is that the provision of the appetite for attaining immortality is supernatural in origin; that without a supernatural dimension, mankind could not have conceived supernatural ambitions; that within each of us, the capacity to glimpse the concept of a superior state exists. That capacity or potential for vision, constitutes the greater part of the abstract device which we generally refer to as the soul.

Of course, an atheistic logician would declare that none of this is rational deduction, but fanciful speculation founded in nothing more tangible than nebulous and optimistic impressions – and he'd be partly right. We return again here to the essence of faith. It's a 'Catch 22' because, by definition, faith demands the absence of logic, it cannot be quantified by arithmetical calculation or vindicated by laboratory experiment, its acquisition is inspired not by scientific research, but by intuition. So it is that the peace which faith provides, so often eludes the grasp of those whose trammelled intellects preclude the notion of the spiritual from their considerations.

The Bible contains a reference to this sad irony where it reports how the truth is hidden from the most brilliant, whilst being revealed to the simplest. If justice is served and we live, in a sense, in a world of equal opportunities, given the handicap system referred to during the buffalo burger speculations in Dodge City, then the truth is not deliberately hidden by God, as might seem to be implied. The truth is something from which the 'clever' insulate themselves by means of an atheistic strait-jacket of their own making, which protects ample capabilities from the consideration of supernatural possibilities.

The fickle quality of faith, and the near impossibility of imparting it, lies with the necessity of its intuitive acquisition. You can't teach faith, you can't learn it from a book or a teacher, though both may help in the destruction of the barriers which obstruct the faith-gaining mechanism. But the development of faith is an abstract process which depends upon abstract stimuli. That is not to say that physical input plays no part; which returns me to the inspiration of these reflections: Grand Canyon, the albatross, natural splendours and beauty in general. It may be argued that we do not need beauty in order to survive as a species; we do not need to be inspired or excited or depressed; we do not need altruism, or pity, or remorse, or any of the human features that collectively constitute what we term our 'humanity.' Perhaps a Darwinian purist would contrive some complex biological defence for all emotions, based on the physical necessity of their chemical influences on our metabolisms; perhaps, but no such discoveries would undermine the concept of their spiritual origin to the mind of the believer.

The perception of truth in the observation of beauty, albeit the simple perception, 'God is,' may be the most potent and gratifying capability anyone can possess. It would be foolish to suggest that one must travel around the world, whether to the Southern Ocean or the Grand Canyon, in order to collect the tokens in the game of life to which I alluded. Such a necessity would be inconsistent with the concept of justice, since few have been blessed with the opportunities I have enjoyed. The tokens and clues must be everywhere if the Grand Plan embraces all humanity, as I believe it does. Nonetheless, I did not feel that my journey here had been wasted; the truth I was glimpsing through my visit to the Canyon in Arizona may have been no more significant than the truth a child might discover from a butterfly in Balham. Perhaps we were collecting tokens of equivalent status, with the difference that I was enjoying the privilege of the deluxe versions in terms of scale, just as my journey might have as easily have been accomplished on a Honda as a Harley-Davidson.

I am grateful for my opportunity of meeting the albatross, and on this desert pilgrimage, to have seen the Grand Canyon. I felt that in travelling to this prestigious square on the great board game of life, I had, by a different throw of the dice, acquired another piece of the jigsaw whose completion leads us to an understanding of creation; if only we can recognize the picture when it is complete. There would be much to be learnt from reflections on what I had seen here, and from an analysis of the impressions which the awesome landscape prompted. Whatever notions my subsequent speculations might derive, one thing was certain; just as years before, I had enjoyed the privilege of meeting that icon of seafarers, the albatross; now, by a different mechanism I had forged an entry into another contingent of the elite, for I had seen Grand Canyon – and now it was time to go.

BROWN PAPER SACKS

I travelled west through the afternoon, watching the sun set behind the mountains of Arizona, the engine running sweeter and sweeter as the humidity rose with the approach of evening. At a liquor/general store, I paused to buy a tin of hot chilli peppers, some meat paste and crackers, I didn't quite know why, but it seemed like a good idea at the time. More significantly, I couldn't quite get over the fact that the storekeeper was wearing a gun. Not the kind of apologetic number tucked away out of view under a wimpy button-down holster. No, this was a proper, don't-mess-with-me, open-holstered piece of macho hardware.

The great novelty of America is that the land of the movies is for real. There is an unconscious assumption that what we see on the cinema screen is a travesty of reality, a theatrical exaggeration. People can't really wear stetsons and bootlace ties; there can't really be a place called Dodge City; people can't really keep saying 'Have a nice day,' or any one of the thousand lines dreamed up by the feverish brains of Hollywood scriptwriters. The truth, however, is nearer to the screen image than might be imagined. My experience way back in that other world of the New York bus terminal convinced me of that. The giant trucks are real too, as are the gum-chewing drivers in their baseball caps. The Rocky Mountains are real, and so is the Grand Canyon, and I didn't doubt that the gun on the storekeeper's hip was the genuine article too.

I paid for my purchases and strolled out with them nestled in a crackling paper sack, wherein the paste, crackers, and peppers were joined by a quart of genuine Budweiser beer. I enjoyed walking out of there with that paper sack. Americans don't seem to use carrier bags with handles. Watch a movie in which some character buys a pile of groceries at a store, and they all end up in a sack which has then to be supported from beneath, rather than suspended from waist height, great eh? So what's so great about it you may ask? Why should this make me feel good? The same reason that wearing white boxer shorts makes me feel good. It's all a question of association. It isn't just a question of liking things because they're American (although the attraction is equally trivial) the attraction stems from a dissatisfaction with the mundane quality of life's familiar features. I don't suppose Americans think twice about walking out of a supermarket with a crackling brown paper sack cradled in the crook of one arm, because it's normal for them. But for me, it was something else; for me it was different and novel because, however modest the association it provided, it represented a tenuous link between myself and the world of the movies. The crackling brown paper bag made me a movie star; well that's ridiculous, that's overstating things, but it made me feel I had something in common with the glamorous world of the movie stars. Why the white boxer shorts? Same kind of thing. Whenever Burt Reynolds gets out of bed, no matter how beautiful the girl still in it, he always has white boxer shorts on. I bought a pair for myself on my first trip to America on a merchant ship in 1977. Thereafter, however awful I felt when I got up in the morning, however hung over, however dreadful the day ahead seemed, if I had a pair of white boxer shorts on, my wretchedness was ameliorated by a theatrical quality which humourized the desperation of my mood, and enabled me to cope with it. Similarly, sheltering from the rain in a doorway, which should, ideally, be a slummy brownstone, one can draw consolation from the recollection that Bob Dylan was photographed in just such an aspect, peering expectantly up the street, for the sleeve of his album *Street Legal*. The common ingredient is the identification of a theatrical element amidst the most mundane and inconsequential of activities. When such recognitions and appreciations can be achieved, the mechanics of life acquire an invigorating colour that can sustain our interest through dramatic interpretation. The successful and subtle movie-maker maintains our interest through the less active sequences of a film, by innumerable devices which have been developed over the years during which the art form has evolved. As with real life, the credible film must, to hold our attention, make things interesting throughout, rather than relying on a collection of stunts or dramatic high spots interspersed with colourless padding. One reason so many people, particularly those in mundane occupations, resent the tedium of their lives and live for the weekends, is that they are unable to enjoy the humour and theatre of routine life. Once you learn the knack of achieving that appreciation, you've got yourself a free season ticket for perpetual amusement. OK, feeling good about walking out of a supermarket with a crackling brown paper sack, might not be everyone's idea of a high time, but when you're looking at a night alone in a motel room, with a TV full of smug realtors and some paste and crackers for company, then it's just a little better than nothing.

As it happened, I decided to cheer myself up a little more with a meal in the local restaurant where I stuffed my face with a substantial salad creation featuring bits of bacon, cheese and mushrooms laced with a lemon sauce. This restaurant was memorable for two reasons, one was the dog, the other was the chef. Throughout my meal a sound like that of a parrot reached me from the kitchen, fuelling my curiosity to the point of acute intrigue. Eventually, the source of the sound revealed itself. With a giant chef's hat tilted rakishly to one side, I instantly recognized the author of the noise as none other than the Swedish chef from the Muppet Show. I was surprised to find him here because, whilst the Muppet Show is meant to be set in America, I was pretty sure that the whole thing was put together in England. It was while pondering this puzzle that my attention was drawn to a slightly wild looking dog that was lurking by the door. It wasn't a particularly large dog, but it had the look of a hound that might do a chap harm for no good reason. It reminded me of an old fashioned border collie that we took to New Zealand from England many years ago, when I was in the merchant navy. It had that same bloodshot, desperate look, which turned out to belie a good-natured temperament which became apparent as soon as it was shown a little kindness. The waitress in the restaurant must have sensed this, for she trotted outside without hesitation to pat the animal, returning a few minutes later with a piece of raw steak which was consumed with predictable enthusiasm. Whilst the waitress and I speculated upon the status of this apparent stray, a young couple at the next table to me maintained an air of complete indifference to the beast and its benefactor, confining their attention solely to the consumption of their meal which they ate in unnatural silence. It was not until they left that the hound's presence was explained, as the man produced a chain which he attached to the dog's collar before the uncommunicative duo departed with their canine charge.

This all seemed a little odd to me, though no odder than the bizarre programme on my motel TV about an attempt to reintroduce captive ferrets to the wild. The crucial requirement of their training, it seemed, was to induce in the creatures a substantial fear of owls which, I imagine, represent their prime natural enemy. To achieve this, stuffed owls with large staring eyes were swung on strings over the heads of the anxious predators, while small stones were catapulted at them in an effort to forge a Pavlovian connection between the feathered assailants and pain. I have never found owls very intimidating myself, but then I'm not a ferret. What was causing me some concern, however, was the clear evidence of serious chiselling around the lock of my door from the outside, bearing clear witness to some villain's felonious intent. Recalling the stark image of the storekeeper's revolver, I speculated on the unsettling notion that I was holed up in a slightly dodgy town. Fortunately fatigue overcame the insomniac influence of this anxiety, and I slept the sleep that comes from covering long distances on an unfaired motorcycle.

KILLIN' JIM SULLIVAN

One thing I like about motels is the easy getaway the morning after. There's no fussing over bills with complications about how many cherries you had in your cocktail. You pay when you arrive, what you see is what you get, no frills, and when you go, you go – albeit with a slightly guilty feeling that you must have neglected to do something important. The morning I left the town of Kingsman, I realized pretty soon that I had; it was my jacket that I'd left behind. My jacket, containing wallet, passport, credit cards, and just about everything that I needed to get me out of every conceivable contingency, starting with filling up at the gas station where I'd arrived before realizing the nature of my neglect; I decided to return to the motel.

By the time I reached the state line, the next state being Nevada, it was very warm. I pulled off the road to look at the Hoover Dam and bought a postcard. The card was based on one of those old sepia photographs, a series of which depict famous characters from the wild days of the frontier, when men were men and, in the case of the wretches depicted on this card, hung by the neck. I don't know why the sight of these lynch-mob victims should have amused me as much as it did, but the picture of them dangling like so many Christmas stockings from the rafters of the barn where they'd been run to ground, tickled me to the core, setting my features into so intractable a smirk as to attract the interest of fellow travellers who, like me, were nosing around the souvenir vendor's emporium. There was in this ghoulish scene, the evidence of a simple justice that, if more generally applied might well deter the indulgent behaviour of a few poisonous miscreants amongst the seedier levels of the motorcycle subculture.

I scribbled a few ludicrous comments upon the back of 'Killin'' Jim Sullivan' and his compadre's pictorial epitaph, posted it to my sister in Ickenham, and crossed the state line into Nevada.

DEATH VALLEY

I hadn't travelled more than fifty yards before I was flagged down by a state trooper who pointed out, good naturedly, that Nevada was a slave state; he didn't put it that way but his meaning was clear, and it was helmets on heads time. Studying the map, I decided that today had to be the day to make a run through Death Valley. No interstate runs through the dreaded divide that presented one of the greatest terrors of the old pioneer route, it's off the beaten track some significant distance from the direct route to LA, at least from the way I was coming. But why do things the easy way when you can suffer the appalling misery of the thermally induced masochism on offer at so celebrated a natural grill pan?

Even before I got to the Valley I was too hot, and had picked up a piece of half molten tar from the road with my boot, which was sticking to the footrest rubber like a piece of tenacious gum. I'd taken Highway 95 north to Beauty, where I topped up the gas and bought two pint bottles of Coke, my sense of intrepid adventure heightened by the simple precaution. The woman who served me verified that my indicated direction of travel was the correct one for Death Valley, her manner betraying a wearisome attitude toward the childish curiosity that propelled tourists to this desolate place. I pocketed my change and set off for the nearest entrance to the valley at Daylight Pass, which my map advised me, was 4317 feet above sea level, a sharp contrast to the lowest point in the Valley at Badwater, were the altitude was 282 feet below sea level, affording it the distinction of being the lowest point on the surface of the United States.

I paused again to check the oil level, a tricky business, as the dip stick was scalding hot to the touch. The tank was full, so I nosed onto the start line.

Sitting on my motorcycle at the head of Death Valley, I experienced a sense of misgiving such as one balancing on the tip of a high diving board feels before taking the plunge. My anxiety, I assured myself, was theatrical, consider the facts, I urged myself. This was 1989, a good road, I was sure, extended throughout the course of the Valley, I had a sound motorcycle, sufficient fluid for a day, in all likelihood, and only seventy miles or so between me and the far end of the Valley. Furthermore, there would be other traffic passing the same way, and who could possibly drive on and leave a fellow stranded in a place like this? There was really no rational cause for concern, and yet, like an intelligent child trying to suppress its foolish fear of the dark, my logical endeavours failed to eliminate a powerful anxiety that soaked my brain with liquid fear as I squinted down that awful gully.

The Valley's awesome reputation, allied to the daunting view from this high vantage point, contrived to unravel the resolve that had brought me to this ominous pass. I was not the victim of pure hype; the picture of the valley from this point is unnerving. A flat-bottomed trench perhaps four or five miles wide, I guessed, stretched before me, lined by the hills that border its lethal track. The air shimmered in its depths above the salty lining glistening along the middle of its course, disrupting my attempt to focus my eyes as they surveyed the macabre divide between the hunched treeless mounds hulking with palpable menace like fresh earth bordering the sides of an open grave.

Easing the clutch out, I slid cautiously forward, pausing a second time at a board bearing details of the Valley and featuring holders stuffed with leaflets bearing survival hints for the benefit of the unfortunate. These token gestures of a responsible society flapped languidly in the feeble breeze like the scant hairs of spitted skulls marking the boundaries of an Indian burial ground. Motivated by childish bravado, I ignored the leaflets and rolled forward into the valley.

As I descended, my anxiety rose in converse proportion to the declining altitude, as the heat correspondingly, increased. Heat at this level provides an experience that is more than just the uncomfortable sensation of extreme warmth; it acquires an asphyxiating oppressiveness that borders on the malevolent extreme of aggression. The sun was no friend in this place, and I made every endeavour to protect all exposed skin from its vindictiveness. Such was the influence of the forces to which I found myself subjected, that I decided to retain my jacket, since I suspected that in shirt sleeves alone I could be burned or roasted through the scant cotton. I couldn't quite rationalize this at the time, but in retrospect, a logic emerges from the recognition that once the air temperature significantly exceeds that of one's blood, the phenomenon of a cooling breeze ceases to exist. Just as pouring boiling water over a body will not cool it, so it is with air. I had experienced what, to a temperate dweller, is a perverse and puzzling sensation before, when in the Persian Gulf in summer, but even there, if my memory serves me honestly, perhaps because of the moderating influence of the ocean, the heat seemed less intense than in this land-locked oven. Besides retaining my jacket for protection, I greased my lips with ointment, that I'd bought in Arizona. Produced by the Navajo Indians, the thick waxy substance boasted an aromatic piquancy that encouraged a sense of faith in its protective capabilities. I lathered my forehead and hands with suntan cream boasting a protection factor of ten, and to enhance the chances of these products retaining their properties in the arid wind created by my own movement, I tied my green army fishnet scarf across the lower half of my face in the manner of a desert-bound Bedouin, while my photochromic prescription lenses completed the gap between it and the shadow cast by the peak of my nominal crash helmet. Resembling, in this guise, a figure drawn from a military manual on chemical warfare survival, I posed for a photograph by an appropriate sign with the camera balanced on the saddle of my motorcycle, the delayed action shutter mechanism having been operated. This obligatory theatre completed, I remounted the motorcycle, started the engine, and proceeded with the assault on my Promethean gauntlet.

Just as later in my eastbound journey I was to be outraged by the ability of the temperature to fall so low, now I was perplexed by its seemingly infinite capacity to rise to such unfamiliar extremes. I struggle for Dante-esque adjectives to describe the heat, but to do so with a bucketful of similes would permit the essential evil to evade its distinctive label. Each intake of breath hurt my lungs, forcing me to sip the air with shallow reluctance as the hungry, from necessity, drink boiling soup. Still the land sank, and, despite the dryness of the air, I blinked the itchy sweat from my eyes in an effort to maintain sufficient focus on the quivering tarmac.

It was a sense of inescapable molestation that better describes the assault under which I felt myself to be labouring. The atmosphere, like a multitude of powerful hands, was curling its thick fingers around my throat, a thermal garotte of lethal intent. The air before and behind, to left and right of me, pressed in on my baking body. I was trapped in a paradoxically open tomb devoid of respite, denying relief in any plane, as a cricked neck withholds all hope of comfort. It was perverse, I was flying down an open road and yet felt caged; though in motion, I felt tethered. Tethered and caged by the intangible adversary of asphyxiating air, a friend turned foe, a necessity mutated into a pain. With each yard I travelled, I felt myself to be moving intractably into a labyrinth of accumulating danger, as if doors were silently closing behind me while deadly foes conspired to block my retreat; I seriously thought about turning around. Few things induce panic quicker than difficulty in breathing and I was having trouble, I was getting panicky. Should I turn back? I eased off on the throttle which was barely cracked open as I was rolling downhill; my fingers hovered over the brake lever, I was in two minds. Just how much hotter could it get? What if I passed out? What if I suddenly became an asthmatic for the first time in my life? I felt that I'd lost my bearing, the experience was so unfamiliar, so hostile, I was scared.

This was the stuff of childhood nightmares, prompted by the frightening predicaments of boyhood heroes trapped in caves of gurgling larva or pits of venomous snakes. Nonetheless this was something different. I had come to America to see different things, sights I couldn't see at home, sounds I couldn't hear there, and sensations I could never feel there. Well I'd got what I'd wanted, this was different all right. Different from a run down to the South Coast, different from a night in the pub or a walk in the woods, different from punting in Cambridge or raking through the celebrated bookshops of Hay-on-Wye. It was totally, unreservedly, and indisputably different to any of those things, and the sooner it was bloody well over the better.

Years earlier I had felt this same sense of panicky desperation when undergoing a Merchant Navy fire-fighting course in Plymouth. On that occasion I, with two others, was sent into a brick building filled with oily smoke to recover several dummies representing collapsed victims of the fire. Each of us wore a cumbersome smoke-helmet, like an old fashioned diver's hat, equipped with an air hose and life-line. We were shown a plan of the building before being directed within via a blanket door. We had, each in turn, to negotiate a concrete tunnel a mere three feet in diameter, beyond which a series of passageways led to the destination where the mannequins lay. Before five minutes had passed we were hopelessly confounded, our life and air-lines a pitiful tangle which thwarted our intended advance, rooting us to the spot like a trio of mating octopuses. Having been gone a long time, one of the firemen came looking for us, equipped with the more flexible self contained breathing apparatus. Pushing his face close upon the windows of my helmet, he shouted advice at me before turning me around to unravel the disabling chaos of lines that had frustrated our efforts. In response to his muted entreaties, I climbed a metal ladder to a platform composed of numerous round bars, which revolved as I struggled for a foothold on their unstable surface. The dreadful disorientation had destroyed any sense of ambition for completing the mission. I cast about in the murk, terrified by the prospect of severing or disjointing my air-line. By chance, my hand fell upon a doorknob which I grasped with ecstatic gratitude, as a drowning man might grasp at a lifebuoy, turning it enthusiastically to effect my escape into the blessed clarity of the outside air. On discovering behind the door, nothing but the blank spectre of a brick wall, a sensation of utter despair overtook me. This was the stuff of nightmares, the very worst kind of helpless scenarios from the tortured realms of childhood dreams. It was at this low ebb, when I feared my resolve could sustain no act more controlled than desperate and undignified flight, that the pulses of air which had flowed down my air pipe with metronomic regularity, now ceased. The pause which separated the last charge from the resumed effort, extended in reality less than ten seconds, a delay whose influence on my disturbed state, was out of all proportion to its duration. The explanation subsequently supplied to me by my partner on the pump, was that his leg had grown tired and he had paused to shake it about whilst standing on the other, a defence for ageing me by several years which did not at the time seem quite adequate to me. The similarity of this experience invoked a disturbing reminiscence.

I paused again to re-wax my lips from the tub of ointment which I'd wisely stowed upright in a small pouch of the left hand pannier. The temperature had reduced the consistency of the contents from that of soft candlewax, to unset yoghurt, which poured over the lip of the vessel as I unscrewed the lid. This time I administered a more liberal application, lining my nostrils also, to protect their delicate internals from the smarting dryness which was affecting them with a curiously cold sensation, the paradoxical inverse of freezing metal which can burn the skin as surely as a hot iron.

I continued along the empty track, stopping occasionally to take a photograph, pauses during which I left the engine running in order to reduce by one, the multitude of unhelpful possibilities threatening me. I did speculate on the fate of the film confined within the metal case of the camera, a concern which I was to learn weeks later, was not unfounded, as all the transparencies which had, for the transit of this valley, endured the confines of the camera, revealed after processing, a variety of streaky scars, as if traced by some insidious flame. I returned one to Kodak, who assured me that the imperfections were not the responsibility of their laboratory, but the consequence of exposure to extreme heat. Since none of the other films were similarly affected, I guess that the film company's interpretation was correct.

It was during one of my photographic pauses, where, for some reason I had cut the engine, that the unthinkable happened. I'd pulled off the narrow road onto the loose shingle of the desert floor in order to photograph a great loaf of yellowish rock apparently bulging under the influence of the sun like fresh baked bread. Even as I was stepping off the machine I recognized a hint of that ominous intuition that cries 'no,' which with characteristic optimism, I ignored to my cost. Before I was clear of the machine it keeled over to an irrecoverable angle, crashing down into the dust like a poleaxed bull elephant. I'd failed to extend the sidestand adequately and had now to risk hernias if I was to escape this damned spot.

A fallen motorcycle encourages in its owner, the same concern and response, as the prostate form of a hapless geriatric who's fallen in the street. The popular instinct demands that the poor devil must be righted, regardless of whether such a tactic is appropriate or desired by the recumbent. Convention prescribes restoration to the vertical, *Homo erectus*, repair dignity and damn the consequences. I foolishly practised this crude logic with a heedless desperation, my back bent over the prostrate machine in a manner depicted in a million industrial safety posters as the one most likely to invite dorsal injury. Pushing as I was, against soft yielding sand, the bike slid from me like a runaway wheelbarrow as I strove to right it, dissipating my effort, undermining its aim, and significantly injuring my back. I knew at once, with the depressing certainty of the mortally wounded, that I done myself a serious nasty, and it was with a gasp of pained and wretched dismay, that I subsided in pathetic blubbering defeat alongside my useless burden onto the stony embers of the desert's unsympathetic

155

ash pan. An increment was added to my state of distress by the observation from my dusty couch, that the left hand mirror of the motorcycle was cracked, shards of glass lying shattered about the stone with which its unequal contest had been held. Remaining segments clung to their grazed frame in a sadistic effort at ensuring that my distress was visually as well as emotionally apparent. Seldom had my reflection appeared so acutely distressed.

As I lay panting from these exertions, I discovered a sense of deep empathy with the courageous pioneers who had trodden this fearsome path. I had no serious doubt that I would resolve my immediate problem sooner or later, but what of those weary wagon trains, short of water, low on supplies, appalled by the unaccustomed hostility of the environment to which they had wilfully come. How often had broken axles sunk into soft sand? How often had recalcitrant horses collapsed in their harnesses? Looking across the heat-haze of the blistering valley from my recumbent position, I could visualize with an intuitive clarity, the pathetic scenes that must have unfolded within the scope of my present vision. I could see the pawing horses, bemused and panicked by their plight, urged on by the desperate entreaties of their masters, as sinewy arms glistening with perspiration, strained at the fractured spokes of sunken wagon wheels. I could hear the awful crunch of splintering timber as a subsiding carriage fell backward into some unseen depression, chaffing the horse's flanks with its retreat as, like a ship sinking stern first, it settled irretrievably into its sandy grave. I could envisage the wretched travellers, exhausted by their efforts and demoralized by their failure, slumped alongside the crippled caravans, their backs against the ruptured planking through which the remnants of grain and water trickled like the crucial lifeblood of a wounded soldier amidst the smouldering carnage of a battlefield. I could see their faces turned upward toward the sun in acknowledgement of defeat, a tacit gesture of suicidal resignation, like that of the crippled deer that turns its throat to the lion's jaws. As I looked around at the treeless terrain, I recalled a signposted warning not to stray from the road as rattlesnakes love the arid heat of this region, but not the interference of the trespassers who disturb their venomous solitude. At this unsavoury reflection I cast my eyes about for some sign of a scaly presence; none was apparent though I could see wavy lines in the sand which I took for the tracks of serpents and the possibility of their appearance stirred me from my recumbence, inspiring me to struggle upright and resolve my predicament.

Disciplining myself to a reasoned tactical strategy, I unstrapped the tent, bedroll and bagged luggage from the pillion area in order to lighten the load. With a firm hand on the left handlebar grip and another on the saddle base, I managed, by the narrowest of margins, to lever the weighty brute upright. Besides the ominously broken mirror, and some irksome dimples in the chrome of the primary transmission cover, there seemed to be no other damage. I restored the luggage, took a gulp of disgustingly warm, flat Coke, and pressed the starter button. A moment's concern ensued as I wondered if I might have caused some damage that would prevent the engine starting. I could not imagine what form such damage might take, but my mind was not riding on the most optimistic of tracks, so it was with a sense of substantial relief that I heard the motor fire and watched it shuddering cheerfully in its rubber mountings before swinging a painful leg over the seat and riding up on to the welcome tarmac of the narrow highway.

The engine pinked a little as I climbed the upward slopes after passing the lowest point of Death Valley, a symptom of the heat I decided, and thought no more about it, a confidence that was justified since the irksome noise diminished with the later evening cool. For the moment though, it was still hot as hell as I headed for the appropriately named Furnace Creek. Here I met a character who, by his expression of one-upmanship, quite overawed the perception I had nurtured of my own stoic resolve in running through Death Valley on a summer's afternoon aboard a motorcycle. Towards me, out of the merciless sun, like a bizarre mirage from the desert, came a man on a bicycle. A man in shorts and T-shirt, wearing sunglasses, crouched over the handlebars and peddling as if all the goblins in hell were hot on his tail. 'Typical,' I thought, just when I think 'I'm the roughest toughest dude around,' some toe-rag has to burst your bubble, shatter your illusions, and totally put you in the shade by kicking you off your pedestal of supreme masochism through going ten better. As far as he was concerned my effort might as well have been a jaunt down to Brighton for the day in as much as it compared with his. Not wishing to seem churlish, I gave the sicko a cheery wave, dismissing him as a perverted disciple of one of those weirdo Californian cults. He returned my gesture with sickeningly energetic enthusiasm as he whirred past, a blur of spokes and coloured stripes – bastard!

At a point somewhere beyond the halfway mark in my transit of the Valley, I came, rather disappointingly, to an oasis. I didn't need gas, I even had enough soft drink, having made adequate preparations at the other end, so this unexpected staging post served only to diminish my sense of adventure, already thrown into belittling perspective by the cyclist. It was interesting nonetheless to discover a place in the USA that looked so convincingly as if it belonged in North Africa. The suddenness with which the harsh desert surrendered its austerity to lush palms, was dramatic to a degree which suggested artificial irrigation. It was rather as if the whole set had been constructed in Hollywood and transplanted to this place. High up on a rocky ledge perched a Moroccan villa, which, in conjunction with the palms, would have made General Gadafi feel at home, at least until he spotted the good ol' Stars and Stripes fluttering over the general store and felt the heavy hand of Uncle Sam on his burnous-wrapped neck.

After sunset the temperature dropped rapidly, leaving a pleasantly cool evening by the time it was completely dark. Furnace Creek and Death Valley lay behind me now, and I was heading south at full steam to pick up Interstate 15, west for Los Angeles. I was still in desert though. Most of California, at least in the south, seems to be desert, which came as a big surprise to me. This image was graphically at odds with that of the lush fruit groves depicted on packs of dates and the legendary orange groves. It was not unattractive in its own arid way though, this desert, at least what I could see of it in the darkness, which amounted to no more than a black silhouette of jagged rock starkly framed against a cloudless star-pocked backdrop of sky. I saw no sign of life besides the increasing swarms of *kamikaze* insects that flowed toward the beam of my approaching headlight with lemming-like fatalism. The density of this assault was such that it was hard to imagine the entire area enjoyed so prolific an occupation of these creatures. I could only assume that they were lured from afar by the solitary light to which instinct compelled them with terminal consequence. I stopped once or twice, to clear the accumulated carcasses from the headlamp glass, as its light was dimming rather as a stream blocked by soldier ants is arrested by the temporary dam of their sodden corpses.

I was travelling faster now, up to seventy and then eighty miles per hour, keen to put Death Valley farther behind me, eager to be away from the wilderness and, shameful though it sounds, back to the highway with its towns and restaurants and people. I felt lonely out there in the dark desert night, there was a spookiness about it that encouraged frequent glances at the fuel gauge and made me especially glad of the reliable engine rumbling softly, even at this speed, beneath me.

I didn't normally travel much above the mandatory fifty-five miles per hour speed limit all the time I was in America, but tonight was an exception. I didn't reckon on meeting any cops out here, and if I did, unless they were hiding in darkness, I'd have seen them coming literally miles away. Since I only passed two vehicles, both travelling in the opposite direction, within seventy or eighty miles, it was no great inconvenience to slow down for both. Besides, I reasoned, even if they weren't cops, they might just be on the wrong side of the road, and I wanted time to manoeuvre. The only other thing that bothered me, not counting the slight spookiness, was the possibility of a large animal wandering into my path. I had seen no evidence of such wildlife, and this country was far too dry for cattle I assured myself, and so I rocketed on, hurtling into the coal cellar blackness with only the company of flies splattering me in a remorseless suicidal sleet.

The road beneath me was invisible, and beyond a few yards of illuminated centre-lane markings the route ahead was likewise coal-black, promoting a sense of total isolation from reality that had developed in the darkness. The clock showed a steady eighty miles per hour now, a velocity at odds with good sense, given the limited scope of my vision. I'd succumbed to an academic detachment which curbed all anxiety. I felt above and beyond the limitations of my situation, immune from the consequences of my indiscretions, a false confidence that I had sometimes experienced when studying a marine radar screen, forgetting, in my tiredness, that these dots represented ships hundred of feet long, and weighing thousands of tons, inhabited by dozens of people, people like me. They weren't confined to the screen, they were out there on the ocean, all around me, some coming toward me, invisible in the fog, invisible, menacing, but vulnerable, just as my ship was vulnerable, its fate resting in my hands, the fate of all the people on board in my hands, subject to my decision. Three possibilities: turn to port, turn to starboard, or do nothing – only remember that the dots on the screen are not just dots on a screen, keep track of the reality, don't lose concentration, remember it's all for real, real ships, real lives. I used to find it hard sometimes, to discipline myself, to keep track of the reality. I've never been that hot on facing reality, I should never have been a ship's officer, I wasn't sure I should ever have taken up riding motorcycles. The darkness of the warm night reminded me of the cosy darkness of the ship's wheelhouse, always blacked out after sunset, the dimly illuminated chart room screened off with curtains, but the wheelhouse inky black so the navigator can see other lights on the water. This was not a wheelhouse, this was a desert. I wasn't sailing now, I was riding, riding through a desert. There was something surreal about my circumstances, a paradoxical comfort born of unfamiliarity had induced a sense of fantasy upon which rested a dangerous confidence in a perceived invulnerability.

The air about me felt tangibly close, just as the hot air of the afternoon had felt close by virtue of its humidity; so the darkness cocooned me in a capsule identified by the warm luminosity of the instrument dials and the stunted questing beam of the headlamp sticky with its gelatinous mausoleum. Despite my velocity the warm air felt intimate, matching my progress with irresistible persistence as an electric hare forever outpaces the greyhound. Had a hand reached steadily out from the darkness and latched upon my shoulder, surprise would have formed the lesser part of horror, such was the convincing tangibility of my environment. And so it was that with the accompaniment of these abstract feelings I hurtled on, a missile of optimism trusting to the unwavering nature of my track, just as the faithful navigator pursues a course across the featureless ocean toward an invisible destination.

I attributed to that road the same unwavering quality of consistency with which the navigator, in setting his course, credits the unfaltering dependability of his compass. And so with faith, if not quite blind, at least myopic, I roared across the empty desert, as wild improbabilities consumed the vacant potential of my imagination. With the stars for bases of uncertain reference, the terrestrial trappings of my immediate consciousness had fallen quite away, as I rode an astral freeway into the infinity of the cosmos.

Perhaps there was no end to this road, or conclusion to my interminable transit? Perhaps I had died in Death Valley, like the legions of my equestrian precedents and was now fulfilling the fate of an eternal voyager as the wages of my itinerant lust?

Still the figures of the odometer ticked steadily on, sustaining my faith in the reality that I was really getting somewhere. Like fruits revolving in a gambling machine, displacing their forebears at the windows of chance, the numbers climbed and climbed, until, with statistical inevitability, the welcome bells of the jackpot rang. Up ahead the silken blackness surrendered to the illuminated lacerations of light moving perpendicular to my lonesome track. Thank God: Interstate 15, the road to LA.

LA

I felt pretty good this morning. The weather was dry and clear, my back didn't seem too bad, and even the surly Mexican in the motel office seemed friendlier than he had when I'd booked in the previous evening. Out on the parking lot an elderly couple in a sleek grey Pontiac smiled at me as I pulled the fat pannier straps tight, and buckled them down for the last stretch of my westward journey.

'Nice bike,' commented the old boy, nodding appreciatively at the motorcycle, which despite not having enjoyed the benefit of a clean since passing into my ownership, still glistened with an eye-catching compulsion that belied the thousands of miles travelled. I, however, failed to identify any part of the motorist's goods and chattels upon which I could with sincerity, bestow reciprocal applause, the greater part of my attention being consumed by the appalling nature of his trousers, which were, quite simply, very yellow. Why do Americans wear yellow trousers? Nobody else does, so why do they? Are they all colour-blind? If it was all a bit of a joke, and the comedians rushed home and changed them after raising a few laughs, I could understand it. But no; Americans walk around all day in yellow trousers, they go into shops wearing them, and get served. They walk into bars and order drinks wearing them, and aren't slung out. They drive cars in them and they frequently drive golf balls in them. It's a wonder they aren't disqualified for causing an obstruction. Why do they do it? Arabs have a reason for wearing white robes, hikers have a reason for wearing plus-fours, Eskimos have a reason for wearing animal furs – but what reason can Americans possibly contrive in defence of their patronage of yellow pants?

It took me two hours to reach the outskirts of Los Angeles, a ride throughout which I was puzzled by the question – when am I going to get out of this desert? The colour of the hilly landscape around me was as uniformly brown as the Pontiac driver's trousers were remorselessly and unapologetically yellow. My preconceived notion of California as a lush green paradise of well-covered horticultural opulence, was being dismantled by the parched reality of first-hand observation. It is to be remembered, however, that I was in Southern California. California is a pretty big place, and extends through significantly diverse latitudes. I didn't feel like complaining anyway, I was enjoying the sunshine, the bike was running like liquid butter, and I would shortly be among friends. Not that shortly though; it took me three hours from the time I reached the outskirts of LA, to locate the law offices of Richard M Lester in Ventura on the south-east corner of the vast metropolis.

Dionne Warwick was right, LA is a great big freeway. L.A. has roads like Venice has canals. LA has such a superabundance of roads it's a wonder there's any room left for a city. With so many people moving so much of the time, it's surprising there's anyone left static anywhere to actually do anything, let alone any space left to do it in. Leaving aside, for obvious reasons, gas stations, I imagined all other retail outlets, homes, parks, and beaches, must be devoid of people, since they were surely all busily engaged in travelling somewhere. I began to suspect that, had I pulled over, assuming I could see how to pull over, in order to make some mundane purchase from a store, I would have found its closed door decorated with a sign bearing a corruption of the old fisherman's excuse – 'Gone driving.'

A movie released a few years back, drew for its title on the critical significance of being at the site of happenings, when they take place. The movie was called *Being There*. Hollywood should make a follow up as a testimony to the philosophy of Los Angelinos, which surely subordinates arrival to the more important prerequisite of travel; it could be entitled, *Going There*.

I'd been told I would hate Los Angeles. I like small compact towns with clearly defined centres and identifiable boundaries. LA has neither, but I did not develop negative sentiments about the colossal metropolis. Perhaps it is a feature of the instinct to challenge the ability of others to predict one's taste, that compelled me to form a benign perspective on the City of Angels.

Provided you take the right freeway exits, navigation in Los Angeles is probably simpler for a stranger than it would be in London, and for motorcyclists, the infinitely more disciplined driving style makes life a lot less hazardous. It is probably a feature of the purpose built roads that encourages lane discipline. By contrast, the bends, inconsistent widths, and unclear sense of priority imparted by the labyrinthine folly of London's roads, promotes a degree of artistic interpretation which has steered the evolution of our driving habits. The American road system may not have eradicated bad driving, but its clarity robs the offender of the wealth of excuses to which his European counterpart has recourse. Beyond these mechanically engineered influences, there are at work forces of commendable decency, reflected in wider passing distances and less cavalier behaviour at road junctions. On occasions I found myself puzzled by the appearance of cars a hundred yards distant, static at intersections for no apparent reason, thus inviting the suspicion that their drivers had either expired at the wheel or were levelling shotguns barrels at me. Their movement, subsequent to my passage, would dispel both theories whilst confirming my opinion of Stateside drivers as refreshingly considerate. I exclude New York from this general assessment, as the aggression and near homicidal lunacy displayed there, approaches the Italian standard, a distinction which may not be unrelated to the incidence of pasta people domiciled in the Big Apple. Over most of the country, however, the lack of congestion obviates the competitive spirit which characterizes the Continental motoring style. In America, a more patient attitude prevails, to the particular benefit of the more vulnerable road user. This road user was certainly more sinner than sinned against, as I executed erratic lane switches upon belatedly sighting exit signs that sounded familiar from my perusal of the hastily scribbled directions I'd taken over the phone.

By the time I'd left the freeway and was in a part of what could be called a city, as opposed to an infinite asphalt strip, I was low

164

on fuel. Pulling into a filling station, I unscrewed the gas cap and lifted the hose off its pump body. A large, gusseted rubber boot extended almost the full length of the nozzle, like a substantial yet inadequate contraceptive. I pushed the nozzle into my tank and squeezed the trigger – nothing. I suspected the out-sized prophylactic to be the author of my frustration, but could not imagine what it was I was supposed to do with it. I strolled over to a pay booth where a short Mexican explained that you had to push the nozzle right in, so, armed with this advice, I renewed my efforts, but with no more success than before. The toad-like character in the kiosk, repeated his advice from afar, with accompanying gestures which emphasized the need to retract the rubber sheath further. My failure to overcome an incurable ineptitude excited the tutor to more vigorous efforts of graphically demonstrative mime. Like some demented charade player unable to fathom the incomprehension of his team mates, he repeated his visual advice with a frenzied repetition of reciprocal motions that bordered on the comically obscene. It crossed my mind that it was fear of robbery that persuaded him against abandoning his post, though as it did so, the mustachioed homunculus burst out of his glass cell and crossed the forecourt in a series of squat bounds to where I stood lamely gesturing at the sky with the pistol grip. Snatching it impatiently from my hand, the Latin instructor demonstrated the workings of this fangled hardware.

'*Si, Si*?' 'Ah, *Si*,' I understood now. The adaption was designed for cars; when the nozzle was pushed a long way into the gas tank, the rubber boot contracted sufficiently to activate the mechanism that released the gas. Not having sufficient depth in my motorcycle tank to accommodate the required length of nozzle, I needed to simulate that minimum penetration by withdrawing the sheath by hand, all rather complex really, though the design had been conceived with the best of motives in mind. It seems someone in the environmental lobby calculated how much gas evaporates into the atmosphere whilst escaping through the gap between the nozzle and the filler access during the time it takes to refuel an automobile. When you multiply the individual pollution from a single car by the millions of vehicles in America each day, then apply a factor of 365 to the equation, you end up with some environmental statistics to impress the legislators with and ensure that rubber sheaths are mandatory, whatever the Pope says to the contrary. Of course if Americans made do with engines slightly smaller than the ones Europeans associate with buses they could make far bigger savings, but hey, let's not get sacrilegious.

Tanked up, I took to the freeway once again in search of Ventura Boulevard. Now the address I was seeking was 15910 which I had always assumed was some kind of code – zip codes, I believe they call them over here. The original idea of a zip code I was once told, is to discipline the exodus of populations from urban conurbations when it is known that a nuclear bomb is about to explode on them; the anticipated effect being an orderly departure with no shoving. This always struck me as a highly optimistic plan, notwithstanding the pessimism that contemplated the need for such contingency arrangements in the first place. 15910 is not a zip code however, it's a street number. This had not even occurred to me when I first wrote the address on a letter I was mailing there. No street, I thought, has almost sixteen-thousand numbers in it. I was of course wrong. Ventura Boulevard goes on and on and on, not unlike a Barry White record, though the duration blessedly, is not matched by the big man's tedium. Why do people buy Barry White records? I suppose one might as well speculate on why Americans wear yellow trousers or what the Sphinx is smiling about?

Ventura Boulevard 15910 is a twelve-story office block, the seventh floor of which houses the law offices of Richard Lester. Richard Lester is an enthusiastic entrepreneur of remorseless vigour and infectious optimism. Richard's colourful *curriculum vitae* includes the collection of wild animals, principally poisonous snakes, which kept him occupied for some years in South America, though his principal claim to fame in the natural world derives from having trained Clarence the boss-eyed lion of *Daktari* fame. Subsequent to this, he built an empire based on the sale of water beds, a venture which, luckily for motorcycling, sprang a leak, prompting another change of direction. The law practice which Richard now runs, operates to represent motorcycle riders who have been involved in accidents. AIM is the name of the game, standing for Aid to Injured Motorcyclists. It costs nothing for riders to join the scheme, but, in the event of an accident in which they suffer personal injury, attorneys appointed by Richard Lester endeavour to negotiate the best compensation deal possible. Part of the profits from this activity are bled off to finance the efforts of the National Coalition of Motorcyclists (NCOM), a body which co-ordinates the efforts of the numerous riders' rights groups in their campaigns for justice from legislators, which principally amounts to resisting pressure for the introduction of mandatory helmet laws and repealing those already in place, though other issues are addressed. At the time of my arrival in LA, the coalition was primarily concerned with orchestrating opposition to the Chaffe Bill. The Chaffe Bill posed a fundamental threat to the partial autonomy of the states, which illuminated the character of the American political system. Chaffe's Bill, if it had been successful, would have enabled the Federal government to withhold highway maintenance funds from states which failed to introduce approved federal safety programmes. Those programmes included compulsory seat belt and crash helmet wearing requirements. The emasculating flavour of this threat with its big stick ingredient, encouraged its opponents to dub it 'the Blackmail Bill'. Through threatening the sacrosanct autonomy of the states, the whole Federal constitution was jeopardized, thus enabling the motorcycle lobby to mobilize support from a far broader political field than would have been the case had a more selective attack on motorcycling liberties been made.

When I arrived, key members of the committee debating the dreaded 'blackmail' bill were being targeted for treatment. Frontline lobbyists were being contacted, and flights arranged for them to meet the critical people by recognized deadlines, it was all very impressive. Richard Lester is a demonically enthusiastic leader with the single-minded resolution of a General Patton, issuing directives from the turret of his lobbying tank, and puffing on a large wooden pipe that shares a rack with a collection of others on the large oval desk in his sumptuous office.

My stay in Los Angeles was hosted by Pepper, Richard's then chief of staff, at her ritzy apartment a mile from the NCOM office. The contrast with my humble asbestos prefab opposite the scrap yard in Bethnal Green, where Pepper had stayed when in England, was stark. Nice though Pepper's place was, however, I wouldn't have traded it for what I had. There's something about having your own detached place, however humble. It's all a question of entrances. A shared entrance is a shared home, that's the psychology of it. Pepper's apartment escaped that shared common entrance feel of the tower block, partly because it wasn't a tower block, and because there didn't seem to be any other front doors in the vicinity of her's which was approached from a broad Spanish-style patio. The prefab, however, had a garden, let on to by means of a back door where I could sit and absorb the atmosphere of rural illusion created by the plants and trees beyond which, less than a mile distant, glowed the lights of the 600-foot NatWest Tower. It was excruciatingly novel, this post-war oasis of scruffy huts with their ivies and rose bushes, surreptitiously lurking in the shadow of the towering financial maelstrom that hovered like a fiscal ogre two-minutes ride from its leafy exclusivity. I seriously would not have swapped it for the ritziest Knightsbridge flat. Where else in London, I often pondered, could you buy self contained convenience in such a location, for twenty quid a week? Madonna, by contrast, or so I was reading, was having trouble with her neighbours in the New York block where she feverishly works out on an exercise bicycle at all hours of the night; the peddling, it seems, can be felt through the floor, which must be pretty aggravating when you've stumped up a million dollars for the space it occupies. No problems like that for me in Bethnal Green.

THE MONGOLIAN BARBECUE

Los Angeles is a gourmet's paradise of multinational diversity, which for me started with an exotic-sounding Mongolian barbecue, courtesy of Richard Lester. The procedure here was to join a queue moving slowly along a counter loaded with miscellaneous Oriental vegetables, and bowls of meat sliced to a thinness that bordered on the transparent, curled into slim crisps like sun-dried potato peelings. I was concerned that the meat looked rare to the point of rawness, and hesitated at the pork with thoughts of food poisoning unsettling my mind and discouraging an otherwise excellent appetite with graphic images of desperate retching into the porcelain idol. No one else seemed to be hesitating, however, and considering the rigorous health standards boasted by the American restaurant trade, I placed my faith in my host's judgement and loaded up. Maybe, I thought, the meat just looked raw under the bright lights of the food counter. Like a greedy child I piled up my bowl with copious quantities of the multifarious ingredients with a generosity bordering the embarrassing side of enthusiastic. As the precarious pyramid reached unstable dimensions, rogue bean sprouts tumbled off the edge like unwelcome survivors overcrowding a packed lifeboat. I had anointed the omnivorous menagerie of colourful ingredients with a selection of spicy dressings ranging from the mundane to the malevolent, and was just speculating afresh upon the rare nature of the meat, when the whole caboodle was snatched from my hand by a robust Oriental of what I took to be Mongolian origin. A moment expired before I realized that I was not being mugged by some culinary highwayman. No threats had been issued, no demands made, no bold cries of, 'Your noodles or your life,' had rent the air, and though I'd been divested of my dinner by a man with a knife the length of the average sabre, it had not been brandished with the menace of which this malignant mandarin appeared frighteningly capable. As the contents of my bowl were emptied onto a convex hot-plate, five feet across, and attacked with a swift series of lacerating blows, the penny dropped, and my fears of succumbing to uncooked swine fever receded as the spiced shavings of deceased mammal sizzled reassuringly on the frying dome, like victims of an Aztec sacrifice.

As is my way, I'd overdone it with the hot sauces. Gastric retribution requiring the passage of time to exact its penalty, afforded me the opportunity to compound the investment in distress with increments of further indulgence. Bowl number two was no smaller than its predecessor, but since the deal on the meal was 'as much as you can eat,' I could not be accused of over-stressing my host's generosity. Over-eating is a vice which I have cultivated to a point that has astonished my peers, without compromising my waistline. I am convinced that obesity has far more to do with metabolic rates than calorific intake, a fact to which my ability to button myself into thirty-inch jeans bears compelling witness.

CLASSIC & ROMANTIC

From the restaurant, we drove to a bar where Richard was planning to address a local biker group with a talk on his AIM programme and the efforts of the National Coalition. All the bikes outside the bar were Harley-Davidsons without exception, a coincidence which is not a coincidence if that makes sense, which it doesn't so it isn't. Why should people who ride a particular type of motorcycle hold certain views on what we might call social politics? That is to say, the sort of legislative manipulation of people's activity that requires them to be strapped into cars or helmeted when riding motorcycles. The truth is that the riders of different types of motorcycle are as different from one another as the operators of totally dissimilar transport forms. The pilot of a sophisticated Japanese superbike, with state of the art performance and handling characteristics, is as likely to be as different from the rider of a raunchy and comparatively prehistoric Harley as he is from the motorist behind the wheel of a pre-war Bentley. On reflection, the Harley rider and the Bentley driver may well have more in common than either would have with the high-tech Japanese jockey. It's a question of classical and romantic values. Pirsig, in his intensely bewildering novel, *Zen and the Art of Motorcycle Maintenance*, returns frequently to an examination of the classical and romantic components of all items. The classical qualities he describes as those provided by features which fulfil a practical role. In the case of a knife, for example, its classical qualities may be said to be represented by the hardness of its steel, the durability of its edge, or the arrangements for retaining the blade within the handle. Its romantic qualities, by contrast, might include the engraving on the blade or the grain in the wood of the handle. The overall virtue of a knife might be measured by the blend of classical and romantic qualities.

The Harley-Davidson which I owned for eight years before I bought the one aboard which I undertook this journey, had good romantic qualities. It was lean, low, black, and radiated a threatening masculinity which I, by virtue of my close association with it, hoped to share. People would stop and stare at the *Black Pig* in the street, where its prehistoric proportions would evince a variety of emotions from astonishment and curiosity, through to awe or horror. It was an emotionally-charged machine with a compulsive attention-grabbing soul, by which only the most indifferent spirits could fail to be aroused. Like a traction engine, a World War I bi-plane, or a sleek, varnished sloop, it possessed a potent universal appeal that elicited enthusiastic responses from people for whom motorcycles in general held no interests at all.

A notable exception to that generalism is a friend whose ignorance of motorcycles has been refined to an art form. She scaled the peak of her career in indifference one day when I encountered her in the street astride a smouldering two-stroke, ring-dinging, phut-phutting 250cc MZ, an East German machine of such utilitarian modesty that, like the sensibly sexless, Polish-made shoes of a Hackney social worker, it aspired to the inverted pretension encapsulated by the paradoxical title of the pop song, *Hip to be Square*.

My friend failed to notice that, for the first time in several years, I was travelling by means of a motorcycle other than the distinctive *Black Pig*. Seeking to embarrass her by exposing her limited powers of observation to ridicule, she resorted to a defence based on her unapologetic lack of interest in motorcycles. My counter attack drew for inspiration on my minimal interest in, horses. Suppose, I postulated, that I had spotted my showjumping niece on a camel, I might just have said something – I would certainly have noticed that it wasn't a horse. Threats and violence being the last resort of the out-manoeuvred, my friend sought, with implicit menace, to know if I still wanted her to cook me my Sunday dinner. I lapsed into smilingly silent resignation at this point, as among her virtues, of which I am wont to make scant reference, she is a culinary adventurer of commendable ability.

The slight on my proudest possession and the incomprehensible insensitivity that the unintended snub represented, rankled with me like the bitter injustice of a cricket match, destined to conclude in inevitable victory, that is terminated by the intervention of heavy rain. There are times however, when magnanimous victors must respect the adage which recommends silence as the better part of valour, and in deference to my frequent trough-in, I suspended hostilities.

My new Harley, the one I was riding on this trip, possessed much, though not all, of the romantic charisma which the *Black Pig* exuded in as much abundance as the oil, which dribbled incessantly from the engine. What didn't leak from the greasy iron horse was sprayed into the atmosphere via the exhaust pipe after a brief sojourn in the engine, at a rate matched only by the more extravagant airborne insecticide dispensers. What was viewed, before the advent of environmental awareness, with benign, albeit contemptuous humour, was soon to become the butt of serious criticism and the object of legislation prompted by the increasingly powerful Green lobby. The sheathed gas nozzles I'd experienced bore witness to that power, as did the pollution controls specified on my latest bike. This one scarcely leaked or burnt any oil, a feature that owed much to the vibration-free Evolution engine with its simplified construction, rubber mountings, and belt driven transmission. It also ran on unleaded gas, with silky smoothness enabling higher cruising speeds and greater comfort – attributes that were complemented by appreciably enhanced handling.

Thus it was that, in classical qualities, the new Harley measured far higher up the scale than its predecessor, though a number of cosmetic initiatives definitely operated to the detriment of the evolved brute. The plastic fuel cap, tackily lacquered fender struts, and narrowly spaced forks had all been short listed for attention, whilst the obscenely incongruous instruments balanced obtrusively on the handlebars looked as if they'd been bolted on as the result of a hurried after-thought by a negligent design engineer as the machine was rolling out of the factory door. The seat height was also in need of drastic lowering, not only to achieve that ground hugging quality which traditionally distinguishes Harley-Davidsons, but in order to ensure that my 28-inch legs reach the ground. On aggregate then, the new Harley lost on the romantic scale, but won on the classical, which in view of the considerable demands made by a journey across America and back again, was the more important consideration. If a man's character can, as is claimed, be read in the shine of his shoes, how much more accurately may it be divined by the qualities of the transport he patronizes or the house he lives in?

HATS OFF

The universal patronage of giant American V-twin motorcycles by those attending the meeting spoke volumes about the romantic bias of the owner's philosophy, the campaign for the defence of which, provided the motive for this, one of innumerable gatherings across the country. The compulsory helmet issue, which represents the primary motorcycling concern for American riders, is one that is misunderstood by most in the motorcycling world, as much perhaps as those outside it who view bare headed riding as mere irresponsibility. Those with a more fundamental grasp of the essence of libertarianism however, have little difficulty in identifying the significant assault upon civil liberties which helmet compulsion represents.

There are many pertinent practical, or classical arguments associated with this issue, regarding the realities and misconceptions surrounding the limited or counterproductive role of helmets in accidents, but it is the issue of principle which not only underpins the commitment of the perennial campaigner, but poses the more profound implications for the style and quality of our society. For the purpose of maintaining a focus on the ethics of compulsion, as distinct from it's efficacy, it may be useful to assume what is improbable, ie, that compulsion is responsible for significant savings in life, so that we can deal with the issue as an exercise in balancing the value society ascribes the quality of life, where the preservation of that quality conflicts with the preservation of life itself.

Laws like the one requiring motorcyclists to wear helmets represent the inevitable extrapolation of social welfare policies that have characterized the prevailing trend of post-industrial revolution politics. As long as exploitation has been a feature of human behaviour, there have been those who have sought to resist it. Likewise, since the earliest expressions of evil, sin, and crime first manifested themselves, opposing forces have arisen to resist their influence. It's all part of the equilibrium of life that all forces enjoy, or elicit, equal and opposite forces, well at least opposite ones. Where altruistic motivation by the world's benign defenders of the weak operate to protect them from the gratuitously malignant or selfishly indifferent, then those efforts warrant

174

applause. One of the fundamental differences between man and the animals with which we share this world, is the peculiar instinct for protecting rather than rejecting the lame and inadequate. This is really what humanity is all about. It is the abstract ingredient absent from the superhuman foes of science fiction; the inexplicable factor which does not compute, virtuous by its irrationality. The refinement of humanity is tantamount to the cultivation of the human soul it represents, and is the most commendable enterprise of mortal man which paves the path of ultimate aspiration to immortality. In short, caring for others is a good thing.

Up until fairly recently, most laws were framed to protect the vulnerable from the predatorial. Certainly very few laws could have been credited with the motive of protecting people from themselves. There has, in the past, existed an unwritten understanding, that if man owns nothing else in this world, at least his body is his own responsibility, and how he treats, mistreats it, uses or abuses it, is his business, and his business only. It is critical to the sense of human dignity and independence, for that right to be respected if we are not to transform society into a perpetual kindergarten.

Margaret Thatcher once declared that, 'Freedom of choice is essentially what life is all about, dispense with freedom of choice, and you destroy human dignity.' It was a very convenient quote for the anticompulsion lobby to employ, since it precisely encapsulated the essence of the issue. What did Thatcher mean when she said that freedom of choice was what life was all about? One hopes she was referring to the highest aspirations of mankind, the quest for spiritual perfection, the attainment of ultimate goodness that leads us to immortality – one hopes. These high flying motivations may seem absurdly remote to invoke in the context of a discussion on whether motorcyclists should wear helmets, or rather, be forced to, but there is a common thread connecting these levels of human appetite and ambition.

A consistency of rationale needs to be respected for a government's conduct to be credible. On a spiritual level, the existence of choice is imperative to the development of the soul, whose upward progress depends upon the selection of spiritually good options in favour of bad ones. If the purpose of the world were to achieve perfectly ordered mechanisms that functioned with the precision of an infinitely accurate timepiece, then all humanity might have been created equally perfect with identical programmes preset by a higher authority to unfailingly select the correct options. The objective end result of the actions of all would duplicate the actions and intentions of the good minority now. The result might appear to be Utopia, since no dissenters, disrupters or malevolents would exist to thwart the efforts of the apparently righteous – but it would be a mechanical perfection, based on a world of automatons following instructions rather than making decisions.

Science fiction, whilst seeming to distance itself from such ethereal unfathomables as the supernatural and spiritual, frequently hints at the critical significance of these factors to the meaningfulness of human existence. The artificial societies of smiling perfection, devoid of crime and disease, which visiting earthborn spaceman commonly chanced upon in the sci-fi comics of my youth, always turned out to be flawed. The plots frequently unfolded along similar lines. First impressions of the earthling visitors would invariably be great, they would find the meticulously well ordered society a joyful contrast to the struggling chaos of the world they had left behind. There would always be however, one doubting Thomas, one unquiet soul who would smell the rat from the outset, some Dr Who with the perceptive intellect necessary to recognize the absence of ingredient X. He it is, who creeps into the laboratory of Dr Diabolical and catches him fitting chips into brains, the soul sapping electronic gizmos that effectively determine, or rather, undermine choice, by deterring wrong options, these are the mental manipulators that, in the view of the mad controller, obviate the need for souls. Of course the mad scientist may be benign in his motivation, failing to acknowledge the possibility of spirituality or immortality, he perceives the cultivation of well ordered physical well being, allied to the maximum extrapolation of the physical life span, as representing the only goals worthy of pursuit.

The duped earthlings eventually detect the chilling sense of indefinable wrongness about their new-found Utopia as their nagging doubts crystallize into fearful convictions. Despite the frequent reassurances of their spiritually-gelded hosts the visitors have sussed the plot and must be neutered into conformity for retention in the artificial paradise. As the moment of intellectual castration approaches, however, our human adventurers demonstrate their laudably imperfect spirituality by kicking seven shades of shit out of Dr Diabolical.

The message of this familiar theme is - we need law makers, just as we need spiritual advisors: Popes and prime ministers all have their role to play. What we don't need is puppeteers.

There will be those who think it absurd to compare the curtailment of what are viewed as mundane liberties such as helmetless motorcycling, to the evolution of the human soul, but there is a relationship and a relevance in exploring the role of law making, and the limits which must be applied to curtail the excesses of over-zealous administrators. Without a sense of the purpose of life providing a spiritual dimension to complement the temporal elements of government, the ideal alloy from which to machine desirable legislation will not be found. It is for this reason that religious ideology can never be completely separated from the political mechanism of government. Since all good governments expound the promotion of moral as well as material values, the reconciliation of religious faith with state legislation is as desirable as it is inevitable. While one might not want a government biased toward a particular religious sect how can an atheist administration deliberate on issues such as capital punishment or abortion without reference to spiritual values? An entirely objective government might sustain a rational argument for culling the deformed and in the absence of any spiritual element how could one ultimately oppose them? Life is not just about efficiency and perfection and numbers, it is more subtle than that.

To focus more specifically upon the libertarian core of the helmet issue, it is significant that most of the support for the free-choice lobby within parliament, comes not only from the right, but conspicuously, the extreme right. The left, in politics, is generally associated with a benign caring philosophy, reflected in the humanity that characterizes laws emanating from that side of the spectrum. Laws reducing working hours, demanding safer industrial practices, better state housing, minimum wages, and controlled rents. The kind of laws that seek to protect the vulnerable from the predatorial, or exploitative, have traditionally enjoyed a closer association with the left than with the right. The right, conversely, has sought to liberalize restrictions that inhibit trade, commerce, and profit for the entrepreneurial factions, sometimes to the detriment of the working classes, or to be more general, non predatorial classes.

The problem with benign doctrine, is that it is outreaching its conceptual remit to protect the prey from the predator, by proceeding to protect the prey from himself. Having done what it can to save the rabbit from the fox, the altruistic dictators are now telling the rabbit that dandelions are dangerous things to eat without an approved salad dressing. Ironically it was a Tory government which introduced helmet compulsion, but the forces of motherly social politics that concoct transport policy, inhabit a strip of overbanding which occupies both lanes of the political highway, and though 'protective' legislation is more red than blue, the road safety lobby has acquired an apolitical identity that is maroon. If the unwelcome minders exhibit a confused political complexion, their opponents in the libertarian team tend to be far more predictably tarred with a right-handed brush. The mentality that opposes the interference of do-gooders whose regulations threaten capitalist profits, will also tend to resist those same forces when they operate to manipulate the hazardous indulgences of an individual's private life. Of course what is in contention is the extent to which anyone has a private life, and the degree to which he is responsible to society for the actions which, at least directly, impinge only upon himself. The generalization that used to enjoy a broad acceptance as a base line over which legislators did not step in framing their laws, was that one could do what one liked, as long as in so doing, one did not harm others.

The 'rule of law,' which is not just a vague expression, but a guarantee of legal rights, requires that a man be allowed to do as he likes as long as there is no law against it. Thus it required the enactment of legislation to prohibit for example, the use of marijuana. Of all laws, those governing the restriction of drugs, are probably the closest neighbours of helmet or seat belt compulsion, though there are significant differences which are worth considering.

The government's fear of derestricting popular illegal drugs like marijuana, leaving aside the political propriety of sustaining public confidence in itself, which is no minor factor, stems from the belief that the widespread use of the drug would undermine the stability of society. The worst imaginable scenario involves large numbers of the population stumbling around stoned out of their crates when they should be getting on with work to keep the country's infrastructure and economy intact. Exponents of the liberalization campaign would argue that this picture is an unrealistically pessimistic one, and they may be right; however the fear that relaxation would foster a general malaise at best, and widespread decline into hard drug use at worst, provides the rationale for supporting the status quo. Society does have a responsibility to protect itself from influences which it believes will unravel it's fabric, and about this point hinges the critical difference between drug laws and helmet laws.

I have never heard anyone suggest that the fatality rate of motorcyclists represents a threat to the cohesion of the social fabric or the economy, and it would be a damned fool who would try. In fact the fatality rate worsened slightly in the first full year after the introduction of compulsion in the UK. We shouldn't read too much into that, but it's useful to cite if supporters of compulsion start trying to claim that society is seriously threatened by the loss of young working people to the labour pool through motorcycle accidents. It may sound like heartless indifference to say that the numbers that die are insignificant, but it isn't heartless, it's just a fact. Are the losses to the labour pool of motorcycle accident fatalities a significant factor? No of course they are not. Even if we took the total numbers killed every year on motorcycles, which are in the hundreds rather than thousands, it would still be insignificant. It is to be remembered however, that the relevant figure is not the gross one, but the net, which represents the influence upon the fatality rate that helmet compulsion might represent. Given the improbability of sustaining a defence of helmet compulsion based on the threat to society posed by absenteeism from the labour pool using gross fatality rates, the chances of waging the same argument on net figures, would be not so much verging on the bizarre as epitomizing it. Now the emotionally irrational might at this point accuse me of an insensitive endeavour to denigrate the value of human life, whereas my intention is merely to separate the objective factors from the subjective. Of course there is an emotional aspect to this issue, but it is illogical to use it for the purpose of clouding a pragmatic argument.

A popular tactic of the intellectually neutered, is to suggest for example that if your son were killed in a motorcycle accident, you'd think differently.

If, in that situation, my altered opinions vindicated their predictions, it would in no way undermine the validity of the logic I am currently propounding, reflecting as it would, merely the sad decline of my own impartiality in the presence of misfortune. If I knew I would die in an air crash on Thursday, I might, if empowered, ban civil aviation on Wednesday, even though I respected the value of the public's access to air travel. It would be unfair to exercise that selfishness however understandable it might be. The essential point here is that the truth is the truth, irrespective of its exponents or opponents, and what is right remains right, however many of its champions defect under the influence of personal experience. So when one's views are tested against the stresses of dramatic hypothesis, and found by dint of honest admission to appear flexible, this in no way affects the quality of the original principle. A Christian denying the existence of Christ in the face of a hungry lion, does not by his faint-heartedness cause Christ to vanish, though he may resolve a personal dilemma of immediate concern.

Another characteristic bleat from the camp of the incurably emotional, is that if it saves one life it's worth it. This is of course the kind of pseudo-sagacious claptrap that bottom-league politicians are fond of doling out like punishment lines to a schoolboy. As an exercise in logic, it is just as tiresome and about as useful, providing, as it does, a basis for prohibiting all private transport, with motorcycling at the top of the list, if extended to its logical conclusion. The irksome reality is, that it still gets trotted out in TV discussions, at which audiences nod sympathetically and applaud with a Pavlovian predictability.

Leaving the patently unsupportable social collapse theorists, there remains the more general issue of social burden to be considered. Since almost ninety per cent of UK riders wore helmets voluntarily, and post compulsion fatality rates failed to vindicate the need for legislation, no pragmatic argument exists to counter the libertarian one. It is, however, insufferably hypocritical of those who support compulsion to ignore other indulgences which represent incomparably greater social burdens. The cost to the nation of smoking, excess drinking, and over-eating, and, if I dare say it, the AIDS epidemic, throw even the gross cost of the motorcycling burden into a belittling perspective.

So why pick on bikers? Well the difference between the public perception of the dangers posed by the health threats mentioned, and that posed by the motorcycle, is provided by the dramatic nature of motorcycle accidents. People who die from smoking-related disorders do so quietly in the privacy of hospitals or their own bedrooms. There's no drama, no ambulances, no police, no debris, no shocked crowds, no pools of blood or press photographers. The road, however, is as public a place as any that can be found, an elongated amphitheatre open to all, where gladiatorial contests between motorcyclists and automobiles are as spectacularly messy as they are unequal. So it is that chain-smoking lard-arses, whose daily exercise involves shuffling round to the shops to buy their streaky bacon and chocolate biscuits, will squat self-righteously on their sofas sucking on Marlboros, and pontificating between coughing fits, on the appalling hazards of motorcycling, comparatively safe from the spotlight of public criticism.

A further indictment of those who chastise the indulgence of the dangerous sports contingent, whilst committing slow suicide, rests with the certainty of the damage they do themselves as distinct from the risk, which in the case of the unhelmeted motorcyclist is nothing more than that. A bareheaded rider who returns from a ride that has not resulted in an accident, has suffered no impediment to his health, unlike the smoker whose lungs are a little dirtier for every cigarette he smokes. Hopeless addicts may endeavour to sustain, against any amount of evidence, the belief that smoking does not cause illness. What seems transparently obvious, however, is that if you take a membrane that is designed to operate as a medium through which gases are supposed to be exchanged, and coat it in soot, it is not going to work so effectively, and you don't have to be Her Majesty's Government or the American Surgeon General to work that one out. This false perception of risk is a great problem for libertarians in that their battle is not so much a contest of facts as a battle with public prejudice, on the basis of which governments frequently frame policies. I have spoken to MPs whose assistance I have sought in the effort to reform the helmet law, who have plainly stated that they fully agree with my stance, but insist that the political feasibility of reform without a substantial shift in public thinking is nil. The simple reality is that few if any MPs want to stick their necks out and be branded as 'Mr Loony,' particularly if their majorities are slim.

The social burden argument goes beyond the direct burden represented by injured riders; it extends to the postulation that by utilizing medical resources, injured motorcyclists (and logically we should specify head-injured, unhelmeted motorcyclists, as no others are relevant to this debate), are depriving others of the attention they might otherwise receive. Even were we to believe, for argument's sake, that this was a problem of more than infinitesimal proportions, it opens up a frightening Pandora's Box of repressive controls based on the same premise. Smokers and swimmers, drinkers and drivers, gluttons and hang gliders, climbers and cavers, parachutists, piss-artists, and gays all could be charged with the same offence of burdening society with the cost of their hazardous indulgences, and accused of selfishness in threatening the medical welfare of which other more deserving cases might be in need.

In an interview I conducted some years ago, Dr. John Adams, a past chairman of Transport 2000, and author of a contentious volume entitled, *Risk and Freedom*, made a statement to the effect that, those who seek to limit by law, the risks to which people may expose themselves, must assume a responsibility for identifying the point beyond which the right of authorities to regulate people's conduct ends. It is an optimistic expectation but a good point nonetheless. The MP espousing the virtue of helmet compulsion for motorcyclists should determine whether or not he considers that horse riders should be subjected to the same restriction, or rock climbers, canoeists, push cyclists, or, for that matter, motorists, who far more frequently die from head injuries. No doubt, particularly in the last case, the MP would argue that the discomfort and unacceptablity to motorists, of helmet wearing, were overriding factors, in which case his judgement would reflect more political expediency than justice, which is a dubious basis for the moral element which one hopes characterizes the evolution of our political system.

It is a useful tactic for the libertarian to demand of his opponent the identification of Adam's 'point,' since it persuades others to view their own liberties or lifestyle in a threatened light, thus encouraging sympathy with the intended 'beneficiaries' of their compassionate controls. This question of sympathy, or lack of it, lies at the root of much of the libertarian dilemma. Motorcyclists suffer from it particularly badly, as their image is poor: noisy, dirty, dangerous machines ridden by yobbish young working class louts with poor manners and unruly or violent dispositions. That, until recently, was the stereotypical view held by a large section of the public – though it's largely out of date now. Nonetheless, the shrieking two stroke is unlikely to ever appeal to a majority of mature adults, and the beefy tourer, though infinitely more acceptable, will always be considered by the mass, to be not for them. To most people, big powerful motorcycles are just terrifyingly dangerous machines whose riders should welcome the helpful intervention of authority on their behalf. Since the do-gooders perceive motorcycles primarily as dangerous devices, rather than instruments of fun, they are most unlikely to reach acceptable compromises with the rider lobby. In the view of the safety lobby, every item of equipment available for use in conjunction with the motorcycle will be instinctively evaluated in terms of its potential to reduce risk, rather than in a manner that reflects sympathy with the aesthetic aspects of the item. 'How long does it take to put one on?' the uncomprehending will ask, as if that was of some relevance. How long, one may ask, by way of reply, does it take to don handcuffs?

Transport departments are capable of similar insensitivity in viewing motorcycles simply as transport units, as opposed to instruments of pleasure, let alone of artistic self expression. When I spoke to former Roads' Minister, Robert Atkins, on the subject of conspicuity devices, he expressed surprise that a veteran of over twenty years riding, as I was, should be wearing a dark jacket with no colourful component. As a minister charged with promoting road safety, at least partly through the promotion of what I would term, safety gimmicks, he found my 'neglect' in this respect, inexplicable. Leaving aside the practical arguments pertinent to the value of conspicuity aids, the simple reason for my disdain, rather than neglect, of these colourful 'solutions', is that I don't like them. This may sound like the petulance of a child who refuses to wear spectacles because he thinks they spoil his looks, which in a sense, it is, with the important difference that spectacles are demonstrably useful and conspicuity aids aren't. The point is, that for the 'lifestyle' biker, his appearance when on or off the machine, forms an integral part of the experience which may, for him or her, be ruined by dayglo or helmets. However self indulgent or frivolous that may seem, a very good reason is needed to deny him it.

Atkin's predecessor at the Department of Transport, Peter Bottomley, struggled to recognize the importance of this concept of the motorcycling experience as a form of self expression. In an attempt to encourage his sympathy, I advised him to visit the Kent Custom Motorcycle Show where, at that time, the largest number of 'lifestyle' bikers in Europe gathered for a weekend party. My intention was to demonstrate as graphically as possible, that to many of us, motorcycles are far more than simple transport units, they are instruments of self expression, every bit as valid as paintings, sculptures, or architecture. An artistically sensitive biker might feel the same outrage at having his artistic expression inhibited by needless legislation, as others might be by government regulations dictating the colour of private living rooms or the cultivation of rose bushes. Peter Bottomley came to the Kent Show where he toured the site wearing a fluorescent 'cut off' modelled on the design of the host club's 'colours' which, in lieu of the words 'Hells Angels' read 'Peter Bottomley' and in place of the word 'England,' the designation, 'Dept. of Transport.'

I am not sure if he came away persuaded of the need to preserve the lifestyle he'd witnessed, but he had demonstrated a sense of humour that was as widely appreciated as it was surprising.

So to pursue this subject of self expression, one would not expect a city gent to attach luminous stripes to his charcoal grey suit in order to prevent him being run down when crossing the road. Certainly you could present a case for adopting such measures in view of the fact that people, unlike vehicles, are not required to display lights after dark, but would it be a reasonable requirement? Should not a motorist be proceeding at a speed such that he can identify even a darkly clad pedestrian? And if, due to the inadequacy of his vision, or the excess of his speed, an accident should occur, should the onus of responsibility be transferred to the pedestrian whose failure to adopt the available conspicuity options might be constructed as contributory negligence? Furthermore, should such a 'negligent' pedestrian be fined for failure to adopt such measures in the event of their mandatory introduction, and would society be prepared to imprison those who failed to pay such fines? Such a fate has, incredibly, already overtaken a number of motorcyclists who have pursued a belligerent path, one such even dying in prison.

Fred Hill was an exceptional man who endured thirty-one prison sentences imposed under 'contempt of court' regulations which were invoked in response to Fred's refusal to pay numerous fines levied for his failure to wear a crash helmet. Fred finally died during his thirty-first sentence, his longest ever at 60 days. It was a sentence imposed by barbaric magistrates who would, in my view, have made far more worthy occupants of Fred's cell than the man who suffered a heart attack during his seventy-fifth year. This was an extreme case, but it serves to highlight the fact that when society imposes highly intrusive laws that disturb people's sense of individual expression, it must consider both the morality of imprisoning those who pursue campaigns of opposition, and the feasibility of doing so should large numbers walk that path. In the case of Fred, the government were extremely lucky that the newspapers almost totally blanked the case. With the exception of the late Auberon Waugh and the then MP, Matthew Paris, a veil of silence was drawn across Fred's death. Of course a seventy-four year old man dying in custody during his thirty-first prison sentence on an issue of principle is not a powerful human interest story is it? Herein lies an issue in itself, but we shall return to the more general question.

As regards the self expression reflected in the machine itself, it is self evident that some minimum design criteria are necessary to protect the safety of other road users. The custom builder who decided that the appearance of brakes disturbed his artistic concept could expect scant respect. Similarly in the home, is it reasonable to demand, if only for the sake of neighbours, that minimum fire prevention criteria are met? Again, it is the person's indulgence in exposing others to danger, that justifies legislation. What the exponents of helmet compulsion fail to provide, is evidence that a threat to the common good is presented by the bareheaded rider.

There are those who make the point, in defence of helmet compulsion, that we must have laws to protect society, as if the acknowledged acceptance of laws in general was a justification of laws *per se*. Implicitly, in their estimation, opposition to any law betrays a manifest anarchy in the motivation of the protester. I have argued with those who maintain that we don't tolerate self-expression in the form of murder and therefore should not tolerate people trying to kill themselves, which is, of course, why bikers want free choice on helmets.

I mention this absurd 'logic' in passing to remind myself of the danger from bewilderment, which in the pursuit of logic can derail one's train of thought through the employment of perfectly refined nonsense. As an example of anti logic it rates alongside the unsustainable claim, that since all monkeys have tails, all animals with tails are monkeys.

A relative of this homespun logic, is the gem of reasoning which implies that, because a practice, precaution, or device has merit, the legal enforcement of its adoption is automatically justified. In the case of the crash helmet, the unqualified benefit of its employment appears, under scrutiny, to be at best, open to debate. That aside, to proceed from a recognition of the helmet's virtue which, for the sake of argument we shall assume is unassailable, to the conviction that we must enact legislation demanding, on pain of punishment, the uniform patronage of helmets, represents a monument to simplistic presumption. It would be as just to demand the mandatory carrying of umbrellas on the basis that they will protect the user from possible pneumonia should it rain.

What the argument may be distilled to in the final analysis, is the question of what kind of world you want to live in. Once the facts and perspective of this issue are clarified, the decision must be made, as long as the right to make decisions survives, are we going to control people's lives to an infinite degree as far as technology in the form of surveillance equipment, court time, and public acquiescence permit? Or, do we allow a more liberal society in which people can indulge potentially hazardous activities, thus incurring inevitable costs? Dangerous activities provide society with a safety valve like that on a pressure cooker. As the population, or pressure, increases, so the necessity of the valve becomes greater. There is, at least for free-spirited souls, an asphyxiating claustrophobia about the curtailment of personal freedoms, that the most humane of motivations does not justify.

E M Forster's novel *The Machine Stops*, presents us with a view of the restrictive option extrapolated to an extreme by portraying a society characterized by ultimate indolence, in which the lethargic population live out their entire lives in individual rooms. Everyone enjoys the privacy of their own luxurious capsule equipped with all the necessities for comfortable existence. Any food from the culinary gamut of all cultures can be conjured at the touch of a button, all music likewise, all films ever made, all educational programmes, any book ever written may be summoned up on a video screen or read to the listener on request. Sickness is dealt with by robotic medical analysts with which all rooms are equipped, the necessary medication being provided without the need for the patient to be inconvenienced by leaving his comprehensive apartment. The machine controls everything. The machine is an omnipresent mechanism that represents the ultimate expression in automation, even repairing itself without human assistance.

People seldom travel in this world of effete cushioned effortlessness. There is no need. People can communicate with each other by means of video screens, private transport has long since been abolished as being far too dangerous. Those who do wish to travel about the world may, but few do, and the exceptions are regarded with suspicion by the controlling authority. Adventure and exercise have become foreign concepts, moods are adjusted by drugs. It is a society of such conformity as to make Hitler's Third Reich by comparison resemble a state of anarchy.

Perhaps to some idle sloths, this padded world of listless opulence represents Utopia. It would not, I am sure appeal to the majority, since the human temperament demands a level of adventure, of which danger is an essential component. To be fulfilled, humans need danger just as they need other abstracts such as affection. Some theorists claim that all human emotion influences the body physically through the stimulation of hormone-producing glands. The balance of the chemical products of these glands are, it is postulated, as important to human welfare physically and mentally as a balanced diet. It's a theory in which the greater longevity of married people over single for example, is cited as evidence of the unhealthy stress of loneliness.

Different individual's appetite for danger varies enormously, but since distaste for injury is universal, the admission that there is a foolish or irrational dimension to risk-taking enjoys a similarly broad based recognition. This reluctantly apologetic stance of the risk takers, gives the concerned majority a lever with which to work the ratchet of restrictive legislation inexorably toward the goal of a risk-less society. The luxurious Hell of Forster's novel, emphasizes the need to urge John Adam's duty of identifying the limits of social control. It is of course a boundary which the exponents of safety laws will be unenthusiastic in establishing, since the appetite of their breed for discipline is infinite. Even if the pacemakers of the present contest accept the concept of a finite level of social engineering, the subsequent runners who grasp the baton of anxiety from their tired hands, will set new times in the insidious sport of libertarian erosion, proceeding from baselines provided by their political forebears to which they can refer in search of precedents.

As the campaigning players succeed one another, the game evolves, and for the foreseeable future the score seems certain to continue accumulating against the 'irresponsible' members of 'Team Risk.' The nightmare of the machine-run world may be remote, but the ideological sapling from which it might grow, is alive today.

On an optimistic note, we may draw confidence from the fact that, as in nature, politics experiences pendular oscillations which we must hope will stem the flood-tide of coercion before we forget what it was like to draw breath without a filter strapped to our faces.

ABATE

So, as I was saying, before my train of progress was diverted into that shunting yard of libertarian speculation, Richard and I had arrived at a bar in down-town LA for an ABATE meeting. ABATE stands for Association of Bikers Aimed Toward Education or more extravagantly – A Brotherhood Against Totalitarian Enactments, a catchy little name that typifies the less-than-minimalist titles for which Americans display a conspicuous enthusiasm.

Inside the bar a dozen bikers had already gathered for the meeting. With the exception of the one I took for the local ABATE rep, they were too tall. The exception was about my height, though his body looked a shade too short for his legs, a disproportion that I attributed not so much to a natural physical imbalance, as to the employment of a pair of well-heeled western boots. I hesitated over the decision to drink beer as I was riding later that night, but Richard assured me American beer was very weak by British standards, and I'd need a gutful to get anywhere near trouble. The version of their own beers which the Americans ship to this side of the Atlantic is substantially stronger than that commonly available on the home market. Frankly I find very strong beer absurd. The joy of beer is that you can pour loads of it into your face without tumbling over in a heap. One hears much about the glorious Belgian beers brewed by monks and invariable sold in little bottles of which one is invited to try a variety. Insanity! You might as well ask somebody to punch you until you can't see properly – and they taste awful. I prefer the moderate strength American beers that give you some hope of socializing before you vomit all over yourself.

I drank slowly, something I have to discipline myself to do, taking in the character of the bar and the clientele as I did so. The interior had a cosy, clubbish informality about it, cultivated by the exclusive use of timber, to which posters and notices had been attached at the behest, I imagined, of the patrons, the overwhelming majority of whom were bikers. Twenty minutes after we arrived, the meeting began with a pledge to the flag.

I'd noticed a large Stars and Stripes on a pole over against the wall, which gave me cause to reflect upon the conspicuous nationalism of American bikers. I recalled an old man in Ohio pitching the flag in his lawn on the Thanksgiving weekend at the beginning of my trip. Something about the self-evident pride in the gesture gave me a good, rather than ominous feeling, and I felt similarly about the ABATE group's demonstration of respect. Before the meeting proceeded all stood to attention, hands on hearts for the recital of lines with which they were all clearly familiar. We don't really have an equivalent ceremony on this side of the Atlantic, unless it's the singing of the national anthem. I can't imagine getting many MAG groups to sing the anthem at the beginning of meetings, the anthem having steadily diminished in general usage to a point where nowadays it has become an exceptional rather than a regular feature of life.

When I was a young child in the late fifties and early sixties attending Saturday morning pictures, the anthem was always played before the programme started. At adult showings it was played after the performance, thus prompting that great tradition of exhibitionist disrespect – legging it out of the auditorium before the national anthem. The prevailing exodus provided patriotic stalwarts with the converse opportunity of demonstrating their conviction in the principle of monarchial respect, by standing obstructively in the pews like fearless generals vainly endeavouring to reverse a spontaneous retreat by holding ground in the midst of a military rout. I recall the numerous compromises that were struck by the guilty escapees who, having failed to make it to the lobby in time, would be frozen in their tracks by the evocative drum rolls preceding the melodious metaphor of patriotism. Most would turn and stare at the curtained screen as the familiar tune rolled through its course, before resuming the enthusiastic stampede for the nearest pub or bus stop. The most pernicious ringleaders of desertion would demonstrate their perceptive impatience by recognizing in the text and tone of the dialogue toward the end of the film, the imminent conclusion of the drama, and pre-empt the titles by rising prematurely from their seats to ensure a place in the vanguard of the exodus. Of all examples of impatience, I used to find this the most aggravating. If there is justice in this world, then when the reaper wields his grisly scythe it will sweep most accurately in the cinema foyers to which the unspeakably vulgar have fled on their hooves of hasty disrespect. There was no such disrespect in downtown LA, where everyone played the game to the rules with a total absence of fidgeting, giggles, and contrived flatulence. Interesting that a country as young as America should have so much more self-respect for its traditions than one as old, and with such a history, as Great Britain.

The meeting proceeded, like many minority political meetings of my experience, with exhortations from the key characters to write letters to their political representatives, urging them to support a variety of motions, the advice being occasionally interrupted by a raised hand from the keener or more imaginative members of the flock.

Richard proceeded to deliver a talk on his AIM programme, whilst I gave one on the European biker scene, which I wound up by expressing the hope that Californian riders would enjoy success in their effort to resist helmet compulsion indefinitely, emphasizing the confidence that their triumphs gave us on our side of the great water. This seemed to go down well and induced many present to step up and wring my paw, which made me feel the effort had been worthwhile.

With the serious part of the meeting concluded, a tall bearded character, who had slunk in earlier, raised a hand and requested to know if it was necessary to own a bike to become a member of ABATE. No such condition prevailed it seemed, and when the newcomer announced his intention to join on the spot since he was going to buy a bike, the news was greeted with hoots of delight. '*Yeahhs*' and '*Ryyyyyatts*' punctuated the murmur of enthusiasm like rockets spurting out of milk bottles amidst a ground-level, static firework display. In response to this encouragement, the stranger produced a bag full of linen patches embroidered with Harley-Davidson insignia, a fairly safe batch of products to field in this sympathetic environment of patriotic bikers.

There probably isn't a single vehicle that can match the Harley-Davidson for the near idolatrous devotion which its patrons afford it, and fortunately for the patch seller, most Harley riders want everyone to know what they ride. The man that buys a Harley does not just buy a motorcycle, he buys a legend, and to advertise his respect for, and pride in that legend, he needs all the trinkets, accessories, and embellishments that complement, qualify and re-assert the supremacy of the world's greatest motorcycle. There are T-shirts emblazoned with eagles and pictures of Harley engines, hats bearing the name Harley-Davidson, scarves likewise, cigarette lighters with the distinctive monogram etched into them, wrist and headbands. You can buy throw-over panniers with the name burnt into the leather, wallets for your pocket, tool rolls for your tools, there are belt buckles and bandannas for the serious image cultivators, there's even Harley-Davidson beer and Harley-Davidson oil. The thing about owning a Harley, is that everyone has to know it, not just when you're riding the machine, but when you pull out your wallet at a bar, light a cigarette or cut something with a knife (the sheath will be marked). If you take off the Harley jacket you can have a Harley sweatshirt on underneath and a Harley T-shirt beneath that. On the way to serious intimacy, your partner needs to be impressed by a pair of underpants decorated with the name of your prize possession, and when there's nothing left to impress her with, there is always the option of a Harley-Davidson tattoo, and there are plenty of people around with them.

'Harley-Davidson No.1' – 'Born To Ride/Harley-Davidson' – 'Harley's Best Fuck The Rest.' From the witty, through the corny and hackneyed, via the alliterative, to the obscene; the common ingredient remains the assertion of supremacy. An assertion that enjoys a degree of repetition which the uninitiated or sceptical might sacrilegiously interpret as a deep-seated sense of underlying doubt or inadequacy. Psychologists would have a field day amidst the disciples of the metallic messiah from Milwaukee where the factory that turns out the revered marque is based. The Harley Riders clubs would provide living models that so perfectly fitted the psychologist's perceptions of textbook stereotypes, that their pupils, if not better informed, could be forgiven for believing that the exhibits paraded before them for their critical analysis were parodies whose exaggerated features aspired to cartoonesque extremes in order to illustrate the outer limits of a scale against which all real world personalities could be measured.

The trouble with psychologists, however, is that they have to attribute deep-seated subconscious motives to the most trivial act and most transient thought in order to sustain their own credibility, or that of their questionable profession. The only shrink I have ever met, was, by the popular assent of everyone else who met her at the time, clinging to the merest thread of vestigial sanity by a hand that shook with the tremulous uncertainty of a limb terrified by the frightening instability of the mind to which it was attached. My lasting impression of her is one of a figure, sodden with alcohol into a state of unconsciousness, slumped in a chair with daffodils sprouting from her confused head. So much for shrinks.

The vendor of the patches, however, was a different kettle of fish. He reminded me of the bicycle salesman in the film, *Butch Cassidy and the Sundance Kid*, the one who capitalized on the sheriff's failed effort to raise a posse by advertising his 'rolling horse.' I suspected the tall stranger with the patches of a similar financial motive. America however, is the land of opportunity, and I invariably admire a fellow who, upon sighting the passage of a bandwagon, leaps up to oil its axles rather than moaning about the noise it makes. I was very glad of one thing at that meeting, and that was that I was not there on a Japanese motorcycle. If there is one thing that American Harley riders dislike almost as much as helmet laws, it is Japanese motorcycles. The antipathy owes its conception to the steady encroachment of the Japanese into the American motorcycle market during the sixties and seventies, by the end of which the future of Harley-Davidson was looking seriously threatened with extinction. Americans feared their motorcycle industry would go the way of the famous British marques which had struggled vainly to survive against the overwhelming economic might of the Orientals with their inscrutable efficiency and colossal investment programmes. As public indignation at the industrial invasion of the Japanese grew, so too did an industry which fed off this resentment by producing a variety of products which, like the array of accessories available to proclaim one's dedication to the all-American freedom machines, served to advertise the wearer's emotive opinions of motorcycles from the land of the rising sun. T-shirt slogans such as- 'I'd Rather Eat Crap Than Ride A Jap,' began to sprout up in magazine adverts; there was one bearing a large picture of a hand grenade alongside the legend, 'Japanese Motorcycle Repair Kit,' and the questionably tasteful, 'Two Bombs Weren't Enough.' At bike rallies, at least at Harley rallies, smashing a Japanese bike to pieces with sledge hammers became a popular game. Entrants were charged a sum of money to take a swing or two, until the whole vehicle was reduced to a useless pile of twisted junk, whereafter it would be burnt to a cinder amidst shouts of vengeful glee. I witnessed such an exhibition of the mechanically macabre once, and though I sympathize with the sentiments of resentment that inspire them, my attitude softened a little, as the condemned contraption bounced and writhed to the merciless punishment of the heavy hammers. I have always suffered from an irrational affection for inanimate objects which encourages a ludicrous sense of pity for articles that suffer neglect or abuse. I can remember feeling that way in childhood about a chisel that was thrown away when its handle split, or a china mug with an amusing design that was cast into the rubbish bin because its handle broke off. I still sometimes pick up dented cans in the supermarket in case nobody else does and they languish neglected on the shelf.

The bike smash I witnessed was held at a Harley Club rally in England where the victim was a small Honda. While still in running order, it was drained of oil and kicked into life with the throttle wound open whilst onlookers laid bets on how long the engine would last before it expired. The mechanism actually endured for a credible eight minutes before throwing in the towel, whereafter the hammers of the Harley men fell upon it with gleeful wrath. There occurred, toward the latter stages of this mechanical crucifixion, a poignant moment when, against all odds, amidst the crippled carnage of misshapen metal, a lone indicator bulb began to flash. There was, in that final expression of improbable resilience, a taste of the indomitable spirit of humanity, struggling to the last and carving in the process, a respectful epitaph for itself on the memories of all who witnessed its terminal gesture. I photographed the scene, and, on having the picture enlarged, noticed with some interest that whilst nearly all the adults present wore expressions of light humour, the children in the photograph, appeared uniformly melancholy, thoughtful, or even disturbed.

It is difficult to generate too much sympathy for Japanese sensitivities to this disrespectful treatment of their products, since I doubt that they enjoy the same affection at home as British and American-made motorcycles do in their respective countries. Vehicles, to the Japanese, provide the means to accumulate wealth, they're units of barter, like tape-decks, CDs, radios, cameras and televisions. They are useful to the industrious little fellows as a means of elevating their materialistic standard of living, but they have little relevance to the soul of Japanese culture. Paper houses, geisha girls, sumo wrestlers, sushi, saki and cherry blossom, are all essentially Japanese features, but not motorcycles. It is widely claimed that in their ravenous quest for industrial and technological supremacy, the Japanese have lost their own culture, and up to a point, I'm quite prepared to believe it. It's little wonder that many Americans resent the influence upon their lifestyle of these Oriental clever dicks, to whom so often, they, like us, come a very poor second in the trade war. The fact that the faithful diehards are surrounded by millions of their own countrymen deliberately choosing foreign goods in preference to their own, rubs salt into a bitter wound that festers in the bewilderment that a country a fraction the size of theirs, with minimal resources and all natural advantages withheld, can conceivably stand a chance of competing with it on any level, let alone knocking it into a cocked rice-paper hat. The steady Japanese infiltration of the motorcycle market from the sixties onward, now stemmed by Harley-Davidson's astonishing renaissance, might be compared to a zombie invasion, in the face of which, friends and relatives mysteriously shift their allegiances under the influence of intangible forces, to which the faithful few remain valiantly resilient in their bitter perplexity.

In the worst days of the Japanese motorcycle trade war, it must have seemed to the 'lifestyle' American bikers that the very soul of their nation was being poisoned, starved, and perverted by the 'evil aliens,' for though motorcycles might not be part of Japanese culture, they most certainly are part of American culture. Little wonder then, that at some open (all makes) events, untended Japanese motorcycles are occasionally set alight by vengeful agents of the angry home guard.

There is, in America, a fierce sprit of resentment against all countries that have the audacity to penetrate their home markets, and against their fellow countrymen, who, by the exercise of purchasing priorities, facilitate it. Even their old allies, the British, provoke evocative displays of resentment through acquiring American companies. In fact, Britain is the biggest investor in America, and whilst most British people know that companies like Ford and IBM are American owned, and accept that, they probably don't realize how many substantial concerns in the New World are controlled by British money. I am sure though, that as a target for US irritation, we come a long way behind the Japanese. The relationship between those two countries in the financial joust of trade and industry, is like a boxing match between two contestants of disparate size, in which the giant's blows swing wide of their elusive target, who cunningly weaves and snipes to astonishingly good effect, leaving his opponent enraged and bewildered.

In a sense, the colossal military supremacy of the USA lends a greater poignancy to the situation, by exacerbating the potential frustration that is there for the feeling. Fortunately, the delicacy of the contemporary international political scene is such that the frustrations of the militarily muscular can not be as easily exercised as once they were.

By contrast, in the heyday of Britain's colonial power, unacceptable irregularities in trade would have been resolved by the likes of Lord Palmerston, using the simple expediency of a gun boat. Take the Opium wars in China. A war waged by ourselves in response to the outrageous resistance displayed by brother Mandarin to the perfectly reasonable arrangement worked out for him by HM Government, whereby we scooped up shiploads of expensive spices and silks in return for copious supplies of opium. Had Bob Dylan been writing at that time, his talents may have earned him a Queen's commendation for the lyrical opportunism embodied in his memorable line, 'Everybody must get stoned.' Words which, whilst frowned upon by the establishment as encouraging unhealthy behaviour in the twentieth century, formed the core of government policy in the nineteenth.

To return to the comparative present. In the eighties, Ronnie Reagan came to the rescue of Harley-Davidson, not with gun boats, but with a punitive tax on Japanese bikes which gave Harley the competitive edge they needed to develop new models and pull themselves back into the running, so that by the late eighties they again dominated the large-capacity motorcycle market in America. Interestingly, in Japan an American or British motorcycle is regarded with tremendous respect as a status symbol of substantial mystique, in the same way that Cadillacs and Jaguars earn their Oriental owners heavyweight points on the street-cred scale. It's an appreciation of quality that hints at the Nipponese sense of their own inadequacy, just as wealthy Japanese women pay large sums of money to have their eyelids surgically altered in order to look more western, so Japanese men would really rather be driving their Jags and riding their Harleys. Perhaps it's true that they are a nation which has, at least superficially, lost sight of its culture – unlike America.

We left the bar as the meeting was breaking up. Outside in the parking lot, motorcycle engines were exploding into life, a pride of lions stretching their limbs to signal the end of an afternoon's siesta, shaking their manes and bellowing indiscreet warnings to the lower orders to back off or watch out. The clunk of engaging gears heralded the first departures as others stood chatting under the orange glow of the illuminated bar sign.

The zipping of jackets and flexing of fingers in gloves sounded the opening chords in an overture for the motorized orchestra's departure, as ignition keys turned, and starter buttons were pressed, whilst the more spartan traditionalists stood on kickstart pedals, levering the ponderous engines into motion with Herculean effort. Motors running, handlebars were turned full lock to manoeuvre the cumbersome mammoths out of their hangers as the pilots paddled them around the confines behind the bar, before nosing off toward the gap in the urban breakwater and the open seas of the busy highway. Pausing at the kerb like paratroopers at an open aircraft door, they studied the nocturnal stream of automobiles. Taking their cues from the gaps, they peeled off into the warm night air, pillion riders grasping for support against the beefy acceleration of the torquey motors. Growling leopards of locomotion, rocketing into the night on unspoken missions, they departed like jets catapulted from the deck of a carrier.

LOST IN LA

A spectator from the front seat of Richard's Jag, I sat in the soft glow of the instrument lights illuminating the natural swirls of the walnut dash, envious, despite my comfort, of the riders disappearing into the night. The silent colossus of the V12 engine pressed me firmly into the comfort of the sumptuous leather seat, as we joined the brigade of motorized recruits streaming down the neon highway toward south-west LA. Back at the NCOM headquarters I forsook the luxury of the tasteful motor for the sparser appointments of my own wheels patiently waiting in the subterranean parking lot beneath the office where I'd left it under the watchful supervision of the resident security force.

The uniformed guards nodded at me with genial courtesy as I weaved past them and ascended the steep ramp to the side street which led on to Ventura Boulevard. Blatting along the brightly lit main drag, switching lanes and twisting the throttle to pass gurgling Trans-Ams and curb-crawling Stingrays, I felt very much the boss. I was told I wouldn't like LA, and was prepared to do just that, but as I chicaned my way down mainstreet Ventura it didn't seem so bad to me.

It was late evening now but the town was alive. Pizza parlours, wine bars, pavement cafes, drugstores, delis, and drive-ins, all shone their simple messages into the midnight air: 'open for business.' It was a good place to go profiling up and down on a ritzy Harley with the warm wind in my hair and the staggered gargle of the pipes responding to the whims of my throttle hand like a dutiful Rottweiler. Almost running a red light in my cheerfully indulgent distraction, I screeched to a halt outside an open fronted bar from within which the familiar lyrics of the Beach Boys' classic *Good Vibrations*, spilled out into my helmet-free ears; good vibrations, good vibrations indeed. The length of Ventura Boulevard is such that it's easy to ignore the navigational necessities of life, and bumble aimlessly along without the need to turn left or right. So it was with me that I travelled three or four miles before it occurred to me that I hadn't the faintest idea where I was going.

Despite having been employed as a navigating officer in the British merchant navy for many years, subsequent to which I was a despatch rider in London, I am not very good at finding my way about, and tend toward the optimistic assumption that things will somehow turn out OK if I just keep on keeping on – an assumption from which I am still inclined to draw confidence, despite innumerable disappointments.

Pepper had given me directions that morning which sufficed to get me from her apartment to the NCOM office, but since they were simple I had made no written note of them and my memory provided no clues as to how I might trace a reciprocal route. Bewildered by my predicament, and aggravated by the familiar repetition of my own stupidity, I drew into the curb, cut the engine, and considered my situation. I was lost in one of the biggest cities in the world which numbered amongst its millions of citizens just two people that I knew; Pepper and Richard. I didn't have Pepper's address or telephone number, neither did I have Richard's, and the NCOM office would be closed, I'd seen Richard driving away from the building twenty minutes earlier. These were the negative considerations. On the positive side, I had transport, money, and, I could speak English, which, was the language spoken by almost everybody in this part of the world. These were significant cards to hold but they did not appear to comprise the bones of an immediately recognizable plan of repatriation. Several more moments of speculation passed before an idea pierced the web of dismal confusion shrouding my immediate prospects. The NCOM office operates a twenty four hour helpline for the benefit of injured motorcyclists. I wasn't injured but I was in need of help. I would return there.

An Oriental security guard escorted me through the building to the NCOM suite; a friendly character, he seemed impressed by the length of journey I had undertaken, which surprised me. My impression of Americans' attitude to travel, was that it was something in which they were perpetually and joyously engaged. Is the USA not that huge country across which those folk heroes of the road, the truckers, are forever rolling their solitary way to the plaintive chords of a mournful ballad? Are the deserted heroines of tear-jerking tragedy not forever wakening to the roar of a disappearing engine and the sight of a farewell note from a departed lover? Did not the author of just such a note, record the projected itinerary that unfolded half the states in the union before his wife fixed breakfast? Were not Peter Paul and Mary, 'Leaving on a jet plane,' as Bob Dylan was getting his kicks on 'Route 66,' while Elton John boarded a southbound train on his journey from 'snow to sunshine,' sometime after Muddy Waters was 'walking to New Orleans,' preceding Scott McKenzie on his way to 'San Francisco' where Tony Bennett 'left his heart,' clearly indicating that he was already somewhere else when he was singing about it. If Americans aren't going somewhere or coming back from going away, then they're encouraging others to do so, whether it's 'North to Alaska' or 'South of the border down Mexico way,' the consistent theme is one of ceaseless motion.

Perhaps it's the restless ambition born of the American competitive ethos that breeds a dissatisfaction with location as well as circumstance, fostering the conviction that the grass is always greener on the other side of the state line, thus justifying the need for travel. The collage of titles here cited, are proffered in support of the notion that Americans are the footloose nation of Gypsies their music proclaims them to be, but is this really true? My experience did not bear out the minstrel's implicit claims. The security guard seemed genuinely impressed by the scope of my journey. He had never, he told me, left the state of California. The comment triggered a recollection of others cast in the same mould of physical intransigence. The tourist on the aircraft who hadn't travelled outside New York State – he'd been to Europe, but in America he had confined all movement to the boundaries of his native state. Chip's mate in Ohio, who suggested that I ride half way across the continent and call my friends on the West Coast to fly out to rendezvous with me. The curious motorist in LA, who'd pointed at my registration plate in surprise, and now this home-loving security guard. It would be crazy to infer from this handful of examples that Americans are a bunch of stick-in-the-muds who hesitate to venture beyond their timber porches, but the mobile excesses of *Vanishing Point*, *Easy Rider*, or Kerouac's *On The Road*, are not, I felt, as commonplace as the ballads might lead you to suspect. Certainly the notion that all Americans think nothing of driving fifty miles for a meal is fanciful twaddle.

I liked this in a way. I liked the attitude of surprise in the comments that were laced with a flavour of undisguised envy. It enhanced my sense of belonging, my sense of Americanness. In one simple respect, I felt I'd out Americanized the Americans. They are the people who are popularly perceived as the loud mouthed, 'I've been everywhere' globe trotters, making jokes about the diminutive size of Britain, from which we may infer an allegation that we are somehow incapable of comprehending the scale of their own country, let alone riding across it by motorcycle in little more than a week. There was a smugness to be had from the achievement of having run across more state boundaries in a few days, than some Americans manage in a lifetime. I hadn't lived in, worked in, and absorbed the spirit of the lands I'd raced across, and it would be foolish to present my whistle-stop tour as anything but that. It would be equally foolish, however, to deny the reality that a degree of mystique attaches to the traveller's exploits. A mystique that survives the criticism of superficiality to which my own efforts could be fairly subjected. To cite the most extreme example, an airline pilot listing his brief stop-overs, will enjoy a measure of envy from those for whom a weekend in Blackpool represents a major excursion. The mystique intrinsic to an experience may be rationalized out of sight by the insufferably objective, but it cannot be destroyed because it exists, as an independent abstract entity. I have sustained long arguments with people about war in its relevance to this subject.

Is war romantic? Is war glamorous? Most people respond to the notion in the negative, with an alacrity born not of conviction, but of a sense of obligatory revulsion that is automatic to a Pavlovian degree. Those of us who grew up in the sixties, amidst a tide of international pacifism, were forever having thrust in our faces the grisly evidence of the Vietnam conflict's miseries, as graphically recorded by the daring photographers of the day. A TV programme about the exploits of one such photographer, whose record of persistence in the face of danger was extraordinary, was screened in the presence of an audience whose critical interrogation posed the allegation that he was guilty of glamorizing war. The audience were, or at least affected to be, startled by the blunt response that parried the questioner's postulation. 'War IS glamorous,' insisted the photographer, 'you can't destroy the glamour in war,' and of course he was quite right.

Those who deny the glamour in war, endeavour to assert that the pursuit of morality not only defeats horror, but eliminates the curiosity about its form. Those who thrust gruesome photographs of mutilated bodies in our faces, demanding with irrational emotion, the identification of glamour, totally miss the point. It would be absurd to assert that every facet of war exudes glamour, but the total experience of which the grim horrors are components, provide the source of the glamour, just as the collective contributions of an automobile's parts provide the means of locomotion. A sceptic thrusting a fan belt under one's nose, and demanding to know how one was going to get anywhere on that, would be treated with ridicule, but when a zealous pacifist brandishes a portrait of a napalm burned child, and demands the recognition of glamour, his sagacity is applauded by a circle of nodding heads. One may as well deny the existence of pleasure in sex by conjuring up some gross example of the diseased consequences of indiscretion.

Glamour and romance survive as abstract entities independent of human censure or moral indictment. To insist that there is no glamour in war, is to assert that there is no drama in a hurricane because the overall effect of the force is destructive. A common mistake in trying to divine the truth in this matter, is to assume that he who has been most closely associated with it, is the person best equipped to provide the correct answer. There will be critics of these academically detached comments who will dismiss them as meaningless speculations from an armchair, invalidated by the absence of first-hand experience. Such critics might well favour the opinions of one who had suffered the hardships, tragedy, and wretched squalor of war. 'Ask HIM if there's glamour in war?' they might advise, and it may well be that his caustic response would involve an unequivocal rebuke of the claim I am labouring to make. Does HIS personal involvement validate his conclusion in the same way that a mechanic, labouring to repair part of a beautiful, but ineptly manufactured car, will be blinded to its aesthetic qualities by the frustration of trying to repair what, to his objective perspective, is an infuriating junk heap? On another level, one might be tempted to ask the wife of a man killed in an air crash, if civil aviation were a good thing. It is often the way, that those with their noses closest to a painting, fail to identify the elements which stubbornly survive its prevailing image.

There is a fascination, a mystique, which attaches to those who have endured things out of the average man's experience, particularly when those experiences involve drama, danger, and violence – and especially so if they enjoy the historical distinction of determining the course of national ambitions. The man sitting quietly in the pub who is known to have been in Korea or Vietnam or the Falklands conflicts, wears a shroud of mystique whether he likes it or not, and whether he talks about it or not; especially if he never does, in fact, for silence enhances mystique the way premature death immortalizes movie stars. The veteran may deny the romance, and urge his questioners to think themselves grateful they were not there and do not carry the scars of his nightmarish experiences. We may acknowledge the sincerity of his words, we may not want to go where he has been, we may agree it was all dreadful, but a part of us may wish we had been and come back to savour the ghoulish mystery that survives pure horror, to ferment in the imaginations of the inexperienced. Like the case of the boy who peeked behind the curtain at the fairground freak, or the adolescent back from the brothel, the others always want to know – what was it like? No level of censure, no demonstrations of moral revulsion or protestations can ever eliminate the curiosity or erase the reluctant envy. It survives the realities, the horrors, and the disappointments, because like a dream, its home is the abstract territory of the mind. As long as man has imagination, as long as he remains an animal of curiosity, then despite the denials of the warriors, the entreaties of the pacifists, and the admonishment of sages, there will remain an indestructible romance inextricably entwined with war, and those whose lives have been embraced by it.

Similarly, the romance of travel may be diminished by its brevity, but it is not destroyed. The security guard whose comments indirectly prompted these tangential reflections was short and Oriental. Was that, I wondered, why he had never left California. Perhaps he felt a little insecure, who knows, maybe there was a more simple reason, maybe he was simply happy where he was. As someone who has spent half his life travelling around, twelve years of it in the merchant navy, I have always thought people who are content to stay in one place very strange. Plenty of British people are like the security guard of course, some enjoying or enduring the confined distinction of never poking their noses beyond the boundaries of their home counties. There was the case of the old Yorkshire lady who travelled to London for the first time in her life, the rest of it having been spent entirely within the county of her birth. I imagine she must have been very happy there. In one sense I envy these people who are happy where they are, happy with what they're doing, happy with who they are. How can people be so bloody contented? How can they be content with one home, one job, one wife? How can they have such a mono-residential, mono-employed, monogamous, monotonous existence? I don't know. Perhaps it's the restless traveller who is the insecure one, the indecisive one, who doesn't know where he wants to be, what he wants to do, or most importantly who he is. I have a great suspicion of settled, contented, confidently self-assured people, people with nice homes, successful careers and happy families. They worry me almost as much as enthusiastic rugby or football players with their mud and their shouting, their camaraderie, and their confidence. I am reminded of a laudable line from the film *Charge of the Light Brigade*, when Lord Raglan, viewing the disappearing form of a young cavalry officer, played by David Hemmings, commented, 'That young man has far too much idea of what he's doing, it will be a bad day for the army when there are more men like him in it.' True words indeed.

I had my directions supplied by a member of Richard's night staff and was on my way again toward Pepper's apartment, armed with a scrap of paper on which I'd scribbled the necessary instructions. I found the place without difficulty. Pepper was in, which was just as well, and as it wasn't late, we took a walk around to the local deli to get some beer. Above her apartment block, almost directly above it, a helicopter circled, its searchlight scouring the rooftops like some inquisitive dragonfly seeking out its prey. Pleasantly affluent though the immediate neighbourhood seemed, less than a mile away was a district notorious for heavy drug trafficking with all its associated evils. This is one of the strange facets of America's social problems. It is not quite so easy to identify a dangerous part of town, at least not out here in sprawling suburban Los Angeles. In New York the dangerous areas look dangerous, but in leafy LA appearances are misleading. Towns on the West Coast are more spaced out, and LA is about as spaced out as towns get. The neighbourhood I saw depicted on the TV news looked like nice middle-class suburbia to me. The broad street was lined with variously painted timber houses, all detached, with their own gardens and trees, and yet this was one of the prime drug-dealing areas where local vigilantes were endeavouring to clear the pushers off the sidewalks through tactics of direct confrontation.

The campaign against drug abuse was gathering substantial momentum when I was in America. President Bush (Snr) was publicly designating substantial federal funds to finance the efforts of the Central American republics, principally Columbia, in their efforts to run the cocaine barons to ground, prompting counter offensives from the bad guys who, according to the national press, had put out a contract on the new president. The true scale and organization of the drug trade was acquiring a public awareness at this time which it had not hitherto enjoyed. Tales of the threats and assassinations to which the Columbian judiciary were exposed vied for space in the newspapers with the overly enthusiastic denials, admonishments, and entreaties of all-American celebrities competing to advertise their clean living God-fearing credentials aboard the 'just say no' bandwagon of zealous purity. America at this time was riding a wave of moral fundamentalism on a tide of outrage against the decadent and ruthless polluters of its youth. Advertising hoardings, embellished with graphic warnings of the consequences of indulgence, punctuated the streets and highways; newspaper and magazine space by the acre was devoted to the subject, radio and TV phone-ins, talk-ins, walk-ons, all made their contribution. Rock stars were queuing to issue their emphatic condemnation of drug abuse, and assert their resolute commitment to the 'straight and narrow.' Essentially, the necessity of such a purge can hardly be denied, but the transparency of some of its catalytic exponents serves to illuminate the endemic hypocrisy of one level of American life.

It would be unjust to infer that few Americans perceive the fraudulence of their overtly righteous countrymen. The media moguls who provide the platform for the proclamations of innocence, are as enthusiastic in erecting scaffolds on them for the subsequent sacrifice of the unwary who, despite their claims, succumb to the temptations of *Miami Vice* to suffer the indictments of *LA Law*.

If there is one thing LA is not short of, it's law; or more precisely, lawyers. The young man in the deli who packed our beer and groceries into a thick paper sack was studying law by day and holding down this evening job to pay his way through school. He knew Pepper and offered this intelligence in response to an enquiry about his current projects. 'I have decided,' he proclaimed with gravity, 'that LA needs just one more attorney.' It has been estimated that one person in three hundred of the working population of America, is employed in the legal profession, a figure which does not lend credibility to the claim of the man in the deli, but who can blame the pedestrian standing on the platform, from attempting to board the gravy train when it comes rattling through the station with all seats taken, aisles jammed and roof rack a tangle of clutching bodies, hell there has to be a chance that someone will fall off and make a space.

EASYRIDERS

The day I rode out to interview the editor of *Easyriders* magazine started well, a man on the radio forecast blue skies and 86 degrees Fahrenheit. Americans don't seem to bother too much with decimalization, they even persist with measuring their engine capacities in cubic inches, and why shouldn't they? Though it seems surprising that in a country so closely identified with change and progress, a strong vein of traditionalism should so conspicuously survive.

God seemed to be in his heaven as I took the freeway exit for Agoura Hills, that mythical address I'd read a thousand times inside the cover of the magazine, which, to my impressionable mind in the early seventies, constituted an icon of the motorcycling religion to which I had become an enthusiastic convert.

The directions I'd received were perfect, terminating at the smart two-story building whose brown wooden frames and matching tinted windows blended subtly with the dry earth of the surrounding hills. I turned around in front of what appeared to be the main entrance, and backed down toward the kerb with the cheerful gurgle of the twin exhausts announcing my arrival. Kicking down the chromed sidestand, I cut the engine, pushed my shades up on to my forehead, rubbed my eye sockets for theatrical effect, and looked around to see who was taking note of my landing. The one-way glass provided no clues, but I convinced myself I looked pretty cool as I swung a leg over the saddle of the huge machine which, for the second time in a week, tumbled ignominiously onto its side.

There are times when the injustice, improbability, and seeming impossibility of what has just happened, appear so acute, that the conscious mind has difficulty in acknowledging the reality. An attempt is then made to refute the facts through erecting barricades of denial which frequently resolve themselves in hysterical outbursts of manic repetition, in which the word 'no' features with monotonous regularity. Under other circumstances I would have righted the bike, started the engine, and departed with as much nonchalance as I could muster. In this case, I had an appointment at the very scene of my embarrassment, and short of reappearing in disguise on a different motorcycle, I could see no way of avoiding the music which had now to be faced from the inevitable audience behind the smoked-glass windows.

Recalling the injury sustained the last time I grappled with this prostrate leviathan, I hesitated this time in order to frame a plan of action that offered the best union of efficiency with dignity. With regard to the latter, the important preliminary requires the correct appropriation of blame, which in the case of my mishap, clearly rested with the motorcycle. It had, after all, fallen – I did not push it. But would others realize this? To ensure that they did, I stared for a few seconds at the recumbent beast, as one might at a recalcitrant mule, its hooves rivetted to the ground with obstinate determination against the pull of its reins. This is a tactic I invariably employ whenever some mechanical indiscretion disturbs the preservation of cool, a missed gear, a clumsy take off, a deranged bungee chord, in each case the offending apparatus must be subjected to a superior scrutiny of puzzled inspection in order to distract the focus of the casual observer from the true source of the error which invariably lies between my shoulders. My silent visual rebuke administered, I took a hold of the bars, and, bracing a knee against the side of the saddle, levered the machine upright whilst fishing out the mischievous sidestand which I blamed for the disaster. I now stood back to study the machine for any sign of a relapse, before circling warily around the rear wheel, my eyes directed low to avoid the critical scrutiny to which I feared my efforts may have been subjected. And so with bowed and humble demeanour, I headed in the direction of the office entrance.

Inside the air-conditioned cool of the shady interior, a receptionist directed me to the editor's office on the first floor. I felt hot and flustered from physical effort and embarrassment, so that by the time I'd mounted the stairs, I'd totally forgotten the simple directions I had been given twenty seconds earlier. As I stumbled along the softly lit corridor, still breathing heavily from my exertions, I sensed movement behind me, and, turning, discovered the lofty form of the editor, Keith Ball, setting out on a mission of exploration, no doubt prompted by my delay in reaching his office from the reception area. My host was a tall athletic man of movie star appearance, that gave a clue to his exceptional marital record – three wives, the third still in harness, and he not much older than myself. The editorial office into which I was led, was a large room featuring a wide desk at one end decorated with Harley-Davidson models, while a huge picture of one covered most of a wall. From here we went on a tour of the offices, one of which, I noted with some embarrassment, overlooked the street where I had endured the unstable drama with the motorcycle. Here I was introduced to a profusely bearded character, whose exuberant moustache screened the orifice one assumed lay beneath it, much as the eyes of an old English sheep dog are obscured from view. My erstwhile friend Maz had a description for these people, he coined it some years back when studying a photograph I'd taken depicting a brace of compadres similarly hirsute of face; namely Wol and Hairy Flong. 'These are men without mouths,' Maz declared, an expression which he retained for future use whenever the possibility of that duo being somewhere arose. 'Will men without mouths be coming?' he would ask.

The fellow before me now, was a definite candidate for the 'mouthless' title, but there was no doubt that he had eyes, and a tongue.

'Was that you who pulled up on the Evo Harley?' he enquired. There seemed little point in denying this, and I owned up without further comment. The silent smile I sensed playing around the invisible lips, hinted at the awful truth, but he passed no comment on my parking skills, and we moved on to other departments. Back in the editorial office, the subject of lunch climbed on to the agenda. Considering my last three meals had involved red hot enchiladas, spicy Cantonese, and a ring-stinging Mongolian barbecue, I was now in the market for something a little nearer the bland side of poached-eggs on toast. A friend of Keith who had appeared in the office, offered a suggestion.

'How about some good spicy Mexican?' he proposed, rubbing his hands with enthusiastic innocence, 'you like Mexican?'

'Sure,' I replied, sensing an involuntary twitch of apprehension in the hind quarters at the thought of some more nosebag de la furnace, what the hell I thought, out of the barbecue into the burritos, as they say.

Before lunch we took a ride over to the *Easyriders'* ranch to look around and see the twin-engined motorcycle that was being prepared for an attempt on the world motorcycle speed record. A huge cigar shaped tube over twenty feet long, the ambitious vehicle consumed three-quarters of the building housing it, where a pair of mechanics crouching on the floor, worked feverishly with spanners in an effort to meet a deadline barely a week away. Why is it that man, in the pursuit of epic endeavours of this nature, seems destined always to be struggling against some improbable deadline? To be fair, my slate is scarcely clean in this respect. In my seafaring days I would invariably postpone packing for my next voyage until the night before I was due at an airport or train station, and I still, many years after leaving the sea, have nightmares about arriving on board a ship with half my gear missing. Joining ship without all one's gear is a concern that bothers a lot of seafarers, the problem being that you can't just nip home and get something that might make the difference between happiness and misery. An old friend of mine from Liverpool once summarized this feeling when leaning on the ship's rail studying a merchant vessel steaming in the opposite direction. 'I'm bloody glad I'm not on that ship,' he remarked with considerable feeling.

'Why's that I asked innocently?'

'Because', he replied, without a trace of mirth, 'All my gear's on this one.'

Leaving the industrious wrenches to their Herculean task, we set off at a spirited pace set by Keith on his retro-styled hardtail chop, for the Mexican restaurant, where we seated ourselves in the conservatory annex amidst a jungle of tropical vegetation. It was here that I'd decided to conduct the interview, and produced a mini tape recorder that looked splendidly effective with its shiny push button controls peeking purposefully out of the snug black leather case, making me feel very much the professional journalist. Sadly the device failed to work. I pressed all the right buttons, shook the machine about, tapped it on the table as if it were a magician's wand, and then pressed them again. When this failed to produce the desired effect, I pressed all the wrong buttons, in the hope that their movement might encourage the others out of a sense of mechanical competitiveness; it did not. My interviewee was looking on patiently as I removed the leather case, extracted each of the batteries, rubbed their terminals on my napkin, and replaced them, checking carefully that the positive marks on the cells corresponded to the same marks on the plastic interior of the battery compartment. I have never been a wizard with electrics, but I can follow things this far; the flat ends went up against the springs, and the ends with the protrusive nodes went up against the flat plates, that seemed to make sense, and matched the positive and negative coding, which convinced me that everything was hunky-dory, a conviction disturbed only by the irksome reality of total inaction. The spools would not turn around.

Lunch had arrived now, and my endeavours were suspended

whilst I arranged the various dishes and got stuck in. Nothing, no problem, however monumental, should stand in the way of food. In a perfect world, time should stand still for meals, phones should not ring, traffic should not move, babies should not cry, precipitation should be suspended, and the wind subside to the merest napkin ruffling breeze. Of all the daily human exercises that should enjoy a sacrosanct respect, meal time tops the list. In the case under consideration, food provided not only the physical pleasure which it invariably affords me, but also the inspiration to solve the riddle of the inoperable cassette player. The problem was simple enough, some clown had left the pause button depressed. Once released, the tape rolled, and my dining companion's face relaxed, as did I.

I was particularly keen to conduct this interview with *Easyriders'* editor. *Easyriders* is more than just a magazine about motorcycles, or rather Harley-Davidsons, which it features to the virtual exclusion of all other makes, and the deliberate exclusion of the Japanese. *Easyriders* is a piece of uncompromising American culture with a capital A and a Stars and Stripes flying alongside the great American freedom machine for which it provides the publishing world's most unreserved promotion. Critics of this colourful tome might describe it as a piece of elitist, sexist, nationalistic bigotry, masquerading as a motorcycle magazine. The content of *Easyriders*, besides bike features, includes social events, news of political developments in the unending war against helmet laws, plus letters, fiction, cartoon and photo spreads, and the occasional political comment on some topic of contemporary significance. The last area was the one I wanted to discuss immediately, in order to draw some kind of commitment on how the editorial department perceived its political orientation.

A hot potato which at this time was being tossed around Uncle Sam's political kitchen, was the evocative issue of whether or not to prohibit the burning of the American flag in public. *Easyriders* had taken a firm stand on this, by publishing an unequivocal statement, in their emphatic style. *Easyriders* supported the viewpoint that such acts constitute an affront to the patriotic sensibilities of the population, amounting to a kind of insult to the nation, which overrides the libertarian respect for free expression. As someone with both strong libertarian and patriotic instincts, I found my own attitude to this question somewhat equivocal. In common with other tricky subjects, the flag burning issue might be described as a victimless crime, in that, assuming that no one is wrapped up in the

211

symbolic cloth when it's torched, it is difficult to determine a clear case of suffering, at least on a strictly physical level. How then does a legislature quantify the subjective injury inflicted by the exercise of insensitive or provocative acts? Whose sensitivities are to be respected and whose ignored? What is offensive to some people is obviously not to others. I, for example, hate the sight of gambling machines in pubs, I find the sound of them additionally offensive, and the demeaning spectacle of human beings playing them, pathetic to an offensive degree. I am sure that a lot of people think the way that I do, yet I can see that it would be overreaching itself for the government to outlaw them. Certainly it would be exceeding its authority to outlaw game machines which might not represent the same compulsive gambling threat. I find the sight of flabby trollops pushing prams down the street whilst cigarettes hang limply from their lips, disgusting, but again it could arguably be construed as over-zealous enforcement of public standards to prohibit such slovenly behaviour. The dividing line which separates the merely irksome from the deeply offensive, must be determined by a measurement of the majority feeling. In many Arab countries, the sight of a woman walking down the street in a bikini is considered unacceptable, while two men walking hand in hand like a couple of lovebirds is commonplace.

If majority opinion is not respected in the framing of laws however, then the outraged may take the law into their own hands in the conviction that right is on their side. For this practical reason no doubt, the law tends to endorse the prevailing public feeling, particularly if it is rooted in some religious principle. For the sake of maintaining law and order, therefore, the overwhelming sense of public morality simply has to be appeased. An example of the kind of endeavour guaranteed to outrage the sense of general propriety in Great Britain, was the attempt, some years back, to release a film portraying the sex life of Jesus Christ. Predictably the film was branded as blasphemous and offensive to the standards of absolute decency, and consequently banned from public showing. The decision was reached amidst a hurricane of protest which was joined, most exceptionally by Her Majesty, presumably in her role as 'Defender of the Faith,' which certainly did the prohibition lobby no harm.

The burning of the flag could be said to fall into the same category of concern, since the state probably comes second only to

God as a focal point of respect. It is reasonable to expect, that in a healthy democracy where people achieve approximately the kind of society that they want, the State, as represented by the law of the land, should warrant a high degree of respect. The law, after all, represents the collective conscience of the population. I am, admittedly, presenting an idealized model of State and population in order to assess the general viability of prohibiting acts which offend people through insulting the State for which they, ideally, should have respect. I am in a way perhaps arguing against the concept of anarchy in placing respect for the State above respect for the right to express disenchantment with the State – although that is not really the object of those who would prohibit flag burning – and if that does not seem clear it is because that statement is not only a simplification, but a distortion of the argument. We are not considering the abolition of public protest *per se*, only one specific manifestation of that protest. Protest by civilized and peaceful means is broadly recognized as a healthy feature of a tolerant society. When protest becomes violent or gratuitously insulting to the State it is endeavouring to influence, then it becomes the physical equivalent of an argument that has degenerated into a slanging match. A TV debate that collapses in this way is invariably terminated once its constructive potential is perceived to have evaporated. In seeking to prohibit flag burning, the exponents of censure are assuming the stance of the editor who seeks to confine disagreement to an intellectual plane by preventing the exercise of words and actions which serve only to inflame passions and excite breaches of the peace.

When I asked Keith Ball how he reconciled his magazine's libertarian stance with its anti flag-burning policy, he maintained that freedom in art and literature had to be viewed distinctly from the freedom to destroy. While there is no doubt that the burning of the flag destroys it in an immediate sense, I think Keith was implying more than the superficial physical destruction of the material on fire in his criticism of destruction. Given however that the burning of the flag is destructive, could not paintings with sufficiently provocative themes, have the same charge levelled at their artists? Does not a painting of a man burning the American flag, enshrine the same symbolism and manifest the same provocation, as the man actually burning it in the street outside the gallery where it is hung? No doubt the legislature, in debating this tricky issue, must have considered the implications for art and free expression, and in coming to their decision, which was to tolerate flag burning, the fear of a string of repressive demands to censor art, with the nightmare of the subjectively orientated bureaucracy which that would have required, stayed their hand. If there is a practical rather than an emotional argument for permitting this incineration, it is this, though the possibility of a compromise emerges from the perception of what is deemed public.

A distinction could be drawn between a street and an art gallery with some justification, particularly if the gallery, or specific rooms within it, bore signs warning persons of the provocative nature of some of the exhibits. Even within the confines of a contentious exhibition, it could be argued that the same anarchical forces of subversion would be at work upon the population, but there one has to respect the right of individuals to sift and judge all the arguments put to them, and credit them with a measure of ability to chose, as well as a right to view, what of their own free will they chose so to do. There is in short, a distinction between the art gallery and the street. In burning a flag on the street, a protester is thrusting his insult unavoidably into the faces of the population at large as he condemns not just a particular policy, but a nation. Supporters of this liberty might argue that you have to shock people in order to force them to consider issues. That may work with a poster of a laboratory animal being tortured, but in the case of flag burning, the consequence is far more likely to be a polarisation of existing viewpoints, with the possibility of violent retribution.

Most people's attitude on this issue is likely to be determined simply on the basis of whether they feel a sense of pride, or a sense of shame in the quality and conduct of their country. I have always felt antagonistic toward people who abuse Great Britain *per se*, particularly when that criticism coincides with the support of some unfriendly state where 'freedom' is dirty word. There is, in this misplaced affection, a naivety most commonly associated with the adolescent, that owes more to fashion and peer pressure than to sound logic. It displays itself in the fond patronage of figures and philosophies opposed to our own, on the dubious assumption that since we are so wrong then whoever criticizes us, must be right. There is almost an affectation of liberalism in defending, or at best failing to condemn, the acts of terrorists of whose actions our people are the victims.

In their enthusiasm to evade association with our establishment, the gratuitous critic may promote such figures as Mao, whilst conveniently forgetting the annexation of Tibet and the persecution of counter-revolutionaries.

Bikers are just as likely to be guilty of this hypocrisy as anyone, however. There have been cases where outlaw gangs have tried to defend their display of swastikas as legitimate free expression while ignoring the sensibilities of the majority who find Nazi regalia deeply offensive. The trouble with some people's idea of freedom is that they don't qualify it with any limits or sense of responsibility or sensitivity.

We didn't get into this one over lunch, but we did discuss *Easyriders'* attitude to women in connection with bikes, an enquiry prompted by the amusingly chauvinistic approach consistently employed by the magazine, to an extreme which may be thought to parody the archetypal male chauvinistic pig. *Easyriders* makes a virtue not only of putting down sexual deviants, but women *per se*. A letter of complaint from a woman reader protesting about the subordinate status to which her sex was confined by the magazine's abusively discriminating tone, and running to a full column of well reasoned, if petulant rebuke, elicited the unequivocally blunt editorial retort: 'Screw you bitch.'

That kind of wittily economic response is not designed to inspire universal respect, but it serves to establish a clear sense of editorial identity, which happily fails to deter the incurably outraged from concocting more doomed missives of protest, thus providing excellent sport in the letters page. Sadly I can't remember what Keith's defense of the politically incorrect stance of his magazine was, but from memory it was a little tongue in cheek.

Half-way through our lunch, a waiter appeared to ask if everything was OK. 'A little more sauce please,' replied my host, and therein demonstrated another difference in behaviour between us and them. My experience when eating out, is that the British, when asked by the restaurant staff, if everything is all right invariably reply in the affirmative without even thinking about it. The enquiry is simply acknowledged as a polite ritualistic gesture by a dutiful restaurateur. The American response by contrast, reflects a sensible recognition that the waiter is not simply wasting his time by coming over to dispense niceties, but actually wants to know if: a) everything is all right, as opposed to being a pile of shit; and b) is there anything else you need, for example, as in the case in point, a little more sauce.

The heat of the dish was not excessive, and my stomach felt like retaining a state of balance, so I accepted an offer to trade plates as we were half way through our respective meals, another practice less common in the Old Country, and probably one that would be frowned upon at the RAC club in Pall Mall, but not a bad way of assuring yourself of variety.

The interview proceeded to areas more directly concerned with the factors responsible for the magazine's success. It was selling six-hundred thousand copies worldwide at that time, a credible figure that grew from modest beginnings at the start of the seventies when *Easyriders* was something which, in England at least, was obtainable only from rare, dubious outlets outside the main distribution networks. In the USA, which accounts for the majority of sales, the magazine received a body blow some years back from the puritanical lobby, when legislation threatening retailers with prosecution for stocking any magazines displaying nudity loomed over the horizon. In fact an announcement had been made by an authority in advance of any change in law and with typically American hysteria, the retailers panicked and heaved everything showing tits and bums into the garbage. It was all a false alarm because the legal mechanisms were never in place, but the damage was done and some hefty losses had to be footed by a number of publishers.

Americans seem more prone to these hurricanes of reactionary morality than do the European races from which they are primarily descended. Does the comparative infancy of American culture fail to sustain the confidence upon which its stability depends, does this soul-searching introspection reflect an insecurity that demands frequent examinations of the map to ensure the walkers have not strayed from the route? Like a huge tree that has grown at unprecedented speed with the infusion of multifarious composts and the influence of a host of horticultural advisers, it seems that its very cosmopolitan character inspires self doubt in the integrity of its trunk and roots, thus prompting the periodic pruning purges of the legislative secateurs. The ascetic endeavours of the prohibition era, followed later by the vigorous witchhunts of McCarthy, provide a historical reflection of religiously motivated austerity in Cromwellian England, and the alternate persecutions of Protestant/Catholic rivalry.

Like geologically youthful landmasses, it seems reasonable to suppose that countries take time to solidify, in the process of which the turbulent vacillations preceding the steadier simmer of later life, throw up some quirkily unstable compounds. Perhaps partly because of this, and partly because of a substantial regional enjoyment of power delegated from the federal authority, legislative mavericks which a more lethargic political mechanism might reject as patently frivolous, have crept onto the statute books of America, where idealistic fervour has triumphed over common sense. Laws forbidding the carriage of beer in automobiles, even though the bottles are sealed, for example, are commonplace. Then there was my experience in Kansas, of state law requiring all bottles of beer to be put into bags before they could be taken out of the liquor store. In the Mormon-controlled regions of Utah, alcohol is still prohibited altogether, whilst a plethora of driving regulations infect the entire country. There is at least one state that even has laws forbidding masturbation.

Britain suffers less from rampant looniness in this respect, largely because the more centralized mode of government cannot, for want of time, accommodate the more freakish demands of the legislatively avaricious. Localized responsibilities being confined by more parochial boundaries than in the American state system, all of the more tendentious issues must endure the critical scrutiny of Westminster's seasoned mechanisms including, of necessity, the solemn examination of the Lords.

The retention of our own House of Lords, sadly diminished as it now is, is frequently defended on the basis that the collective age, experience, and wisdom of that institution's members imbue it with a moderating potential that acts like a benign damper to inhibit the frivolous excesses of the junior house's more excitable evangelists. Protected from the vagaries of political fate by their unassailable positions, they are at liberty to exercise their powers in the absence of party or constituency pressures. If a hand of restraint does rest upon their venerable shoulders, it is born of the recognition that failure to maintain the standards of moderation which characterizes the nature of their power, will further encourage the reformist elements who view the undemocratic authority with jealous disdain.

As genuine and reliable restraints may be measured by their effectiveness rather than by the theoretical ambitions of their architects, this simple unframed threat of extinction operates to maintain the political dinosaur of the Lords on as sane a footing as many political institutions in the world. Besides the constructive and stabilizing role with which the House of Lords is credited, there is a wonderfully refreshing eccentricity in the improbable survival of a political institution within a democracy, the membership of which depends not upon any democratic mechanism. The privileged members of the upper house, the hereditary ones at least, earn their position by no demonstration of business, political, or military acumen; wit, wisdom or honesty play no part in their guaranteed ascension to the red-leather benches, nor are education, academic prowess, or the possession of oratorical skills, essential prerequisites for membership of this most exclusive of clubs. No, the one unearned, unjust, non-negotiable factor that bestows upon the nation's elite, the right to sit in judgement upon the mother of parliaments, rests with a simple quirk of fate, the ultimate expression of old-school-tie philosophy. The venerable majority whose well-heeled feet step through the historic arches, do so in the confidence that they are their father's sons. Theirs is a privilege which the ablest, cleverest, most energetic, popular and sagacious intellects of our nation are conversely unable to indulge, purely because of who their dad wasn't.

Those who cannot rejoice at the hilarious immorality of this priceless anomaly, clearly deserve no place in our sceptred isle, and deserve no better fate than exile to the monastic equality of an institution for the terminally humourless.

I am sure Americans would profit from an institution similar to our own House of Lords, but sadly they remain enamoured with an idealistic notion of equal opportunity which precludes the establishment of a duplicate system, besides which they have no titled people on whom to draw for the establishment of such a chamber. It's all rather sad.

By the end of the meal I had filled an hour's worth of cassette tape with which to compile my interview. Keith produced a credit card in order to pay the bill, an effort to which I responded with a shamefully insincere remonstrance, in a half-hearted endeavour to pick up the tab myself. This embarrassment over, we returned to the bikes, and set out for our different destinations; he back to his office, I to Ventura to meet up with Pepper in her seventh-floor office of suite 731.

CRUSTY BREAD AND THORNY ISSUES

Gourmet indulgences were not over for the day, and I decided to shed my leech outfit by treating my hostess to a meal out. After freshening up at Pepper's apartment, we took a lengthy walk down to 'Le Cafe' where the food, predictably, was French. A pleasing continental atmosphere prevailed in the restaurant's conservatory extension which protruded into the sidewalk, providing diners with a sense of involvement in the street life drifting by.

I ordered a beer to start with, by way of an appetizer, picking a European lager which was exorbitantly priced well above the home brewed alternative, for I was afflicted with an uncharacteristic extravagance, and determined to affect an air of Bohemian indulgence secure in the knowledge that my accent would protect me from accusations of total fraudulence; given, that is, that anything which is not American, must be slightly Bohemian when in America. I noticed in the midst of this reflection, that I had developed a less antagonistic attitude to the notion of being perceived as a European, rather than purely as an Englishman. I didn't used to feel this way. When Britain voted by referendum to remain in the Common Market back in the early seventies, I was appalled. How could the proud British race surrender the sovereignty which it had so many times fought to preserve? The insolence of a Brussels-based legislature telling us, the great imperial colonial power, the mother of parliaments, the country on which so many others have modelled their own governments, how to run its affairs, seemed to me the most intolerable ignominy. With the passage of time, however, and the establishment of friends in Europe, coupled to a greater awareness of environmental concerns, my sense of priorities has shifted, and my outlook become more global. As for the environmental problems, it would seem that the best chance of getting to grips with them, lies in the adoption of more co-operative schemes, whereby the success of the more ambitious projects will be enhanced by the mutual recognition of priorities to the exclusion of selfish minority concerns. Rather as a group of exhausted walkers will bolster each other's resolve in pursuit of a universal goal, so the petulant protests of minority industrial interests will enjoy a less receptive hearing from a mechanism propelled with the momentum of a morally rather than financially inspired crusade, than they might have from the more corruptible predecessor with which selfishly motivated lobbies might have enjoyed a more intimate relationship. At least that's the theory. Of course there is the danger that such a remote institution might, in the quest for uniformity, be less sympathetic to the individual characteristics of the member states in the framing of common laws.

Since the dawn of science, the logic of standardization has always been supported by compelling arguments, with the thirteen-amp, square-pin plug and the universal bayonet fitting light bulb providing good examples. When that same harmonization invades the subtler regions of cultural expression, however, the necessity of the intrusion must be called into question. In requiring of the European Parliament, that it exercises its strength to trample the baddies, whilst restraining it in deference to the sensitivities of the goodies, I may be demanding to have my cake and eat it; but to what other use, one may ask, may a cake be put?

Speaking of cakes or rather bread, one thing conspicuous by its absence, at least in my experience of this country, was decent crusty bread. Whereas every country town in Europe has its baker, offering an assortment of different shaped loaves with a variety of colours, textures, and decorative or nutritious embellishments, every retail food outlet I'd found in America seemed to confine its wares to dull, soft, sliced bread wrapped in polythene and indifferently bundled into a general shelf of the local supermarket. It is one of the great culinary success stories of our country, that the individual baker has made the comeback that he has and long may he thrive say I.

This lack of interesting bread was a factor in deciding me against home-made picnics on the road, in preference to patronage of the innumerable cafes, truckstops, and diners, that lined my route for the greater part of the journey. It is glaringly conspicuous absences like this that lead me to believe that America is still a land of opportunity for someone with the gumption to get out there and fulfil a need which damn well ought to exist, even if the people with the latent need don't know it. I dare say there are decent bakeries in the big towns and cities, but if that is so, why don't they open up outlets in the provincial regions?

Since I was now in a restaurant with enough cosmopolitan pretension to call itself 'Le Cafe,' I thought I must be able to get some crusty bread. I explained the problem to Pepper who bought the matter up with the waitress. 'Do you have any crusty bread, he can't get crusty bread anywhere in America?

'We'll get him some crusty bread,' the waitress smilingly assured us, and strolled off to fetch it, along with the escargot I'd ordered, leaving me feeling a little like a petulant child who, on having trouble finding an ice cream of his favourite flavour, threatens tears if it isn't provided. The crusty bread shortly appeared, and the meal was great. I love escargot, I love the paraphernalia of tongs with which to worry the encamped molluscs out of their buttery confines, the aroma of garlic, the smooth rich exotica of it slithering down my gullet in the wake of copious volumes of dark red wine, the effect of which was turning a balmy autumn evening, pleasant in itself, into a magnificent experience of bacchanal indulgence. There is definitely something more civilized about getting drunk on wine in preference to beer. For me, it must be red, and consumed with food, preferably involving plenty of crusty bread and a good deal of soft cheese. I'm no wine connoisseur, and I resent the superiority of those who can order a Chablis or a Burgundy with a confidence that suggests that they know what they're ordering. In a similar way, I resent the talents and sensitivity of those who can play musical instruments.

In the seventies I accompanied friends on innumerable trips to pubs on the London 'rock circuit,' which flourished at that time. I knew what I liked, and what I didn't like; my preference based more on what the band was playing than on the technical competence of the musicians. My companions on these outings would come away bemoaning the ineptitude of the sax, or the brilliance of the lead guitar in tones of decisive authority which left me feeling like some culturally-inarticulate peasant. Fortunately, one of my more frequent comrades on these excursions was a small good-natured fellow who I would threaten with extreme violence should he irritate me with his infuriating discriminations between the relative merits of the musicians observed. The more extreme variations of my diabolical threats were never executed, but I was not above turning a scarf around his throat and throttling him into silence, a reward for his enlightening conversation which was frowned upon by those unfamiliar with the ritual, as representing ingratitude as well as inexpediency, since the victim of my frustrations was usually driving a car at the time, in the course of giving me a lift home. Happily the musical critic took all this in good spirit for the merry jape it was, and besides, I would always release my grip before he lost consciousness, whilst maintaining a steadying hand upon the steering wheel to which I anchored one end of the scarf.

I guess it's the sense of being an outcast, that lies at the root of my irritation with those whose cognisance of social graces or art-forms is so superior to my own. It is as if they have formed a club or secret society from which, by dint of ignorance, I am excluded. How did they come to join, where did they get the membership forms, where was I when applications for enrolment were announced? If you've ever tried to park a car in the West End of London, you will have had the same experience. How can those parking bays all be full? Not half of them, not three-quarters of them, not nine-tenths of them, but all of them. How did the last guy into a space know there would be one left? Somebody had to be the final piece in the jigsaw, but how did he achieve that distinction? Everyone knows you can't park in the West End, you can go up there and drive around hopefully for an hour, but you can't park in a meter bay because they are always full. But who fills them, that is the question? At what time of day or night, or year, did they manoeuvre their vehicles into their positions of smug incumbence? They're like anonymous horror movie villains, these phantoms in their Fords, always one ahead of the innocents, like insider dealers from the Stock Exchange. I feel the same way about people who can tell when the drummer's out of time, the sax is off the rails, or the claret's not French. Bastards, the lot of them.

I don't know what the meal in Le Cafe cost, and I didn't want to know. Too many meals have been spoiled by the sobering shock of the bill at the end of them, and in the case of this establishment, I was spared the misery of the details by the discreet presentation of the bad news inside a slim black folder, between the covers of which I slid an even slimmer credit card. Signing the slip without looking too closely at its contents, I rose, a trifle unsteadily, and tottered out into the warm Los Angelian night, leaving a generous cash tip on the table as a testimony to my irreproachable munificence.

It was a mile or two back to Pepper's apartment, a distance which we covered at a leisurely pace since, besides the warmth of the evening, and the weight of food and wine in our stomachs, particularly mine, our progress was limited by the concentration necessary to sustain a heated argument.

My mistake was to discuss the old chestnut of Anglo Irish relations with an American of Irish decent. The chance, therefore, of a cool and rational discussion on the subject of the IRA, was about as high as that of successfully floating an Iraqi package holiday company holiday on the New York Stock Market. Once this particular ship of contention was underway, however, I was constrained by my own perverse appetite for exasperation, allied to a moral responsibility, to stay aboard...

Of course it would be absurd to suggest that either side in the dispute has a monopoly on justice, but it would be equally absurd to contend that the present partition is a feature of British neo-colonialism, and yet that is how some Americans see it. For America to have extended, by means of the lethargic, reluctant, or obstructive interpretation of extradition procedures, a measure of passive assistance to the murderous perpetrators of infamy who have sought sanctuary in that land, does them no credit at all. For Americans to have financed, through covert donations, the provision of guns and bombs which have been used to kill and maim the innocent citizens of a friendly democracy, is as severe an indictment of the American conscience as any that springs to mind. It is in pursuit of a reassurance that the mental stability of this nation enjoys a steady balance that one strives to believe that those who support the means of the IRA are confined to a tiny minority. Once, in Florida, I had cause to doubt this belief, when a hotel sign fell within the scope of my incredulous gaze, 'Welcome IRA,' it read. I subsequently discovered, to my relief, that it was an invitation to members of the Interstate Rodeo Association.

Walking back to Pepper's apartment, the argument raged over a hundred intersections. Now, I enjoy a good argument, particularly when it has as its base, a subject on which the views of my antagonist are a source of unfathomable mystery to me. As mentioned earlier, there is a strange enjoyment to be had in confronting attitudes diametrically opposed to one's own, especially when the champion of those views is a member of a breed rarely encountered in such stridently uncompromising colours. 'American speak' is a good language in which to conduct arguments. The extravagant use of language allied to the hysterical inflections of voice and vigorous gesticulations which owe their origin, no doubt, to the Latin influence, contrive to produce a finished product that is more theatre than debate. The American's style enables one to blot out an opponent's replies to the anticipated arguments, by creating a preliminary barrage before you've formulated what it is you're actually going to say. Whilst an Englishman might precede the main body of his argument with the laconic, 'Now look' or the precursor favoured by Yorkshiremen of, 'Now then,' an American will launch a preamble that approaches the dimensions of an overture.

'OK, I have something to say to you, are you ready for this? There are a few thing you need to know; excuse me are you listening to me?' This introductory flannel may seem like so much superfluous padding, but it fulfils a scene-setting function like undercoat paint – what follows tends to stick better. Even if the profundity of the ensuing rhetoric does not match the quality of the introduction, the ear on the receiving end is tuned for the opening lines, so, like a movie that kicks off a little late after a string of trailers and adverts, fewer people miss the start.

When I was a junior officer in the merchant navy, an old bosun once gave me a piece of advice. In dealing with the crew, whatever you tell them to do, try to sound very positive, and, assuming that what you have told them to do turns out to be complete nonsense, never admit afterward that you were wrong. This was a policy that I saw practised years later by a huge bull of a captain, appropriately called Butch. Butch was an overbearing, bloated, bearded, boorish fellow of sea-lion proportions who was held, by those with whom he sailed, to possess qualities of seamanship which warranted universal, if grudging respect. I doubted very much if these critics of his abilities based their judgements on any clearly understood specifics of maritime procedure, rather, I deduced, they were simply impressed by the self-confident resolution with which he conducted himself. There was about the delivery of his commands, an unequivocal character which was matched only by the volume at which they were issued, and the bellicose scorn with which he assaulted those who failed to comprehend or execute them to his satisfaction.

The combination of scene-setting preamble, with loud confident tones, establishes the trademark of the American orator, and is as likely to be encountered on a Manhattan street corner, as at a Senate meeting or presidential campaign address.

Deliberately mimicking other people's accents, inevitably invites ridicule, attracting accusations of fraudulence, and diminishing the respect in which the mimic is held. Copying their styles of speech, however, must, at worst, be a less serious offence. During the walk back to Pepper's I suspect I was definitely guilty of copying the style as well as emulating the histrionics of America's sidewalk thespians. The debate, whilst remaining good-humoured, developed an explosive potential from the emotional commitment to opposing viewpoints, that bouts of mutual exasperation threatened to detonate. There were frequent pauses in the progress of our journey to expostulate upon the inanity of the opponent's logic, pauses that mirrored the intellectual impasse of the argument. Hands were placed on shoulders, eyes bored into eyes, as if expressions of conviction could of themselves impress upon the opponent the validity of the arguments they were intended to endorse. Against the ambient warmth of the Southern Californian night, temperatures, in tune with the vocalized efforts of the contestants, rose to unnecessary altitudes in endeavouring to break the strangleholds framed by the forcefulness of the entrenched positions.

'You're not listening to what I am saying.'

'I am, I hear you, you said...'

'You hear but you do not understand, you do not digest, there is no engagement of any mental faculty to interpret what you hear, you hear but you do not comprehend; you see but you do not observe Watson.'

'Look let's get back to the base line; do you think that it's right to...'

The blast of a car horn disturbed the debate. 'What are you doing schmuck, get the hell outta the road!' We had stopped half way across a side street into which the automobile was turning from the main drag. Caught in the beam of his headlights, we were like principal actors centre-stage in a drama that had reached a fresh pitch with this motorized addition to the cast. I liked this, we were involved, we were part of the scene, not just shadowy figures flitting by like inconsequential silhouettes in the night, unheard, unseen, unnoticed, like silent mice creeping beneath the floorboards of a theatre; no we were there, we were alive, we were instigators, setters of trends rather than followers of patterns. We blocked the street, a motorist hooted at us, he'd stuck his head out of the window and shouted, we'd make our mark, signed our names, and sewn our threads into the bright tapestry of street life that relieves the shabby greyness of mediocrity.

We were part of the scene. The scene between pedestrians and motorists, motorists and motorists, storekeepers, newspaper vendors, ice cream salesmen; the creeps and cripples, the winos, whores and hooligans, the Holy Joes, touts and hustlers, the lurkers and lingerers, voyeurs, ponces, pooftahs, perverts, cute chicks and cool dudes, all wolf whistling, gesticulating, waving and weaving their way through the cosmic kaleidoscope that provides the framework of the vibrant organism on which we hang that label of concise convenience – street life.

Street life is great, I like street life, I like being a part of it, rather than just an observer, but to be a part of it, one has either to take or respond to a verbal initiative. Too many British people are afraid of the street level intimacy which street life demands. An Englishman accosted by a wretch on the cadge will hurry by with his eyes to the ground, uttering at most, a dismissive grunt or monosyllabic, 'no.' An American will take a more positive stance, perhaps even moralize a little in his reply, 'Get a job bum.' Americans seem less afraid of the contact of strangers, their language provides them with uniformly recognized stock responses. If a woman drops her glove in the street an Englishmen will be unsure what to shout after her. How can he be sure that the woman will know it is her to whom he is referring. He'll cough, he'll try an, 'Excuse me,' or an 'I say;' he can't bring himself to say 'madam' since it sounds too pretentious, whilst 'woman' sounds too coarse, almost abusive, and the word 'lady' is confused by its aristocratic associations. The result is an irresolute stammer of embarrassment, while his hope is that someone else will have noticed the glove and directed its owner's attention in the direction of her saviour. His fear is of causing a scene, he doesn't want people to turn and look at him. Yobs shout, drunks shout, football supporters shout; he isn't any of these, he is an innocent man burdened with the responsibility of restoring property to its negligent owner. The passage of time compounds the problem as the woman's figure retreats into the distance. The Englishman wishes he hadn't seen the garment fall, he wishes he were elsewhere, like the man at the scene of an accident about which he can do little, but which a sense of duty deters him from leaving.

The American shares none of these inhibitions, his remedy is simple. In a loud clear voice he calls unhesitatingly after the owner, 'Hey lady, you dropped your glove!'

Dramatic circumstances encourage the intimacy on which street life feeds; a heavy snowfall, torrential rain, maybe even just a late bus. All that is needed is a common denominator to focus people's attention on a mutual concern which subordinates the individual consideration to the communal need. Americans rely less on the windfalls of catastrophe than upon their natural intimacy. The market trader from the East End of London would dismiss all this as a load of cobblers, the street life of his professional domain is as rich as anywhere he would claim, and he may be right, but it isn't typical of the country, or even of the whole metropolis. The traditional British respect for good manners erects a barrier of civility, stiffened with endemic reservation to obstruct the expression of street life through the use of the words 'please' and the expression 'excuse me', which pose fences of formality to the rapid exchanges that characterize its form.

Street life survives nonetheless in a multitude of trivial manifestations. Documentary film makers have turned its identification and capture into a minor art form. A pigeon dumps on a policeman's head – two strangers turn and grin – a sensuous girl waggles past a lunching line of construction workers whose heads, in comical unison, follow her retreating buttocks. A motorist brakes violently for a careless pedestrian, thrusts his head out of the window and shouts abuse, the pedestrian thrusts fingers into the air. A newspaper vendor shouts his unintelligible signature across the pavement as a busker smiles at a passing patron. A young man roller-skates down the subway as a gent hails a cab. A child blows a soap bubble which bursts upon the beak of a startled pigeon in whose astonished response the ruffled feathers of human indignity find poignant reflection. Imbued by nature with introvert qualities, I deliberately explore the mechanisms of street life as a curious teetotaller might taste beers. Sometimes I'll buy a paper or order a cup of tea in a cafe, just for the sake of the limited contact it affords. If you spot a bus inspector you're on to a winner; you can ask a question, get an answer and make a complaint, and it doesn't cost you a penny. The chargeless quality of street life is one of its most endearing characteristics; if only you could take it home with you.

A friend of mine regularly experiences street life from an armchair by calling telephone operators with absurd requests until they lose patience with him. After a prolonged campaign of gratuitously abusing these anonymous scapegoats, an inspector from British Telecom called at his flat in an effort to resolve the conflict. After an unsuccessful effort at negotiation, the inspector left the unhappy subscriber with one final question, 'Why operators?' He turned to the departing investigator in incredulity at the stupidity of an intellect incapable of identifying so transparent a motive. Honest simplicity rewarded the curiosity of the retreating inquisitor, who departed baffled by the unassailable logic of the laconic answer. 'They're free.'

Walking back through Ventura neighbourhood was pretty cheap, though I might not have enjoyed it as much without first having spent the money on the wine. The argument reached no recognizable conclusion, and though I'd bowled all the right balls at the wicket, the opposition had pulled up the stumps and changed the rules. I hadn't lost, but in the absence of an independent umpire to provide a decision, I'd been robbed of the ashes. 'Never mind' I thought; but I did.

HOLLYWOOD

I had avoided nearly every man-made tourist attraction in America so far, and so decided to make a concession to bad taste by peering at the houses of the rich and famous in Beverley Hills. Equipped with an appropriate map of Los Angeles, I set out for the fabled neighbourhood of the world's most conspicuously successful inhabitants.

My deplorable curiosity had been anticipated, and in predictable American style, catered for. At regular intervals along the legendary strip that is Sunset Boulevard, sat sleepy Hispanics reclining languidly in deckchairs like basking lizards, their baseball hats pulled low over their eyes against the dazzling sun, as they conducted a slow, albeit easy trade, in the supply of what the chalked legends on the roadside blackboards proclaimed to be, 'Maps of The Stars.' I bought one, and self-consciously unfolded it to pick out a few of the more prominent names. What kind of place did Charles Bronson live in, I wondered, and Burt Reynolds, and Elvis Presley when he stayed here. This kind of fawning curiosity does nothing to enhance one's self-respect, but if some concession is not made to satisfy it, then like an unscratched itch, the appetite remains, leaving one in a state of unfulfilled speculation. Lot's wife had the same problem when she was given the chance to get out of Sodom before the old city and its quirky population were well and truly buggered for the last time, a problem shared by Orpheus who, like Mrs. Lot, just could not resist the indulgence of his appetite for curiosity or doubt; both, like the feline casualties of the old adage, suffered somewhat disproportionately, I always thought, for their mistakes and mistrust. No such calamity befell me for the exercise of my embarrassing indulgence which I abandoned after half an hour of poking around leafy culs-de-sac, as it was far too pathetic for an adult.

Beverly Hills was not exactly how I imagined it would be. As is the way with preconceptions, you don't always have a perfect vision of what you expect, and it requires the experience of direct contact to quantify what you didn't, to lead you to the identification of what you did. Like an eye-witness guided by a police identikit artist, you can't describe the face you saw with precision, but as positively erroneous features are attached to the outline, then by means of elimination, progress toward a fair facsimile is achieved. The mental picture I held of Beverly Hills was under-exposed and out of focus, but my imagination stocked a collection of formless ingredients that I was sure I would be able to identify. The abstract collage of my ill-defined conception anticipated a flash, glitzy, trashy kind of environment, an over-the-top depository of affluent urban excess, where neighbours vie with one another in vulgar contests of material exhibitionism. Exactly what form these exercises in architectural hedonism might take, I was not sure, but upon reflection, I suppose I would not have been surprised to find imitation Disney World castles, plastic colonnaded Roman temple replicas, and hedges trained into the shape of dollar signs. I found no such obscenities, though the neighbourhood was no shanty town. What surprised me most about Hollywood, was how pleasant it was, at least in the hilly neighbourhood. Sunset Boulevard, on which many of the big names have homes, is very obviously for the stinking rich. The houses are big, very big, or palatial. Most have gardens, or rather grounds, which are well tended by professional gardeners. Where the boulevard runs into town, the classy opulence falters. When I was there the huge advertising billboards decorating the sidewalk depicted the unpleasant rat-like face of Sean Penn. With his disconsolate face capped by a netted combat helmet, the snarling weasel-featured youth polluted the street, a ludicrously unconvincing vision of militaristic toughness. This was not my favourite part of town.

The spaced out style of Western towns with their wide roads, forecourts, and distantly spaced business premises, are in sharp contrast to the urban cosiness which one associates with the old districts of continental towns. It requires the physical restraint of land shortage it would seem, to encourage that economy, which, whether by accident or design, resolves itself in the development, over the years, of a pleasing architectural intimacy. The advantages of the Western system are mechanical rather that artistic. There may be more chance of parking an automobile near your favourite cafe in LA, but the convenience seems a poor compensation for sitting on a pavement sandwiched between a car showroom overspill, and a supermarket trolley park.

Up in the hillier regions, the scene changes dramatically for the better. The irregular nature of the terrain has dictated a more resourceful and imaginative architecture which complements rather than dominates the landscape. A pleasing Mediterranean quality prevails here, where the land sets the architectural parameters, and a commendable sensitivity has reconciled domestic necessity with an aesthetically-motivated conservatism. For the first time since leaving the Rockies, I encountered roads that turned and twisted in serpentine endeavours to provide the privileged residents with a means of access to their sumptuous homes. Innumerable trees and shrubs supported the rural quality which has survived the assault of the motor car in a metropolis that is world famous as the Mecca of personal transport. Though the clarity of the view across Los Angeles from the hills, is shrouded by the infamous smog, the air up here seemed clean and pleasantly scented by the aromatic junipers and exotic shrubbery that provided screens of botanical privacy, as well as homes for legions of colourful birds. I was reminded of Greek hillside villages I'd visited, the pleasingly leafy clutter of Haifa on the slopes of Mt Carmel, and the more sensitively cultured rural areas of Japanese habitation. None of these impressions sustained the picture of Philistine indifference to environment that I'd anticipated.

The soft burble of the bike's exhaust made no enemies here. Up ahead of me, an elderly woman pruning an exuberant creeper with a pair of secateurs waved cheerfully at me with a gloved hand; I smiled, returning her wave. No anti-motorcycle prejudice seemed to blight this resident's perspective. I speculated upon the reason for this, which I attributed in part to the growing identity of the Harley-Davidson with the more adventurously affluent. Like two-wheeled Porsches, the Harley has joined the growing menagerie of materialistic accoutrements with which the affluent must advertise their success, whilst simultaneously providing a dash of danger with its connotation of indefinite youth.

The reluctance of Americans to abandon the styles and pursuits of their youth, as they proceed to their maturer years, is a feature I found both entertaining and reassuring. In Britain, though less so now than once, the riding of motorcycles was listed among the hazardous indulgences of the foolhardy young. Motorcycles were toys to be surrendered to the demands of maturity as wives, mortgages, and domestic responsibilities supplanted the priority of frivolous indulgence. Middle age meant cars before bikes, and grey flannels before blue jeans. Increasing affluence must have played a role in preserving the options of two- and four-wheeled transport on both sides of the Atlantic. They are options, however, which a fun-loving appetite inspires Americans to embrace more enthusiastically. The British perception of Americans, is of a slightly childish and less sophisticated race of people, a judgement that is at least partly supported by the unapologetic patronage of motorcycles by those who are old enough to know better.

At seventy years of age, billionaire Malcolm Forbes was frequently seen roaring around on one of his huge collection of Harleys, and why not? One of Forbes' greatest regrets in life, he told journalists, was that he did not discover motorcycles earlier; he did not begin riding until the age of forty-seven.

In lumping motorcycles among life's childish indulgences, I am guilty of equating juvenility with fun. The notion that adult responsibilities mean abandoning youthful pleasure is something which needs to be challenged at every opportunity and Americans are damned good at this.

Cruising around Beverly Hills, I felt the benefit of the legitimacy afforded to motorcycling through its patronage by the adult and affluent. Americans have a name for these well-heeled cowboys of the street – Rich Urban Bikers, or RUBS. I wondered if I was being mistaken for one and the possibility did not bother me. It may be a failing to enjoy people's envy, or assume that their recognition of your wealth warrants it, but in my case at least, it is a fact. People who draw no pleasure from demonstrating their wealth on their sleeve, are as rare as those who care nothing for what others think of them.

There are plenty of RUBS in Hollywood. The exposed nature of the motorcycle makes it the ideal transport for profiling, a popular sport in these parts, where proof of success is presented to the public with shameless ostentation. By the end of the eighties, the Harley-Davidson had become a potent symbol to be insinuated into every kind of advertisement in order to embellish the dynamic appeal of the product. Chewing gum advertisements used it, beer ads used it, jeans ads used it. Magazine profiles of rock and movie stars frequently pictured them aboard their Harleys. Sylvester Stallone rides one, Arnold Schwarzenegger rides one, Bruce Springsteen rides one, anyone who is anyone, and has a macho image to sustain, keeps at least one Harley in the garage. The need to explain or justify ownership has receded; interviewers have ceased their incredulous probings for the motivation that prompts such lunatic indulgence. A picture of the face with the gleaming toy in the background requires no more explanation than the presence of a wife or the backdrop of a swimming pool. The implicit assumption, have money have Harley, has asserted itself with the enquiry shifting direction from why, to why not? So prevalent has the adoption of the legendary marque become, that journalists exploring the source of the fascination have dubbed the world's movie making Mecca: Harleywood.

I felt that perhaps I should have resented this exploitation of a cultural artefact whose acquisition had demanded such sacrifice of me, by people who could buy them out of their small change, but I didn't. Perhaps the recognition of a common appetite provided me with an illusion of kinship with the rich, famous, and beautiful people of Southern California. Sadly pretentious? *Moi?*

I climbed higher into the hills, heading for the giant Hollywood sign set into the side of the rocky LA backdrop, a tacky piece of advertising which, with the passage of time, has acquired a nostalgic appeal that has endeared it to some surprising residents whose largesse provided the necessary funds for its overdue restoration. Alice Cooper whose outrageous stage act earned him the unparalleled accolades of contempt from all but the most broad-minded of critics, made a substantial donation to the appeal, adequate to restore a complete letter to its original glory, which only goes to show that you can't judge a man by his mascara.

The factor most conspicuous by its absence, that I had expected to observe in the Hollywood Hills, was an overpowering omnipresence of security arrangements. Perhaps they existed on a more discreet level than I anticipated; certainly I failed to identify the substantial railings and menacing Dobermans one associates with the self protective paranoia of the wealthy. The sole symptom of anxiety that I observed all afternoon, was a sign bearing a traditionally villainous outline which warned jealous predators of the operation of a neighbourhood watch scheme. I was relieved.

The photograph of myself on the bike with the Hollywood sign in the background was obligatory of course. A low wall of crumbling stone, sprouting flowers and grasses provided me with a makeshift tripod, which I endeavoured to adjust by balancing the lens on small fragments of masonry to establish the correct elevation. My efforts, I was later to discover, had been thwarted by a blade of grass which had fallen across the lens, obscuring the lower half of my body as well as most of the motorcycle. Unaware of this *faux pas*, and believing my efforts successfully completed, I threaded a cautious path downhill through the maze of narrow dusty streets, pausing on a corner to buy a postcard from a genteel shop full of tasteful sketches, complemented by a food counter exhibiting colourful salads and slices of quiche. The woman who served me, recognized my English accent, which made a pleasant change from the customary assumption that I was Australian. I rewarded this astute observer with some heavyweight financial patronage to the tune of a dollar fifty cents for three slightly up-market postcards, featuring the famous movie-land sign to which I committed several lines of ludicrous gibberish for the benefit of favoured relatives and friends back in the Old Country.

The home-bound traffic on Sunset Boulevard was depressingly heavy. A bumper-to-bumper jam extended the whole length of the street to the freeway access. Blessedly, California does not forbid motorcyclists to percolate through the traffic, as in some states, where presumably one is supposed to sit in line pretending to be a car when the traffic is reduced to a crawl. How people can tolerate laws quite as absurd as that is a source of mystery to me. A columnist writing about America in a British motorcycle magazine challenged the claim that America is the land of the free. As he pointed out, there are a multitude of trivial laws woven into the political fabric of American life which would not be countenanced in this country. The reason why these restrictions do not make life intolerable, owes everything to the blessed impossibility of enforcing them. British law, by contrast, tends to be made with some reference to the viability of enforcement, which has the effect of sifting out the frivolous restrictions which represent little more than the self indulgent whims of shallow thinking politicians.

I hadn't encountered any congestion all the way from Ohio to LA, so I hadn't found the regulation a problem, but then I had avoided cities all the way.

It was whilst insinuating myself between the roasting legions of tin boxes, that I was startled to see a sight I hadn't laid eyes on since leaving London. A motorcycle courier, unmistakable in identifying bib, bearing the legend, 'Security Despatch,' a radio aerial sprouting from his shoulder, was slicing through the jam above the car roofs like a shark's fin, with the unhesitating confidence born of experience allied to financial incentive. I wondered if this company was the same Security Despatch that hailed from London's Covent Garden? I wanted to stop the rider and ask him, but my 1340cc Harley-Davidson was not as nimble as his 550cc Kawasaki, and I lost him amid the congestion.

RAW FISH

I found my way back to Ventura District without a hitch, and prepared myself for my next and final gourmet outing before leaving Los Angeles. In conversation on the subject of food, I had mentioned to Richard, that of all the cuisines I had experienced in my travels, the only one I had encountered, which I could positively say I disliked, was sushi: traditional Japanese food. I admitted how it annoyed me that I had been unable to enjoy this Oriental cuisine, and that I remained game to have another try. As a child, my exceptional faddishness was a source of constant irritation to my parents, and to me, as I felt myself to be apart from others, and from this sensitive feeling of inadequacy, grew a conviction that I was being got at by others who couldn't understand me. Though I would eat no greens or anything that looked as if it had been 'messed about with' I did, in common with most kids, eat volumes of chips, an appetite that was conveniently catered for by the permanent supply that had come to rest on my shoulder.

I have since spent my adult life cultivating appetites for every fare imaginable in an effort to compensate for the gastric reticence of my youth, in the course of which I have developed the same impatience for the culinary conservatism of others that I once inspired in my frustrated parents. There is a great social advantage in being able to eat anything, and an added bonus if you can enjoy it. One is spared the embarrassment of having to refuse food, which a considerate host may have spent hours preparing, in addition to which, there's a financial element. On my first trip to Israel, as an officer on a merchant ship employed in the citrus trade, I discovered the olive. The first thing that I learned about olives, was that some were green and some were black; the second thing I discovered was that I didn't like either. This was a great disappointment to me, as olives were one of the few things in Israel, which were free. True, olives do grow on trees, but that alone would not have provided sufficient motive for such largesse. Whatever the rationale, free they were. In the bars I frequented on the streets of Haifa and Ashdod, saucers laden with these small, piquant fruits provided a sight as ubiquitous as the bowls of peanuts which in English pubs make their traditional appearance at Sunday lunch times. That I could not take advantage of this generosity was a cause of great distress to me, and so, like the boy who was ordered to stand in the corner until he believed in the Holy Ghost, I, by a supreme effort of will, trained myself to like olives. Before long I was cheerfully popping handfuls of the tart tasters into my mouth, like a child with a bag of jelly beans. This success enhanced my sense of Bohemian accomplishment, and as the waiter replenished my saucer with fresh supplies, my sense of conquest grew from the recognition that I had overcome the greatest of prejudices.

Suspecting I could achieve the same victory with sushi, I accompanied Richard to his favourite emporium of Oriental cuisine.

This restaurant, Richard assured me, was the best sushi restaurant in the universe. The chef, if you can call a man who serves raw food a chef, was once employed by the Emperor Hirohito himself, in the kitchens of his imperial palace in Tokyo. I was forced to recognize the irreproachable pedigree of a man with these culinary credentials, and accepted my host's offer of a meal at Coogie's.

Coogie's restaurant was not the intimidating temple of ritual mastication I had feared might house the ultimate expression of a nation's nosebag. Fragile bamboo partitions separated the diner's tables, whilst a line of high stools surrounded the bar, behind which the grand master stood smiling benignly by a rack of evil looking blades, like a cheerful executioner. Taking Richard's cue, I levered myself on to a stool and gazed into the cold sightless eyes of the aquatic victims whose fate had led them to this terrestrial terminus. The menu meant little to me, and I deferred the selection of dishes to the superior experience of my host, who ordered several, with a confidence born of familiarity. Whilst we awaited the arrival of the starters, we were offered a small bowl of squid segments each, which, it must be said, I found quite acceptable. With the arrival of the first course I produced a camera and prevailed upon a fellow diner to record my impressions on encountering the food which was suspended near my face by Coogie's obliging daughter.

I had four or five courses in all, each consisting of slices of raw fish balanced on gelatinous blocks of cold rice, and dipped in sauces which were provided separately in a selection of shallow bowls. For those accustomed to the Indian concept of rice, in which virtue is gauged by the independence of the grains, the Japanese policy of deliberately producing a coagulated mass that hangs together like a clump of tapioca, must seem perverse in the extreme. No more perverse however than the chopsticks with which they contrive to eat the gelatinous mess. The reflection led me to consider how Orientals have developed a tradition of making life hard for themselves. Whilst the latin based languages have a couple of dozen characters, the Japanese, like the Chinese, have thousands. This, of necessity, demands keyboards that make the legion of stops on the organ at St Paul's look like a penny whistle. Likewise, though not complicated in themselves, chopsticks provide a ridiculous means of moving food from a plate to a mouth. This isn't opinion, it's fact. The Japanese may have practised the art of eating with sticks until they achieve an impressive degree of competence, but the efficiency is achieved in spite of the ridiculous apparatus rather than because of it. I have met pretentious Westerners who love to demonstrate their proficiency with Eastern eating implements, going as far as to claim that they find them easier to use. Even, in the case of one exceptional snob, claiming he found them easier for eating rice with. These people are all liars. Their eagerness in pointing to a body of opinion represented by a billion Chinese does nothing to strengthen their case. Chopsticks are bloody ridiculous things. I'm very glad they exist mind you, since they assist the cause of variety and the joys of cultural diversity. I always make a point of using chopsticks in a Chinese restaurant and deplore the defeatism of those who, in despair, resort to the Western alternatives. Whilst I believe in the 'when in Shanghai' policy, what I can't stand is the establishment of irrational pretences intended to disarm possible accusations of philistine attitudes. If chopsticks were superior instruments for collecting food from a plate, then Japanese earth moving and digging equipment would, in preference to the sensible pronged shovels manufactured in the West, incorporate some power driven manifestation of chopsticks: they don't.

Those capable of practising a degree of self deception necessary to maintain that they can eat rice more easily with chopsticks than with a fork are the same people who can be conned into believing that there is a man in China who can perform calculations on an abacus faster than the master computer at the NASA space centre. In case you are wondering, there is no such man.

To return to the meal in question, the gelatinous nature of the rice enabled me to pick it up with chopsticks, which is of course, why they make it that way, and therein hangs a peculiar logic. Though critics of the Nipponese might suggest that only they could prepare food in a manner that is disgusting so that they can eat it with utensils that are ridiculous, such sceptics would be wrong, for the Chinese do exactly the same thing, which only goes to show that no nation has a monopoly on absurdity. What the Chinese do not do, however, as far as I know, is eat raw fish. One is told by those who know about these things, that the lack of cooking is less noticeable when the fish is extremely fresh, a virtue for which Coogie's restaurant is renowned. It is this unparalleled freshness, allied to the exclusivity of the sauces into which I was urged to dip the cold-blooded flesh, that sets Coogie's a thousand cuts above the competition. Whilst freshness may be virtue, for me at least, this alone does not guarantee enjoyment. If it did I might rejoice at the prospect of fresh dung served steaming from the body heat of its bestial author; I do not. On a scale of nastiness, fresh raw fish ranks better than dung, but, less nasty though it may be, I have as yet failed to generate any enthusiasm for it.

I am told that one of the most highly regarded of Japanese delicacies is a fish that features an element of such toxicity as to stagger the imagination. The extraction of the edible as opposed to the poisonous fibres is a matter of surgical precision which must be achieved with a filigree blade operated by the most knowledgeable and accurate hand. The slightest mistake may lead to the contamination of adjacent flesh with terminal consequences for the unlucky diner whose protests, if articulated at all, are abbreviated by rapid unconsciousness and death. Surely one must recognize the perversity of a race prepared to take such extraordinary risks in return for such disgusting food. Needless to say this particular fish absolutely must be as fresh as can be without actually swimming into your face. The obsession of the Japanese with freshness where fish is concerned is not without good cause, but for my money I don't care how fucking fresh it is – you can stuff it!

To compound my distress, I was prevailed upon to '*ee all at one*'. The courses were, it is true, small, each constituting no more than two or three mouthfuls, but to jam the whole Mars Bar-sized block into the mouth at once was a tall order from a short man. I tried it nonetheless, and gagged on the excess in consequence. The conspiracy of volume with vitriol, contrived to set my digestive tract into a state of muscular reciprocation that came close to producing a scene of desperate embarrassment. The experience reminded me of my childhood dilemmas when, obliged through circumstance to consume some dreadful vegetable, I had suffered that same frightful nausea. For a moment I felt sure I was going to heave the whole slippery mass of piscean purgatory out onto the floor before the eyes of the smiling proprietor. I felt my throat muscles convulse, sending ripples of revulsion through to my stomach, where the wisdom of total evacuation was weighed against social propriety. With trepidation I awaited the outcome over which I felt my control to be slipping. Blessedly, like a ship which teeters on the brink of capsizing amidst turbulent seas, the lower hold of my digestive tract accepted the caustic cargo in to a safe, if temporary stowage. The temple of Bachus, though emphatically closed to further visitors, had settled comfortably on its foundations. I declined offers of additional courses, and sat out the final stages of play on the sidelines, while my host chomped down a cone shaped desert of sticky rice wrapped in a green seaweed shroud.

'I think you might have liked one of these Mutch,' ventured Richard, as he devoured the delicacy in the manner of a large bullfrog crunching the struggling limbs of a disconsolate grasshopper into its slippery maw.

There was no doubt that the meal had been an experience, but in the face of an opportunity for repetition, I was prepared to display the virtue of patience. I made excuses about having reached saturation point which prevented me eating another mouthful while concocting transparent euphemisms about the food's 'interesting and provocative qualities.' Back at Pepper's apartment I begged her for something to eat as she scoured her cupboards for something to sustain me. Beans on toast never tasted so good.

CALIFORNIA

The longest stopover of my trip had come to an end, and it was time to be on my way, for there were more deadlines to meet. Pepper had contacted John Reid and Arlen Ness, both of whom I wanted to interview, and both of whom were going on vacation a few days hence. There was no time to be lost, and I had to head north without delay. Despite having spent four days in Los Angeles, I still hadn't seen the Pacific Ocean, and now recognized a hankering to at least dip a toe in it. To me, the Pacific coast, the sun and the sea, the sand, surfboards, and beach parties, was what California was all about. My adolescent day-dreams were fuelled by the youthful hedonism of Beach Boys' lyrics, and in reverence to their memory I headed for Santa Barbara. I liked that name instinctively. Santa Barbara – Barbara Anne. There is a Latin quality to the name that I like. Of the foreign languages I felt I would profit most by mastering, Spanish excites me most. French may have a classy soft romanticism to it, but Spanish has a musical machismo that I favour. Just as German is a great language for dispensing orders, so Spanish is ideal for hurling insults loaded with bile-sodden sarcasm. It's also a damn handy language to be able to speak; second to English it must be the most international language in the world. It would be a handy tongue to master if you were living in Southern California or the southern states generally, plus Mexico, most of South America, and Portugal where a similar language is spoken, and, I am told, you can struggle by in Italy with it. To cap it all you can always take a holiday in Spain and speak it there. All around, there're no two ways about it, Spanish is a very useful tongue, and if the success of empire building can be measured by the predominance of the mother tongue, then the Spanish Conquistadors must come second only to the British in terms of success on this score. When I was in the merchant navy I sailed with an engineer who was accompanied by his Spanish wife. I was determined to learn the language. I would, I told myself, buy books and cassette tapes and practise for an hour every day; with a Spanish speaking person to help me, success would be guaranteed. By the time we reached Hong Kong, I assured myself, I would be able to trade abuse with the worst of the switchblade wetbacks from Panama to Puerto Rico. I'd be able to take vacations in the dusty Spanish hinterland, order wine and bean dishes with the casual confidence of a man wise to the lingo. I would wear a hat, squint like Clint Eastwood, and spit like a Brazilian footballer. With this linguistic weapon in my armoury the Latin world would open to me like a castanet. No grinning dagos would have the edge on me with their bi-lingual streetwise talents. They'd have to think twice before they abused me to my face in their foreign tongue, giggling amongst themselves at my ignorant discomfiture as they ripped me off for the price of a postcard or pineapple. I would be *El Mutcho* the man with the lingo.

Hurrah, *Ole*!

When I left the ship three months later, I had learnt one phrase, *Oula* – it means hello – and I usually mispronounce it.

Santa Barbara looked idyllic. Away from the sprawling immensity of Los Angeles, it is a small town with clearly defined limits, pleasant wooden buildings and plenty of leafy trees and palms. The desert stretching inland to the east, whilst to the west, the Pacific Ocean reached out all the way to China.

The town wasn't crowded though the mid-September weather was beautiful. I guess most Californians, like the British, take their vacations in the summer.

I looked around for a seafood restaurant with a veranda from where I could look out to sea whilst burrowing into lobster claws and munching crusty French rolls. I spotted just the place with an outdoor eating area, but, something was missing, there were no patrons in evidence, not one, the place was deserted. I was damned if I was going to pull up outside a restaurant on a Harley-Davidson if there was no one there to see me so I kept on rolling. It's easier to keep going when you travel alone. The solitary mode precludes the arguments which travelling companions inevitably encourage. If I'd been riding with somebody else and we'd agreed that we'd stop at a seafood restaurant, how then could I have explained that we couldn't stop at this one because there was no one there to see me? There is a capacity for self-indulgence in solitary travel that I value, though it does work both ways. Sometimes you need that moderating or encouraging force to make you stop to fill a tank or a stomach. A compadre in Santa Barbara might have persuaded me to stop for lunch at the seafood restaurant. As it was I missed it, and it was to be more than a week and over two-thousand miles before I was to sink my teeth into lobster at Indianapolis, in a restaurant a thousand miles from the ocean.

Cruising beyond Santa Barbara town through semi-rural suburbia was beautiful. Beautiful houses, beautiful gardens, immaculate stretches of lush well-watered lawns stood at the side of a picture-book ribbon of faultless black top, that wound beneath giant, smooth-barked plane trees. I left the main route for a while to cruise along a wooded chicane through which the sun's rays were scattered into a leafy mosaic by the overhanging boughs. I was alone on the road, at peace, in total command. The torquey motor pulled fifth gear easily from the bottom of its huge heart with little more than a thousand revs on the clock, unwinding the smooth curves as a cat might lick cream off a saucer. The scene was idyllic, no helmet, no hassles, a warm breeze in my face, and the staggered orchestra of the soft, powerful exhaust note for musical accompaniment, rumbling behind me like a pride of contented lions.

A Mexican gardener, hose in hand, looked up as I passed, his dark face shaded by the brim of a tattered straw hat. I gave him a wave, to which his hat dipped in polite recognition, a Steinbeckian stereotype framed between a brace of banyan trees before the postcard blue of the ocean backdrop. A classic silhouette replete with social comment. I would like to have stopped to take a picture, but I feared the vulgarity of the intrusion would tarnish the pleasure of the recollection; some memories are best preserved as just that, or translated into the written word, leaving their subjects unmolested. I rode on. To compensate for the loss of a pictorial souvenir, I photographed myself using the delayed timer mechanism, sitting on the motorcycle in front of a coconut palm. This is a process that can lead to embarrassment if anyone sees you legging it back from the camera like a terrorist fleeing a carefully placed bomb, and, of course, regaining the necessary poise in time, whilst staying in frame is the tricky bit, but I did it.

I'd intended to leave Interstate 101 at San Luis Obispo to follow the coast road up to Big Sur, for no better reason than that I liked the name – Big Sur. For me it conjured up pictures of giant rollers crashing on a huge golden beach. I was not to discover if my preconception was accurate however, as I muddled my navigation and found myself taking the inland route east of the Santa Lucia mountains which only appeared, on my map, to be crossed by a solitary road by means of which I might return to the coast. I made two attempts at taking what I thought was the right route. One ended in a military camp; the other in a five-bar gate leading to a farmer's field. I was totally nonplussed by this and made a mental note to pen a letter of protest to the Tourist Board for not signposting the route more clearly. I didn't bother of course, and the mystery has since joined the growing catalogue of incomprehension with which the course of my life is tragically paved. I'd missed my chance of a seafood meal on the coast for sure now, and was obliged to travel through the considerable heat of the desert afternoon, a sharp contrast to the coast road I had been following, on which a surprisingly chill mist had descended.

A trucker's diner appeared up ahead, well-recommended by a line of gleaming trucks, variously decorated with personalized murals, Confederate flags, Stars and Stripes, and graphic maps of the USA. Inside the truckstop, the air conditioning, rather like an American beer cooler, was working a little too enthusiastically for my liking, but the bracing environment served to sharpen my considerable appetite to a razor-keen edge, which I sought to blunt with a plate of fried eggs and the now familiar hash browns. One thing was missing though, as in most of the diners I'd visited; one element which the movie-makers never overlook, but which the real life proprietors of these roadside oasis neglect with a disturbing consistency. Music. That's what was missing, good ol' country rock music. When was the last time Goldie Hawn climbed out of her white Stingray and waggled her exquisite arse through the door of a cafe without the accompaniment of Dolly Parton or Kenny Rogers? Country music is part of the American environment, like Wrigleys chewing-gum, Chevrolets and Coca Cola signs; it's omnipresence is such that you only recognize it through its absence. I know this because I've seen hundreds of these movies. The desperado climbs out of his car leaving his dim-witted gum-chewing moll behind. As soon as the car door slams she turns up the radio which is of course tuned to the same channel as the one in the diner which becomes apparent as her partner opens the diner door to meet the gaze of the rednecks leaning heavily on the bar. There was no music in this diner and I shovelled hash browns and dripping egg yolk into my face to the accompaniment of nothing more musical than others doing the same.

THE CUSTOM KINGS

The evening cooled rapidly after sunset, as I nosed into the unclear boundaries of Morgan Hill on my way to rendezvous with an old friend from England – John Reid. Unlike an English country town or village, the scattered character of the place rendered the determination of my arrival difficult. I studied the directions I'd been given over the phone, but failed to identify the features described. Returning to a major road I parked by a huge supermarket and shopping complex from where I phoned John again. 'Stay there,' he advised me, 'I'll come out to meet you.'

America seemed to have done him some good. Gone was the obscene full face helmet, in which his head had been imprisoned the last time we met at his old home near Oxford. The pair of aviator's goggles strapped around his unencumbered dome complemented the pioneer aspect of the classic 1950s' motorcycle I'd photographed four years earlier in England.

'Hello Mutchie,' he said, 'follow me.'

Besides looking more lined and battered than ever, the fellow was in good spirits and obviously enjoying life in the sunshine state with his pretty French wife Jen, who always seems to me like a perennial schoolgirl. Their house, somewhere beyond the outskirts of town, was a largish bungalow, with a rustic wooden veranda out the back, from where John's little estate of several wooded acres on a steep slope could be viewed. A brace of useful-looking Dobermans trotted around on sentry duty, a reassuring precaution that helped my hosts to sleep more confidently out here in the sticks. Complementing the canine deterrent to insomnia, was a cupboard full of guns, none of which looked like they came free with Cornflake packets. I picked out a meaty looking Magnum and strolled out the back to make some noise.

'Where shall I point it?' I asked.

'Oh over there somewhere,' advised John, with a cheerful indifference that I felt I should question.

'Suppose there's somebody amongst the trees?' I queried. He viewed me with an expression of confusion.

'Well there shouldn't be,' that's all my land over there, if there's anybody over there then they're trespassing.'

Thus reassured that if there was anybody there, then they were fair game, I struck a dramatic pose with both hands clasped around the handle of the gun, *à la Miami Vice*. If, like me, you're unaccustomed to firearms, then the reaction you experience when pulling the trigger is astonishing. The Magnum was, no doubt, an unusually powerful handgun – the most powerful, assuming it was the same one Dirty Harry used. I'm not sure if it was, as there are apparently Magnums and Magnums, but it nearly knocked me over backwards with the recoil, so what would happen to the wretch on the receiving end doesn't bear thinking about.

As the noise of the detonation faded John called out for his hound, Kong. Even before the smoke cleared, a dreadful sense of foreboding overtook me, as Kong failed to respond . I looked left then right and then behind me on to the veranda where I thought the animals had been shortly before the firearms exercise; now however, only one dog could be found. John walked up and down calling Kong's name, whilst the remaining beast ran around distractedly searching for his partner. 'Kong! Kong! where the hell are you, Kong? Anybody seen Kong?' I heard him ask his wife; I couldn't hear the reply, but Jen's Gallic tones were of that familiarly negative quality. Then with the opening of the screen door came the ominous words synonymous with the mounting anxiety of bewildered parents, 'I thought he was with you.' The odds against a tragedy had to have been enormous, but a nauseous sense of acute regret grew as I focused on the dark shape, motionless amongst the undergrowth fifty yards distant, confirming the nature of my fears as I stared, motionless, into the woods where the bullet had pursued its lethal journey. John was beside me again a solitary hound at his heels, earnestly sniffing the ground in quest of his fraternal companion. Following the line of my eyes into the forest gloom, John's voice gave substance to our common dread. 'Jesus Mutchie, have you shot my dog?' The relief as the back screen door banged open, to reveal the bounding form of a familiar canine, coursed through my veins like a glass of cold water to a parched body. It was a relief that bore testimony to the awful pessimism that had overtaken me in those few minutes since the blast of the deadly weapon had echoed about the leafy valley. Of all life's joys, that of relief that tragedy has been avoided must be among the greatest. All pleasure is the antithesis of pain or deprivation and its sweetness stems from the relief that misery has been defeated.

I replaced the gun in its rack and collected my camera to do some shooting with a more familiar tool. I took pictures of John sitting a-top a box on the small veranda of his tool shed, pipe in mouth, flanked by his hounds, whilst surrounded with the rustic implements of rural life which hung from crude nails hammered into the planking of the simple hut. Coils of rope, tins, galvanized buckets, heart-shaped shovels and kerosene lanterns, hung shoulder to shoulder in a living environment which justified their presence as much today as it would have a hundred years earlier.

I envied John this remote and peaceful existence. He had space here, space to breathe, to stretch out, a piece of land to call his own, a house, a wife, dogs, two of them, despite my efforts, and a job he enjoyed. But would I have traded my prefab opposite the car-breakers in the East End of London for this rural idyll? No, probably not. You have to be capable of putting down roots to live out in the wilds, especially when that place is six-thousand miles from where you were raised. You have to be very sure that your roots are in the right soil and are going to take. It amazes me that people can ever be sure enough to make that kind of commitment. Perhaps two people bolster each other's resolve to make the commitment and fulfil each other's sense of continuity. I don't know.

I was to sleep in the caravan, as the spare bedroom was taken by Jen's parents who were over from France. Located half way down the slope where I'd feared the dog's life had, at my hand, been violently concluded, was a cosy self sufficient little abode which my hosts had used as a home whilst they were building their house. As I set off with my torch and still unfinished copy of *Porterhouse Blue*, Jen remembered something important.

'John, 'ave you told Mutchee about the 'orses?'

'Ah yes,' said John, 'just one thing about sleeping down there old boy, come about five in the morning, you'll probably be surrounded by half-a-dozen mustangs; nothing to worry about,' he added, 'they just wander down out of the hills, I go out and feed them, they're totally wild but they'll do you no harm.' I was pretty sure he was serious, while any lingering scepticism I might have felt was dispelled as the soft footfall of unshod hooves heralded the appearance of equestrian visitors some hours ahead of their schedule. Speaking in hushed tones, John and his wife moved among the beasts, stroking their noses and offering them fistfuls of feed.

'Don't get this in England, eh Mutchie,' said John quietly, as he moved warily between the lethal limbs of his powerful guests. He had a point there, although we did have sheep and geese in Stepney, on a small compound reserved principally for the education of inner-city kids. Then there are the cows who stray from the unfenced Wanstead flats into Leytonstone High Street when the fancy takes them – but I saw his point, this was different.

Horses do make me more than a little nervous. They may be great friends of man, and they may well be non-predatorial vegetarians, and I could see no logical reason why they should want to harm me, but there is no escaping the fact that they're bloody big. I don't know a great deal about horses, but from my early childhood I recall being warned never to stand behind a horse, since they can kick backwards but not forwards. I learnt this, despite my suburban upbringing, because we lived near a blacksmiths, to whose premises I would often go to watch the shoeing of horses, which, in the late fifties, were still commonly seen towing the carts of the rag-and-bone men. I enjoyed visiting the blacksmith, whose smoky domain of glowing coals and rustic tools captured the spirit of a passing age which, even in my juvenile years, I yearned to preserve against the rabid encroachment of the twentieth century.

It struck me as a damned risky business, taking a horse's hoof in your lap to wrest iron shoes from its feet, and hammer others on, whilst the huge beasts stood impatiently on three legs awaiting an end to the indignity. Do these indelicate surgeons never get a kick in the groin for their troubles I wondered? Craftsmen, being specialists in acts of demonstrable ability, enjoy a confidence that to the envious unskilled may seem to betray an irksome smugness. It was with satisfaction therefore, that I learned some years ago, that the farrier's trade ranks high on the list of dangerous occupations, since the well-intentioned efforts of these rugged fellows are frequently rewarded with just the kind of violent footplay one might anticipate. There are few things in this world as disquieting to the spirit as the faultless exercise of a perfectionist, and little as satisfying as the observation of their fallibility. It might seem a spiteful reaction to applaud the bad temper of a mighty shire whose petulant agitation wreaks painful retribution on his surgical benefactor, but, whilst wishing these equine chiropodists no evil, the honest man can not but admit to a measure of mirthful reassurance at the pained yelp accompanying the splintering shin of the imprudent or unfortunate farrier.

In recognition of the therapeutic necessity of such tragedies, I say to the malignant mares and surly stallions of this world, kick out noble beasts, let your aim be true.

No sentiment was further from my wishes, as I circulated among the quadrupedal guests at Chateau Reid, where anxiety outweighed curiosity, and it was with a measure of relief that I closed the door on the caravan, outside which the beasts stamped and snorted in accompaniment to the orchestra of the nocturnal forest. I took a last look at their long faces, the broad nostrils blowing steam into the cooling night air, condensing on the windows and blurring their images which blended into the night like ill-formed figures in a dream. Goodnight horses, goodnight America.

It was the horses who were first to greet me in the morning, their big brown heads jostling for positions at the window to view the fresh curiosity that had invaded their world. I felt their eyes on me as I cleaned my teeth, itinerant scrutineers of human behaviour, unbounded by fences, they'd chosen this patch of soil amidst all the miles over which they were free to roam, in order to watch a man brush his ivories. I waved the toothbrush at them in greeting to which they responded with sidelong glances at one another in silent consultation.

The greater part of today was spent in shifting some gear for a pal of John, Frank Kaisler, who I think at that time was editing a Harley magazine with a performance bias. We drove in John's shabby van to the warehouse of Custom Chrome Incorporated where John works, designing custom accessories for the company that makes bits for Harley-Davidsons. The job was to load a heavy lathe onto a trailer in a manner that would guarantee its stability during transit to Frank's. This was the kind of practical problem familiar to me from loading general cargo ships during my years at sea. The problem of what was to go where was as common as the interminable enquiry, 'Where are we?' Sometimes a declaration of simple honesty provided a better response than a pathetic gargle of apologetic speculation, and I would cite a phrase I once heard used by an incompetent physician incapable of diagnosing his patient's disorder. Pressed for a definitive statement on the nature of the malady in the face of protracted prevarication, he made the unwelcome, albeit unequivocal declaration, 'I haven't the foggiest idea.' Now you know where you stand with a character like that, there is a candid simplicity in that kind of admission that warrants universal applause. Applause however, was not the response to my employment of the phrase when my opinion was sought in respect of the problem in hand, namely, how to load a ton of lathe onto a trailer. I made a few comments about centres of gravity and scuttled back and forth viewing the enigma from a variety of angles whilst looking concerned as the operation, largely without my physical assistance, proceeded. With the trailer loaded, we made our way over to Frank's house where it was unhitched, before returning to John's via an outdoor autojumble where we encountered a woman with a hose up her nose.

THE CASE OF THE VENTILATED BUDDHA

The autojumble provided a picture of America at odds with the glitzy portrait of throw-away affluence commonly portrayed in the more superficial visions of the country. Here were rural, dungaree-clad characters, whiskered of chin and calloused of palm, clambering over piles of rusty old iron scattered about a dilapidated barn, around which they stumbled in search of bargains like poachers amongst the corpses of a battlefield. A cry of caution from above, drew my attention to where a youth crouched upon the beam of an incomplete loft floor, from which position he guided a canvas sheet, pregnant with miscellaneous artifacts. A stout fellow whose baggy sweater had grown in all directions to enclose its expanding contents, guided the load earthwards with thick steady hands, as all around squinted roofward into the dust speckled beams of sunlight, with a level of concentration that was comically uniform. There is something endearing about the exhibition of collective concern exhibited by groups of humans at such times. The level of intellect exercised may be higher than that of sheep, but a similar sense of common anxiety invites the comparison, and it is this unconscious connection to the ruminating wool-heads that prompts a benign mirth.

The sheet, with its cargo intact, landed without mishap, liberating a mound of rusty miscellanea to flood beyond the splintered perimeter of the old building, whereupon the tribe of scavengers fell upon it with renewed vigour. Several, on identifying objects of value to their peculiar ambitions, scuttled out into the full sunlight to better examine their finds before burrowing deep into denim pockets for the necessary coins and dollar bills.

Outside, beyond the prime arena of bustle, an elderly woman of substantial proportions was seated on an improvized seat, comprising a strong wooden box covered by a hessian sack. Nearby her, on the ground, stood a squat gas cylinder from which a tube snaked across the sparse grass to a terminus in her nose. Like some fearsome bionic dowager, the ventilated Buddha followed our movements with her piggy eyes as we meandered in the direction of a decrepit diesel generator. Studying the machine with, what seemed to me, a feigned interest, John whispered to me

250

in conspiratorial tones.

'You see that woman over there with the thing in her nose?'

'Yes,'

'The first time I came up here, I was walking past her when I caught my foot in her airline and that contraption shot out of her nostril like a sprung-loaded earthworm.'

'What did she say?' I asked, imagining the appalling embarrassment of the sad but hilarious blunder.

'She called me a bastard,' said John in a tone that indicated he'd found the comment hurtful.

'Didn't you apologize?' I asked.

'Sure, I said I was very sorry,' he continued, 'made no impact on her though.'

'Was that all she said?' I asked.

'Well she spluttered a bit,' said John, 'and then grabbed the hose, plugged herself back in and just repeated herself, "You bastard," that was all she'd say, "You bastard."'

I glanced back at the rotund form with her aspirating appendages. She was leaning forward, her plump hands on her knees, staring after us like some aggrieved dog that recalls the offender if not the offence, sustaining an indefinite vendetta throughout all subsequent encounters. John's enthusiasm for scavenging seemed to have withered against the background of the wordless reunion so we climbed into the van and drove off. Looking back I could see her still, the piggy eyes fixed on us like malevolent lasers piercing our wake of dust and diesel fumes. John drove with a mechanical resolution glancing neither to left nor right, avoiding the mirror and gripping the wheel tightly with both hands, he stared straight ahead through the windscreen – the bastard.

NESS

As the unfortunate woman faded from our view, John launched into a comparison between life in California and the Old Country. Despite the previous evening's encounter with the mustangs, life here, he maintained, is not as different as you might imagine.

'A lot of people think it's all sea, surf and beach parties, but look at what we're doing. I've got a day off and I'm helping a mate shift a load of gear in an old wreck of a van.' I had to admit it, there was a familiar ring to that, and as if to underscore the truth of my reflection, the temperature gauge needle hunched itself up against the top of the red sector as steam curled ominously out from under the bonnet.

Trying to make eight inches of hose fulfil the role of nine, is as tricky under the Californian sun as it is in a Walthamstow drizzle, and herein lies a great and inescapable truth. We spent the next twenty minutes at the roadside, alternately persuading a pair of long nosed pliers with twisted jaws that overlapped like greasy chopsticks, to bully a spring clip back *in situ*. I recognized in the predicament, a familiar theme whose characteristic wretchedness flourishes equally on either side of the Atlantic. *Ping*, went the clip, bouncing off the raised bonnet and disappearing into the oily labyrinth of the engine compartment.

'Where's it gone?' asked John.

'I don't know.' I replied, staring intently into the shaded gloom with all the optimism of a blind man looking for the Holy Grail.

'Just like home eh?' suggested my expatriate host.

'Just like home,' I agreed.

I was running a little late by the time we got back to John's as I was due at the house of Arlen Ness some forty miles to the north, with barely an hour remaining in which to organize myself, make the journey aboard the Harley, and find the place. Before I'd got halfway there it had begun to rain, the dense fine kind of rain that explores every point of access and will sort out the broken zips, missing buttons, loose collars and split gloves of the ill-prepared. The rain was more dense than it was heavy, there can't have been a cubic inch of air that was not hosting a thousand separate drops of water, none of which, under such a state of crowded tenancy, needed to be particularly large in order to make a bloody nuisance of itself. It was that intrusive kind of rain that finds its way down your collar, disappears, and then reaffirms its existence by appearing with chilly dampness half-way down your chest or back, causing you to shout indignantly, 'Hey, where did you come from, how did you get there?' You can't understand it because you're wearing a rain suit that's one-hundred per cent waterproof, there's a legend to that effect on the label. Legend is the right word you think, as you tighten your collar and tuck your chin down to prevent further ingress. Nowhere's safe, a trickle of water reaches your stomach, you feel like a man whose been conned by a bank advertising an infallible safety deposit box system which has just been breached by thieves. The manufacturer of my unbeatable, Teutonically-designed ('Have dry hands this winter!'), gloves, should have had his hands pushed into them and been forced to ride my motorcycle through that downpour, whilst a film crew pursued him. My experience was that after twenty minutes my hands were wet, and after an hour what I was wearing on my hands were of as much use as a pair of carefully tailored flannels, which stored water in order to release it in trickles down my left arm each time I squeezed the clutch lever. By the time I arrived at Arlen Ness's shop near San Jose, I was not only Mr Damp, I was also Mr Late, though my host seemed not in the least perturbed.

It seems childish and naive to make a big issue out of how unpretentious and unaffected the rich and famous are when encountered. Why, after all, should they not be? Everyone likes to boast that money won't change them, why should it not be true of some people? The Queen, we are forever being told, is so nice, so natural, so relaxed – so why not Arlen Ness. He is, after all, known within the custom motorcycle world as, 'The King.'

Arlen was accompanied throughout the evening by his pal Jim, a burly, loud fellow, who asked me innumerable questions about England, the apparent purpose of the enquiries being the gratification of his insatiable appetite for derisory hilarity.

Jim thought England, even London, was pretty primitive, though his justification for this critical assessment rested more on the times the pubs stayed open to, or rather didn't stay open to, than any more culturally-significant criteria. Jim was a straight talking kind of cove. 'Are Americans popular in England?' he wanted to know. I answered somewhat uncertainly that they were reasonably so. If I'd been asked the same question in the sixties with the Vietnam war going strong I would have had more trouble justifying my response. But I didn't feel I was being too patronizing to say that Yanks are popular enough these days. Though perhaps in guessing the perceptions of others, I had in mind my colleagues in the Harley Club who tend to have an instinctive affinity for what, in the motorcycle subculture, is more like the mother country. Jim wasn't convinced.

'I don't think Americans are very popular in Europe,' he replied, which only went to show that he was not as insensitive as his brash facade suggested. Possibly, I thought, it isn't so much Americans *per se* that aren't popular in Europe, but just you. It seemed an uncharitable comment to make in the presence of my host, so I kept it under my hat. From the interview, we travelled a couple of blocks to a photographic studio where one of Arlen's latest creations, a long low black number, inspired by the Batman imagery, was to be immortalized on celluloid. Everyone concerned was pretty hungry, so whilst the photosession proceeded, Jim and I went over to a pizza restaurant to get some carry-outs. The restaurant staff couldn't change a hundred dollar bill, so we placed our order and ran up the road to a liquor store were the bill was changed and booze purchased. Back at the pizza parlour we took seats at the bar and drank a couple of beers while we waited for our orders. Ten minutes passed, fifteen, twenty, with still no sign of our food. Jim went over to the counter to see what had happened. Would you believe it, they hadn't even started cooking, and why? Because we hadn't paid. We were sitting on stools in full view of the person to whom we'd given the order, and he'd just ignored us. This was aggravating, it wasn't typical of American restaurant service and this was the exception rather than the rule. What was typical, and most entertainingly so, was Jim's verbal lambasting of the management which was reserved until after we got the pizza.

'So what's the score with you guys? We come in here, we place an order, you know we got the money cos I showed it to you, you saw the money. You wanted me to change the bill, I changed the bill, you saw us come back in, you see us sitting right over there, right there on those stools, waiting, and you don't do nothing, you don't check with us, you don't do nothing, what the fuck is the matter with you people, are you stupid, are you blind? I'll tell you something now, this is the last time I come into this restaurant, you won't see my face coming through this door no more. I'm gonna take my custom some place else, you hear what I'm saying to you? I tell you, you've had the last of my money in this place, you won't catch me in here no more.' Not satisfied with suspending his own patronage, the vitriolic orator turned to the silent audience of prospective customers waiting patiently in line for the ceasefire.

'Hey, get these guys, if I was you I wouldn't waste my money on these jerks, I'd go some place else, these guys are schmucks believe me, I ain't coming here no more.' Swivelling like a talking gun turret on the hapless staff, he loosed off a parting volley in their direction.

'You know the worst thing about this, you know what really stinks, huh? I ain't heard no one say sorry. None of you schmucks has apologized, not one of you schmucks has said sorry, not one of you, it would help if you apologized, you know it just might help, how much would that cost you, huh?'

With this, the sad face in the soggy chef's hat turned his baleful features on the verbal Rotweiler, his hands turned, palms upwards, shoulders shrugged in tired resignation as he spoke.

'Hey, sorry fellah.'

'Sorry!' stormed Jim, sorry! 'what the fuck good is sorry.'

Back in the car, a large Mercedes, Jim unscrewed a squat yellow bottle full of cocktail which he poured down his throat with one hand whilst steering the car with the other, demonstrating a cheerful disdain for the state law regarding drinking and driving. It was behaviour that reinforced a comment I'd heard somewhere about America not so much being the land of the free, in terms of having few restrictions on personal conduct, since it has infinitely more than, say China for example. What makes the USA tolerable, despite its innumerable nitpicking regulations, is the total inability of the police to enforce more than a tiny minority of them, a small fraction of the time. One can't condone drinking and driving, certainly not drunken driving, but my sense of despair at a country which passes laws preventing even the carriage of alcohol in a car, was mollified by the healthy disrespect superbly exemplified by my host. There are times when one is reassured by exhibitions of gross irresponsibility. Whilst one, in all things, seeks balance, it can be heart-warming to identify, in the midst of oppression, the exercise of a thoroughly indifferent and disrespectful spirit. Watching Jim driving one handed, happily swigging from the bottle of powerful liquor, my gratification at the recognition of such healthy disdain overcame the critically self righteous reservations I might have had over the wisdom of such indulgence. There is, after all, a limit to the amount of respect one should have for the law. Sadly, from our conversation I learned that he had no time for the political activists of the biker movement, who he thought did more harm than good. This from a Californian Harley rider!?

Back at the studio I plonked myself on a chair and stuffed my face with the greasy pizza, which, despite being a little slow in coming, was well worth the wait. I had made a half-hearted attempt at paying a share of the food, an offer that was rejected by Jim, who declared that he was getting his money's-worth out of laughing at the English. Just about every answer I gave to his incessant enquiries about the English way of life prompted a roar of outrageous mirth .

'The bars close at ten-thirty?'

'Well actually some stay open till eleven these days.'

'Eleven! Ha, ha, ha! Eleven, wow, terrific; hey you hear that Arlen, some of the bars stay open till eleven, get that. Terrific. Eleven; ha, ha, ha.'

A less generously disposed person than myself might have found this sustained sarcasm a mite wearing. The limits of my tolerance were not far over the horizon, and I sensed Arlen's response to it

Ness

straying to the patient side of enthusiastic. Arlen though was mostly absent from the discussion, perched on his motorcycle as the photographer postured behind his expensive equipment, crouching squinting and speculating as he endeavoured to cultivate the ideal conditions for the perfect shot.

Gary was not, by profession, a photographer, the practice of law being his principal forte, as he was a lawyer who apparently spent a great deal of his time in defending members of the Hell's Angels club resident in the area of San Francisco. I have always wondered about lawyers, whether their belief in the innocence of their clients is an essential prerequisite to the creation of a convincing defence, as well as the maintenance of a sense of moral equanimity. Perry Mason's clients were always innocent, and he, in common with the viewer, knew this to be the case from the outset, so for him the moral dilemma of compromising his respect for justice with his intellectual manipulation of the jurors minds did not arise. I don't doubt that the Hell's Angels of California are often credited with crimes of which they are innocent, but I wonder whether the credibility of a lawyer who consistently engages in defending the same small group of maligned citizens, is not stretched somewhere near the point of its elastic limit.

The issue throws up an interesting problem for the libertarian exponent who must justify his case for liberalism against a commitment to justice and the common good. There is little doubt that members of that club are charged with offences at a rate which provides them with a conspicuously criminal profile. No doubt an organization as visually assertive as the Hell's Angels, and with as colourful a reputation, is certain to present a nest of scapegoats for frustrated law enforcers eager to identify culprits of unsolved crimes. In recognition of that inevitability, it seems reasonable that someone must assume the task of ensuring the impartial exercise of law; I'm just glad it isn't me.

Gary was obviously not the sort of fellow to pick the easy options in life, for besides preparing legal defences for one of society's most infamous cults, he was, at the time I met him, attempting to photograph a black motorcycle against a black background.

I hesitated to draw attention to this factor, when sounded for my advice, since it seemed so obvious that I imagined there was some subtle logic underlying the tactic. An instinctive faith in superficial commonsense was reinforced, however, by the results of the first Polaroid prints by which Gary sought to anticipate the achievements of the more serious camera. A fine example of 'the black cat in a coal cellar chewing licorice with his eyes shut syndrome,' was exemplified here to a degree that was extremely satisfying. As a modestly-equipped amateur photographer myself, I am substantially reassured to witness the appalling results which it is possible to achieve with the most extravagant of apparatus, the current situation providing a case in point. Further attempts were made to enhance the environment by the adjustment of lamp angles and shades, amidst a debate on the comparative merits of the numerous elements involved. It was a discussion from which I decided to absent myself as far as possible, preferring to confine my attention to the simple indulgence provided by the copious acres of pizza. An earnest well-wisher was now recruited to hold a light meter in front of the bike to measure the degree of reflection from the contrasting characteristics of engine, tank and wheels. While he moved the device around the body of the machine like a Doctor with his stethoscope, Gary checked the readouts on a digital display.

'Good, good,' he muttered. 'That's fine, that should be great.' While all this was going on, Jim persisted with his sarcastic assessment of the British, to which I obligingly provided a ceaseless fodder of facts as the oily mozzarella rolled down my chin.

'Let me get this straight, you got a bunch of dudes governing the country, who nobody votes in, right? They are where they are because of who their pa was, right? And this, is the mother of parliaments? You got to be putting me on.'

'That's right,' I replied, 'it's a splendid system, it's worked for centuries it still works very well, and above all, it's extremely funny.'

'Oh boy, it's that all right,' retorted Jim. 'It's definitely that, yes shit it's very funny, ha, ha, ha.'

I grinned at him over a slab of salami and olive-topped pizza as Gary dropped his hand to order the detonation of the flash guns. A tall stubble faced giant of genial demeanour pressed a red button and the room exploded with light as the mechanical click of the shutter ricocheted around the walls. Arlen relaxed his pose, wearily rubbing his eyes as a huddle of scrutineers eagerly crowded around the tripod whilst Gary patiently counted out the seconds necessary for the Polaroid process to conclude. The results this time were better. The black cat syndrome had been supplanted by something less serious. We were now in the realms of tabbies against freshly creosoted fences. This marked progress, but it was slow. It was at this juncture that, with a perspicacity of vision that has attended the most significant leaps in the ascent of man, the photographer made a startling decision.

'Let's use the white backdrop.'

The photo session terminated around midnight, leaving time to take in a nearby bar for a couple of beers. Outside, it was still raining, and so it was with eager gratitude that I accepted Arlen's offer of his house for the night. My host retired almost immediately, leaving me with the television and an immaculate white Persian cat for company. I sustained a one sided conversation with this animal as it crouched suspiciously amidst the luxuriant camouflage of a deep pile rug, from where he viewed me with analytical scrutiny. In the absence of any meaningful conversation, I attempted to gauge his mood by means of reciprocal observation. The ludicrously fluffy face betrayed little, but I slunk off to my appointed space with the suspicion that I was guilty of trespass in a feline domain.

THE JOHN REID CORRAL

Back at John Reid's, I commandeered my host to assist with an oil change, the only maintenance of the entire trip. In the course of this exercise, the problem of what to do with the old oil presented itself, the resolution of which, John decided, was to let it run all over the earth. This struck me as an environmentally unsound practice, but John postured some plausible defence which involved an argument in favour of soil retention, which sounded vaguely familiar. I recalled reading about an effort in the Middle East where re-afforestation efforts were assisted by covering the soil or sand in oil in a bid to stop it blowing away, whilst preserving the moisture throughout a critical stage of the trees' early life. My conscience thus appeased by this recollection, I let the black gold pour forth, spreading over the ground like a developing cloud.

'It's desert here really Mutchie,' said John, pawing at the ground with his foot. This rain now, is the first we've had since December, if you're not careful the soil just blows away. In this little valley an abundance of trees flourished, but the surrounding hilltops were brown and bare save for a scattering of scrubby bushes, and I didn't doubt the truth of what I was being told. Funny, until last week I'd thought California was pretty well green and lush all over, still I had met an American in Cleveland who had asked if Britain was near London, so there's ignorance on both sides of the Atlantic as well as a huge number of fish in between.

It was whilst consuming our evening meal that the phone rang, bringing news of a fresh dilemma. Jen answered it, and after a few moment's conversation, the majority of which was the responsibility of the unseen party, she returned to the table, an expression of grave concern creasing her pretty features.

'What's up?' asked John.

'It's the 'orses,' she replied, 'they're in Mrs Prescott's garden, she's not very 'appy, she said they're all staring at her through the window, she can't concentrate on the television, John, she doesn't like it.'

John gazed thoughtfully in the direction of his closest neighbour's house some distance away, invisible beyond the trees.

'We'll have to do something,' he said after a pause. 'If they're going to make a habit of this then they'll all end up as glue.' With this ghoulish reference to the knacker's grisly trade, a gloom descended on the dinner table which even copious helpings of ice cream failed to dispel.

'We shall have to build a corral and stop them roaming in her direction,' decided John after a moment's reflection. This seemed like the only plausible plan, and we set to with lengths of redundant flex, rope, string, and anything else that offered the faintest prospect of discouraging the migration of the itinerant beasts. Scrambling down the steep slopes of the wooded gulley, we strung the lines from tree to tree, taking turns around their trunks and knotting together the assortment of contrasting materials.

'What the hell's that?' asked John, peering at the fangled knot by which means I was contriving to mate a length of stiff electrical flex with a weathered length of sisal.

'Sheet bend,' I replied, 'recommended for joining two ropes of unequal thickness.'

'Will the horse be able to undo it?' enquired my partner.

'Indubitably not,' I insisted, 'the turns will baffle them and besides, their hooves lack the necessary dexterity, rest assured.' John stared doubtfully at my endeavour over the bobbing timber of his extinct pipe, before scuttling, crab fashion, down the dusty incline, furiously paying out line like a terrorist with a lengthy detonation wire. By the time every piece of adaptable material had been employed, we had created a thoroughly inadequate barrier of varying altitude and dubious conviction, which represented more of a monument to optimism than a serious obstacle to the nomadic aspirations of beefy mustangs. There seemed little more that we could do, however, beside resting our hopes on the instinctive distrust of the lower intellects for any kind of man-made construction that implied a measure of prohibition.

THE DOG OF THE SIERRA NEVADA

My stay at the John Reid corral was over, and the time had come to head east. My timing could hardly have been more perfect. Jen's parents, along with their daughter and son in law, were off the following day for a vacation to LA, where they planned to make a visit to Disney Land. I had been similarly fortunate in managing a visit to Arlen Ness, just one day before he and his wife departed for the fabled island of Hawaii. Whilst fortune smiled on me in this respect, the elements did not. The weather remained inauspicious with a heavily laden sky, the copious discharges from which could be seen at numerous points around the horizon. Choosing an interval of comparative dryness I set out, *sans* waterproof trousers, which, after a period of ten minutes, I was forced to don. It was shortly after this, that for the first time in the trip, I ran out of fuel – almost. The bike coughed and kangarood for half a mile, as I swung the heavy machine from side to side in an effort to fling the remaining petrol into the side of the tank where the tap was located. By this effort I was able to stagger the last few hundred yards to a gas station in Morgan Hill, a scant five miles from John's home. With the confidence provided by a full tank of fuel, I set out afresh, heading north up Highway 101, skirting San Jose, San Francisco, and Sacramento from where I headed north-east toward the great emptiness of Nevada. Ahead of me lay, or rather, rose, the heights of the Sierra Nevada, from which I imagine the state draws its name.

It sounded familiar to me, that romantic Latin title, Sierra Nevada. I plumbed my memory in search of the time and place that I'd encountered that name before. Rounding a tighter than average curve leading into a steep ascent though pine-fringed heights, I fed the engine a generous measure of fuel which sent the ponderous brute barrelling up the blacktop with a pleasing arm-straightening resolution. The tone deepened as I notched fifth, and, with the location of the cog, my memory slipped sympathetically into gear. Sierra Nevada, I'd seen that name printed on nautical charts of the Mediterranean. It is a mountain range in Spain, toward the south, prominent peaks of which are of possible navigational interest to seafarers. Sierra Nevada, the earlier encounter lent the renewed acquaintance a pleasing familiarity that diminished in proportion to my increasing altitude as the temperature fell.

The scenery was impressive. Tree-clad peaks stood shoulder to shoulder, primeval giants, glumly tolerating the intrusion of the asphalt strip that laced its serpentine path between their burly bases, violating the solitude of these geological sentries. The Sierra Nevada – magnificent. Pity it was so bloody cold.

A restaurant sign, like a desert oasis, appeared to my right; too tempting. I pulled into the stony harbour of its car park, hewed from the rock of the mountainside. Blessedly this was an independent eatery, a refreshing change from the garish uniformity of the giant food chain outlets however 'nice' a day their employees urged you to have. In place of the multiple rows of brilliant fluorescent tubes, a single light bulb breached the darkness of the simple diner. After the glare of the outdoors, the dim illumination of the interior demanded some adjustment of the eyes and I was unable at first to locate the source of the woman's voice that greeted me.

'Bet it's cold on that motorcycle.' Hello I thought, we've got a bright one here, she doesn't miss a trick. I reciprocated with the necessary agreement and hauled myself up on to one of the crude wooden stools that lined the serving counter. The scraping of the stool's legs activated the limbs of a large, heavy-set dog that stumbled out of the gloom like a lethargic nightwatchman. After stretching his legs and yawning hugely to reveal a set of canines calculated to cause substantial distress to ill-advised burglars, he padded across the room to inspect me, his features generously disposed in a light brown face that suggested a benign character. This was a magnificent animal with a generic identity that fell somewhere between Labrador and Rottweiler. He studied me with the fearless nonchalance that beasts of his dimensions have no need to affect; the self-assured confidence of the brute striking a sharp contrast with my own shivering form hunched atop the stool, energetically trying to rub warmth back into my quaking limbs. Like a caustic sergeant major critically reviewing an inadequate conscript, he held me in a protracted scrutiny of transparent disdain for several moments, before opening his hairy mouth, from which, I was convinced, some canine sarcasm was about to emerge.

Go on, say it, I thought, say what you think, what the hell am I doing riding a motorcycle up here in this weather when I could be slumming around in a nice comfy basket chewing a bone. Come on

you smug brute, out with it. Intelligent brown eyes read my
challenge, leaving the implicit enquiry unspoken as the whiskered
mouth closed on unborn words, the hot breath clouding the cold
air in the doorway through which he inspected the conifer clad
peaks for the first sign of autumn snow. The contemptuous pity in
his eyes posed an eloquent substitute for verbal articulation as he
turned to look at me again, their message, as succinct as the most
perfectly enunciated words; 'You tosser,' he said.

I was not offended at this mild rebuke, which bore no trace of
malice from its author, whose muscular shoulders shrugged in
resignation, before propelling him beyond the doorframe to view
the bright chill of the great outdoors.

I have never fully recognized the truth of the expression, 'a dog's
life,' in many cases at least, it doesn't seem so bad to me. A cat's
though, in certain respects, is even better. From my perch on the
stool I could see one now, curled into a smug cushion of whiskered
luxury, a feline exception amongst a row of stone jars on a shelf at
the rear of the food preparation area.

I like to see animals associated with places where food for
human consumption is being cooked or consumed. There is a
hysterical prissiness about the attitude that seeks to isolate the lives
and activities of animals from our own that aggravates me. I resent
the revulsion of the clinically meticulous mentalities that demand
the separation of animals from areas of human endeavour. Those,
'in the interest of hygiene' signs that label the premises of all the
food chains whose corporate policies admit no exceptions,
represent to my mind, the most appalling exercise of prejudice alive
today. For bikers, or gypsies to be barred entry to pubs on the
grounds that they might cause trouble or intimidate other patrons,
is, by comparison, a mild insult alongside the allegation that you
are a hazard to the maintenance of hygienic standards. I mistrust
people whose fear of encountering other living organisms is so out
of proportion to the reality of the threat. Slovenly squalor is one
thing, but this kind of bacterial neurosis is something else. The
pleasure of having animals about us, stems from the sense of
integration that their presence provides. That sense of belonging in
the grand natural world. Once caged and segregated, their status is
diminished to that of convenience and entertainment units, like
televisions and washing machines, to be switched on and off as
required, to be introduced to the arena of human activity when it

pleases us to permit them, rather than enjoying full reign of the *Homo sapiens* environment, through which they can wander freely. To be barred from going into a supermarket or pub, because you're accompanied by someone who might be your best friend in this world, is a terrible restriction of civil liberties. It's not as if a house-trained animal defecates indoors, it would be different if they did. Even I would not relish the idea of sitting down to a plate of *moules marinière* with a Great Dane unloading all over the floor next to my table, but they don't do that. Small children, by contrast, are forever dribbling, puking and defecating in restaurants, and if they're not polluting the air with flatulence, they're assaulting it with piercing shrieks of painful frequency, in spite of which some people, mostly their parents, want to let them into pubs. Give me a dog any day, not only are they more environmentally acceptable, but the larger breeds, amongst which the fabulous Rottweiler has established the most exceptional reputation for violence, reconcile the twin objectives of population control with the promotion of serenity by eating small and bothersome infants. I find it extraordinary that anyone should seek to inhibit the appetite of this magnificent breed.

As for cats, they exhibit the kind of superior disdain that humanity needs to keep its own vanity in perspective; their supremely selfish indifference is something to be applauded rather than resented. The ice cream parlour near my childhood home boasted a resident cat, the presence of which substantially bolstered my faith in human nature. They also served the best ice cream in the world and for want of a better explanation, I am inclined to credit the character in the corner with the velvet nose. I imagine that with the creature's penchant for dairy produce, she operated as some kind of quality control director to ensure the Italian owners maintained the exceptional standard of their product.

Cats and dogs have not enjoyed the recognition in musical spheres which their rightful position in human society warrants, though once, when soaking up culture at the Edinburgh Festival, I listened to an unaccompanied vocalist applauding the virtues of dogs with a song, each verse of which ended with the line 'Sing up for the hound,' and well said too. Cats and dogs, splendid creations; I've never owned a dog and ownership of cats is impossible, but I have had the honour of waiting on them and with a generosity uncharacteristic of the species, they sleep with me, demonstrating a consistency of affection that women, in my experience, are incapable of sustaining. It's an experience I have never regretted.

Besides boasting both cat and dog, the oasis that inspired these reflections served up a superb bowl of genuinely home-made potato soup. A substantial blob of cream the size of a golf ball sat in the middle of the steaming concoction, melting slowly into the scorching solution like a diminishing iceberg in a warm current. The cream lent the earthy fodder a sumptuous smoothness that persuaded me against moderation, and in favour of a second helping. I'd reasoned that I would need the extra calories to maintain my body temperature in the deteriorating weather, and potato soup, accompanied by hunks of home-baked brown bread, commended itself to me as an ideal source.

It was a wrench to leave the cosy comfort of the diner for the unsympathetic outdoors, however beautiful the scenery might be, but I wanted to be out of these mountains before serious snow fell. A drizzly sleet was already dampening the road when I stepped outside with the proprietor's farewells in my ears, and there was no alternative to donning the rather uncool plastic trousers from which an increasing precipitation was soon flowing in chilly rivulets as I romped down the road. My body temperature now began to fall dramatically, as the unholy alliance of wind and icy water bled the heat from me faster than my strained metabolism could convert the potato soup into energy. In the unequal contest of thermal theft versus conservation, I began to shout. I find this outlet of verbal petulance helpful in adverse conditions, and as the roadside signs maliciously confirmed my suspicions about the altitude, I resorted to it with accelerating enthusiasm. Three-thousand feet, four-thousand, five! There were piles of snow at the sides of the road now and sadistic advertisements for ski lodges. 'Come on, come on, up a degree, two degrees if you please, warm up a bit, just a little bit, pleeeease.' Pathetic whining having failed, I abruptly switched to a hysterical dictatorial shriek, 'Warm up you bastard, warm up!' The elements sadly proved impervious to either tactic, and the temperature, despite my imprecations, continued to fall in proportion to my ascending altitude. A sign loomed up on my left, barely visible in the moderate blizzard now blowing. 'Emigrant Gap – five-thousand, two-hundred and fifty feet' Sod it!

I was still climbing. The metal frames of my spectacles were freezing my eyes now, and a steel-fed coldness bit into my face as if I were being injected with liquid carbon dioxide by an icicle syringe, I was very uncomfortable. In an effort to avert what I feared might be permanent damage to my sight, I alternately closed my eyes, hoping that the movement back and forth of the eyelids would impart enough heat to make the critical difference between revocable and irrevocable injury, while in order to sustain morale, I started singing. I began with that stirring number from *Paint Your Wagon*, all about calling the wind Maria. This seemed appropriate enough to me, though the lyrics lacked the searing invective necessary to express my inarticulate rage. Perhaps I'd have been better with one of Ian Dury's more obscene numbers. What I eventually settled for ran along those lines, consisting of a string of Anglo Saxon expletives, varied up and down the scale to relieve tedium, F...F...F...F...! It is at times such as this that I am prone to cast myself in the heroic role of some Homerian mythological desperado, whose wretched tribulations are viewed by the Olympian Gods, through that hole in the clouds from which they observe, with great mirth.

I was introduced to this fanciful concept via the great institution of Saturday morning pictures, where the beleaguered Hercules, labouring through his ten tasks, had the bloated immortals slapping their bellies with glee as he hacked away at the multi-headed Hydra. I reckoned my own tribulations with the elements must have warranted a few minutes of prime time on network Olympus. As I carved my tortured path through the frosty volleys of an indifferent environment, I visualized graphically the portly toga-clad figures crowding around their omnipotent spy hole like viewers about a colossal *camera obscura*. I could hear their sniggers as they pointed out the wretched spectacle to their illustrious peers. A bare motorcycle, dwarfed by snow-dusted, above the sound of which, in tones of pathetic imprecation, the howling wake of invective streaming from the rider's foaming lips: F...F...F...FFFFFFFFFFFFFF! A perverse thought crossed my mind – come back Death Valley, all is forgiven.

Past Reno, and blessedly out of the mountains at last, I left the freeway, and took Highway 50 east for the town of Fallon, where I had decided I would spend the night. My misery was not at an end though, with the rising temperature the sleet had turned to rain, and with it, a fresh anxiety had surfaced to blight the serenity of the damp autumn evening. The fuel gauge, to which I'd paid scant attention for some time now, indicated the glum reality of a near-empty tank. I was exhausted by the ride, and demoralized by the recognition of my own stupidity in not filling up at the last gas station. I pulled over to the side of the road, stepping onto a rain sodden shoulder, cut the engine, and unfolded the map to determine in which direction lay my best hope of obtaining fuel. A huge truck growled by, the driver silhouetted in the dull glow of the cosy cab's interior as, with heartless indifference, the eighteen giant wheels squeezed a strip of road dry, swamping me in a wave of cold muddy water and exciting the unfolded map into a fluttering frenzy like a demented butterfly. The distance from where I reckoned I was to Fallon was less than a finger's width, but on a map that embraced all the territory from New York to LA, a finger's width is a hell of a long way to push a quarter-ton motorcycle. Things could be worse I reflected; if the tank was full it would be a good deal heavier. A dramatic scar of lightning lacerated the sodden sky, illuminating the wet river of road ahead. How could I be so supremely stupid, after all these years, and with no good reason, I risk running out of fuel – and on a night like this. It is just such crass stupidity which, increasingly with the passage of time, persuades me that I am not what I like to think I am, a good organizer. I was reminded of the mute criticism of the dog back in the mountains; his unspoken words returning on me like indigestion, 'You tosser.'

I continued at slow speed, conserving fuel, and praying for a gas station. None appeared, and few cars shared this lonely road with me. It was in the midst of these pessimistic reflections that I felt the engine stagger, for a moment it picked up, and with it my pitiful hope that a speck of dirt on a plug had caused the misfire; in such plights do drowning men clutch at straws. My self deception was cruelly dispelled as, with a depressingly conclusive uniformity, both taco and speedometer needles sank back toward zero. I looked upon those dials as Marie Antoinette might have looked upon the descending blade of the guillotine, had some sadistic wag thrust a shaving mirror beneath her nose at the critical time. It was not a cheerful sight. A lesser man than I might have started blubbering at this point, at least I imagine he would, because I did. I contemplated the prospect of a night under canvas at the roadside in the rain, and looked at the sky. I then looked at the clocks, and finally, forlornly, at the tank which I knew to be empty, whereon my eyes fell upon the fuel tap as, with Archimedean spontaneity, a happy recollection rekindled my dampened morale – I had a reserve. I don't know what made me think that I didn't, perhaps the unaccustomed provision of a gauge, like a car, had made me think like a motorist?

Half an hour later I was in Fallon stuffing my face with pizza. I ordered red wine to lubricate its passage. Like the beer, it was chilled, but the girl who served it to me, radiated a friendly warmth that restored not only my circulation but my zest for life, in a way that only a smile from a pretty girl can. My old friend Reggie once underscored this point about the effect of the mere sight of pretty girls on the male morale.

'What would the world be like without pretty girls?' I once asked him one evening in the pub, as he stared gloomily into his Guinness.

'Life,' he replied, turning toward me, an expression of thoughtful shock knitted into his thin features, 'wouldn't be worth living.' The spontaneous sincerity of his simple response took me by surprise. For a chap of comically muddled outlook and limited eloquence, no trace of hesitation delayed the concise articulation of so appalling a prospect, and, of course, he was quite right. The girl in the restaurant was probably responsible for reaffirming many a young desperado's commitment to life. She had the sort of smile that effused the genuine brand of warmth which McDonald's endeavour, via the training of their staff, to simulate. With cowgirl checked shirt and blue jeans, she epitomized an essential facet of the great American dream. She was the girl sitting on the sun-bleached timbers of the rodeo corral, she was the girl on the roller skates with a tray of milk shakes, she was the captain of the drum majorettes, the cheerleader in immaculately pleated white skirt, she was the girl in the cotton print dress rolling pastry for a Thanksgiving pie. She was 'Miss America'. The talking epitome asked me where I was from and where I was heading. When I told her, her eyes opened to a theatrical width as she poured me another glass of wine. My imagination was working overtime on a theme of improbable optimism, as the radio ground out a familiar Kenny Rogers' hit, 'In a bar in Toledo...' Outside, the crunch of gravel on the forecourt heralded the arrival of an automobile, its identity obscured by the blotchy kaleidoscope of light refracting through the dense rain. The driver left the engine and wipers running, while his radio, tuned to the same Country and Western station as the diner's, provided a muffled monitor of the mournful ballad. From the corner where she'd just hung a tea towel, the waitress looked toward the door which burst open to admit a broad-shouldered, tousle-haired youth, head bowed under a buff Western-style jacket which he held aloft for protection from the deluge. On the far side of the restaurant the waitress grabbed her coat from a peg on the wall, shot me a smile, and dived outside under the protective cowl of her boyfriend's coat. Kenny Rogers' voice droned on as I finished my pizza, 'You picked a fine time to leave me Lucille...'

I was away early today. Nine hundred miles separated me from Boulder Colorado where a photographer friend of mine, Michael Lichter, lived. Michael was off to Utah on a photographic assignment two days hence, so I had to reach him by tomorrow night if I was to catch him at all.

EUREKA

The road before me, by nature of its emptiness, encouraged speeds in excess of the fifty-five miles per hour maximum. Straight as a die, it stretched before me, an infinite black tarmac ruler, its gradations provided by the legions of sentinel telegraph poles whose equidistant monotony recorded my progress with a metronomic regularity. Seeking relief from the soporific influence of these silent marshals, I turned my attention to the countryside, the vast openness of which provided the eye with scant stimulation by way of rapid change in the immediate panorama. This was desert country, but the recent rain had spawned great lakes of grasses and wild flowers, which served to soften a scene that might otherwise have worn a sterner expression. I was riding through broad flat valleys, perhaps twenty miles or more in width, bordered at their edges by mountains and punctuated with very occasional homesteads. These were lonely places indeed. Set a mile or two back from the road, the ubiquitous wind-driven well-pumps bore witness to their isolation. These outposts, which might have been lifted straight from the Westerns, were the focus of brave pioneers' optimistic endeavours; the town-hating loners who struggled to eke a basic living from the uncooperative dust, and felt crowded if they spotted a neighbour's smoke.

Cattle dotted this land, where occasional signs warned the traveller that this was open range. There were no fences, the beasts had the run of the territory, across which the traveller must proceed with caution. Whilst reflecting upon the emptiness of the land, a sign appeared which confirmed my suspicions. 'Welcome to Highway 50, the loneliest road in America.'

I could well believe it. I don't think that at the time I saw the sign, I had passed another vehicle in the last thirty miles. The desolate boast was shortly superseded by another, set at the outskirts of a small town a quarter of a mile beyond it. 'Welcome to Eureka, the loneliest town on the loneliest road in America.'

Eureka is not, it has to be said, the Big Apple. I spotted a gas station, a few shops, a restaurant, a sheriff's office, and a straggle of wooden houses. I rode slowly up the main street which, as far as I could tell, was the only street. With the bike in second gear I proceeded at a walking pace, the pipes gurgling like a brace of

271

leashed Rottweilers. The sidewalks were practically devoid of people, those that there were, turned at my approach, like indignant members of a theatre audience critically surveying the latecomer. Toward me now, stepping bang up the middle of the street, with unflinching resolve, his nose on a line with the centre tread of my front wheel, came a sizeable, geriatric, whiskery old mutt. This animal had one of those humorously unkempt faces sprouting tufts of undisciplined coarse hair that projected asymmetrically from his canine countenance that by virtue of their embellishment, enjoyed a comic quality of which the owner was clearly unconscious. It was the kind of face that, whilst suggesting humour, retained yet a vestigial dignity which discourages mirth. Like an old gunfighter with one decent draw left, he closed the gap between us. Though he wore neither gun nor badge, I sensed with dependable instinct, that this was a character who considered himself to be, beyond any question, the boss. Maybe a little unsteady on his lean legs, but determined, indomitable, assertive, in short, not a mutt to be messed with. A canine Samurai whose pride forbade retreat; 'death before dishonour' was tattooed into the ragged disorder of his bristled jowls. We came to a halt under the cloudless Nevada sky on Main Street as the sparse population looked on. He, the old campaigner, the mayor, the major, the capitano, the man; a four legged Lee Marvin struggling to focus past the influence of a ninety-proof dog chew, at me, the new boy in town.

I stared him down as the dust from the tyres drifted slowly through the forest of spokes into his determined face. He blinked reluctantly to clear his watery old eyes, thus providing a relief from the navigational impasse which gave me the chance to roll forward to the right, just off the line of citizen dog's track. The diplomatic concession worked. As the dust cleared, the honourable hound discharged a solitary bark; which I interpreted to lie midway between a generous recognition of my subservient gesture, and a warning against the clear folly of a renewed challenge. With this, the victor resumed his march, the paws landing with emphatic resolution like the stately footfall of a regent approaching his throne. His authority confirmed, a measure of caution was nonetheless apparent in the orientation of his head which remained pointing backwards at me, while his body proceeded, thus sustaining with gyroscopic consistency, his uninterrupted surveillance of the cowed challenger, until, like a cautious navigator, he was sure that all danger of collision had passed.

Breathing with relief at the peaceful conclusion of this unequal confrontation, I rolled my motorcycle backwards into the curb where it came to rest outside a house of Oriental cuisine run by a pair of gourmets whose hurried movements to restore an atmosphere of bustling normality, betrayed an anxiety which the theatrics beyond their window had evidently aroused. I affected ignorance of their concern and examined the menu with contrived concentration. I like Chinese food, but not at midday, so it was heads down for a plate of hash browns and eggs with a glass of righteous full-cream milk.

I find it very hard to believe that those sun-baked dust blown cowboys who hit town at the end of a thirsty cattle drive ever ordered up whisky as their first drink – and neat whisky at that. Liquid it may be, but refreshing it ain't. Short of a glass full of dehydrated wood shavings, a tumbler full of sand or a tea cup of talcum powder, it's hard to imagine anything much less refreshing to the creaking gullet than the celebrated firewater. I can believe the leathery-faced clients of Western saloons had whisky after they'd quenched their thirst, but not as an opener whilst the saloon doors were still a-creak on their hinges. If the truth be known, as the pistol-shot heraldry of high-spirited horsemen disturbed the afternoon slumbers of frontier barkeeps, they probably busied themselves lining up a row of quart jugs filled with orange squash, plus a few variations for the awkward cusses.

'Shit no, there's Black Jake, he likes lemonade, and Snake-Eyed Pete, always a Ribena man, and Switchblade Sid, he's strictly blackcurrant with soda.' You just try telling that to a movie producer. The nearest you'd approach a concession to reality on this score would be the odd pimply greenstick ordering a lager top to universal mirth. How anyone can drink whisky at the best of times is a mystery to me. It's disgusting stuff. Even most Scots tacitly agree. You have only to watch how many of these hard drinking Celts disguise its abrasive qualities with copious draughts of sugary lemonade to realize how finely tuned is their perception of the spirit's inimitable subtlety. No whisky for me, beer's much safer, and milk is safer still – so long as it hasn't got the word 'butter' in front of it.

Lunch over, I took some photos of the town, and tanked up at the twin pump gas station; the last one had been a hundred miles back down the road, and I wasn't taking any chances. A westbound pick-up, loaded with two motorcycles on its trailer joined me on the narrow forecourt. The driver, a sunbaked old timer, clambered stiffly down from the cab, his work-gnarled claws clinging for support on the weathered door frame as he lowered his emaciated limbs gingerly onto the uneven ground. The oversized cow horn belt buckle exaggerated the scrawny outline of his meagrely upholstered physique that was bracketed at its modest summit by a baseball hat of generous dimensions.

'Howdy,' he greeted me, with a welcome of surprising vitality at odds with his appearance, reflecting the survival of a resilient spirit of disguised potency.

'That's a nice bike son; you going far?' he asked.

'New York,' I replied, hoping the answer did not sound too pretentious. The old man whistled respectfully, his eyes disappearing theatrically beneath the shadow of his overhanging peak.

'Thas-a-lonnnng way son,' he drawled.

'Can't ride myself no more,' he apologised ruefully, gesturing at his chest with a bony digit.

'All shitted up inside.'

I commiserated without further enquiry, as he levered his reluctant bones behind the wheel of the battered Dodge. Hitching my strides, I stretched a leg over the Harley's saddle, its rubber slung engine reverberating in accompaniment to the laden motion of the truck as our respective wheels rolled past the stage front of the gas stop in opposing directions; theatre curtains announcing a fresh act. As I resumed my eastward track, I glimpsed a rugged face glance wistfully backward between the truck window and the chequered sleeve which rose in parting salute. I returned the gesture and twisted the throttle as our dust trails faded toward opposite horizons.

I rode without pause now, for three, maybe four hours, the needle oscillating responsibly about the fifty-five mark with the dutiful consistency of a thermostat, while the rocky panorama slowly surrendered its features to my relentless progress. By late afternoon I called a stop, steering off the highway into the welcome oasis of another filling station which offered, besides the necessary fuel, a selection of chocolate, peanuts and soft drinks. With a fresh tank of gas I parked up to consume a pack of KPs whose gritty passage I eased with a can of Coke. Picking a sunny spot sheltered from the wind, I seated myself on the ground to consume this modest lunch and study the horny calluses that had moulded themselves by dint of motionless tenancy, to the contours of the handlebar grips.

It was pleasant sitting on the stony ground with my feet stretched out before me, the heels of my boots digging shallow trenches in the dust that blew in faint curtains across the empty highway. The air temperature was not high, a fact to which the recent experience of my ride bore shivering witness, but here in the lee of the garage outbuildings, with the sun in my face, I enjoyed the transient illusion of high summer. Beneath slitted eyes, I swallowed by savoured sips, the cool bracing effervescence of the gassy drink, as a burdened semi laboured up to the pumps; the creaks and bangs as it bucked and snorted across the rutted forecourt, arousing the attendant within. With the foolish satisfaction of accurately anticipating trivial developments, I watched for the nod of greeting, the predictable enquiry, and corresponding instruction, as both players reached for their respective props, the vendor for his gas nozzle, the trucker for his wallet. While the mundane mime show unwound its simple plot, my attention drifted to the distant hills where burly clouds telegraphed sobering warnings of impending inclemency.

THE SIMPLE MAN

My brief interlude to 'stand and stare' was through, for my itinerary had already been stretched and it was time to be off toward the brooding hills, from where a wintry challenge could be read in the accumulating cloud. As I headed out of town into the increasing breeze, I sensed the futility of continuing without the protection of my waterproof trousers. As chance had it, I paused to don them by a farm gate, at which lurked an oddly bloated fellow of transparently limited intellect. There being no evident motive for his sentry-like commitment to this bleak post, I pondered the nature of his intentions, as he surveyed me from the ill defined contours of a rubbery face, like a waxen figure melted unevenly into the voluminous cast of his ample dungarees. I checked cautiously for some sign of a weapon about his feet as I struggled awkwardly into the waterproofs through a moment of vaguely anxious vulnerability. With this critical moment survived, I risked a conversational gambit.

'Looks like rain all right,' I ventured, gesturing toward the now not so distant hills. He nodded lethargic concurrence.

'Storm comin,' he agreed, with a laconic economy that I sensed marked the prevailing conduct of his life. This contention-free debate concluded, I boarded the motorcycle, nodded briefly in his direction, and rejoined the minor highway that led to the foot of the hills. Looking back over my shoulder, as I accelerated down the road, the picture of this rural sloth was stencilled on my memory with an indelible emphasis as the quintessential epitome of his kind. Framed against the flat infinity of prairie, with the wrathful sky for a border, and the farm gate to lend perspective to his lofty bulk, he cut a dramatic figure of Steinbeckian austerity; a monument to his breed, chiselled from the insular complacency of modest aspiration.

THE STORM

To the north, huge black cumulonimbus clouds were mating with the earth behind broad black curtains, which they trailed beneath them like the inky tentacles of marauding squid. An examination of the map led me to the conclusion that my route lay in the direction from which these watery bruisers originated, the intelligence lending a grim fatalism to the resolution with which I now pursued my course.

A solitary vehicle shared the single track road, rolling toward me out of the intensifying mist, the headlights a clear herald of diminishing visibility. With its passage, the blast of the storm hit me like a breaking wave, arresting all forward motion as surely as a sand-filled bunker stalls the progress of an errant golf ball. Its force aside, the unusual character of this storm derived from a surprising characteristic – dryness. The hurtling cloud of terrestrial ammo was not, as I had assumed, composed of water, but of dust; I was caught in a dust storm, and all prospect of early advance was suspended. Blinded by the violent hail, I pulled off the road to avoid immediate catastrophe. Ducking my head to protect my eyes which, despite the protection of glasses, were polluted with unwelcome wind driven debris, I kicked down the stand with that side of the machine foolishly turned to windward so that I was obliged to hang on to the motorcycle to prevent it capsizing like a ship beam-on to a heavy swell. Piles of dust rapidly accumulated on the windward side of the wheels, as uprooted bushes of tumbleweed came somersaulting through the air like startled creatures fleeing a forest inferno. The whole surface of the land was alive now, stirred into violent agitation by the vigour of the elements. I was reminded of the experience of being at sea, which develops a similar unnerving drama when subjected to winds in excess of force ten. At this point the water, besides describing the familiar serpentine undulations to which the seafarer is accustomed, begins to move bodily, carrying all that floats before it with an irresistible momentum. What I was experiencing was the terrestrial equivalent of a maritime hurricane, the sky in acute distress, presenting an astonishing picture of turbulent motion as the clouds stampeded across it at a rate I'd only witnessed before in time-lapsed films made to demonstrate natural phenomena.

This was all new to me. Had the earth stopped turning, leaving its atmosphere to spin on at a rate equal to that which it had, of the instant, abandoned, or were the gods of the elements, with omnipotent petulance competing with one another in the exercise of their powers. Fanciful speculations for sure, but ones which the circumstances must doubtless have fostered in the superstitious imagination of the earlier generations who inhabited this land. And so I clung, limpet-like to my motorcycle, eyes shut tight, as several minutes passed before the tempest ran its course, pebble dashing the engine with a remorseless clatter of small stones. When it was over, I felt that I'd been put through a gigantic dry-cleaning process in which every aperture, arch, fold, and crevice of my body, had been filled with dust, squirted with insolent deliberation by some mischievous agent of dismay, to effect my total demoralization. Extracting the displaced vegetation from its unnatural lodging between the wheels and cylinders of my engine, I patted myself down, shook out my congested scarf, and spat copiously, blessing the inanimate indifference of my machine which had patiently withstood the attack, where a horse might have panicked and fled, I restarted the engine. With gratitude for the brevity of the windblown juggernaut which had rolled over me, I resumed my journey.

THE RAIN

By a T-junction at the foot of the hills, I turned north on Interstate 15 toward Scipio where I regained Highway 50 heading south-east for Salina. Towns, the names of which I gratuitously record for the sake of their fluid Latin charisma. I visited neither.

Up in the mountains again now, I was riding on a narrow strip of freshly rain-washed blacktop that cut a discreet course through an exquisitely painted landscape of floral-speckled stone. A great God-sewn, botanical embroidery of multifarious hues extended to the limits of my vision. Every colour of the rainbow was displayed to dramatic effect by this living tapestry, in which acres of blooming bushes collectively monopolized the stony slopes like the uniformed ranks of rival armies massed for horticultural combat in a colossal rock garden.

Rain never felt far away, and as dusk turned to dark, ominous fleets of bellicose clouds sailed over the heights, pregnant with their intimidating cargoes, like menacing bombers. Inevitably, and with a force that vindicated my apprehension, the deluge commenced.

On a motorcycle, rain in the daytime is grim. By night, on a cold and mountainous road, unrelieved by the cheerful respite of habitation, it is wretched. My leather boots, though well impregnated with dubbin, were acquiring a cool sponginess that I didn't care for, whilst the neck of my Gortex jacket was allowing a steady immigration that threatened to breach the manufacturer's boasted water-tight integrity. My gloves, like my boots, having sustained a rearguard defence for a nominal twenty minutes, had now been routed by the damp assailant, to the point where their value approximated to that of a pair of fingered sponges.

If the rain was dramatic, it was matched by the scenery which now exhibited a more rugged character than the rocky pillows of flowers to the north. Here, the jagged irregularity of the land presented a picture more lunar than earthly, its craggy hostility illuminated by the dramatic sheets of lightning which danced malevolently across the sky. At the highest level in my transit of this range, I encountered several miles of roadworks. Half blinded by the rain, I crawled on at a bicycle pace past extensive trenches waist deep, that had been gouged from the ground by mechanical earth movers, whose labours, even at this hour, and amidst such inclemency, persisted still. The lightning painted graphic silhouettes of their toothed shovels as they gestured skyward between bites, robotic hands of mechanical supplication. Beside them, at regular intervals, their feet anchored in the squelching mire, stood a legion of workmen. Caped and helmeted, they swung their torches to clarify the route; a track which, but for their stoic endeavours, would have been unclear to me amidst the dishevelled chaos of the road over which I groped my myopic course. Like the machines, the faces of these guides, invisible beneath dripping peaks, erupted into stark relief as the lightning picked out each with its questing tongues. To a man, their countenances wore masks of grim resolution, like soldiers from the Great War, frozen in the morbid resignation of their trenches as they awaited the ominous hands being shuffled by the grim dealer of unspeakable fate.

There was about that scene, a ghastly apocalyptical hopelessness reminiscent of Benjamin Britten's terrifyingly stark 'War Requiem.' I shuddered to the core and wished myself away from this place but the photographer in me demanded an attempt to capture a picture of the sky. The lightning, unless my tired brain deceived me, was orange, a sight both novel and new to my experience, and I was determined to record it. Parking the bike a little to one side of the road, I climbed a small hill to shelter in the lee of a rocky monolith. From this position I endeavoured to coordinate my shutter release with the spectacular gestures of Promethean excess, as angular skeletons of light stabbed the land with flaming stilettos. I had no idea if my equipment and tactics were adequate to the task, but as Thor bellowed his derisory accompaniment across the mountains, I suspected that they were not, a pessimism that was subsequently vindicated by the darkly vacuous results that were returned by the photographic laboratory some weeks later.

It occurred to me at this time, that I was in a very high place, during a dramatic thunderstorm, aboard a large piece of metal with a high ferrous content. In recognition of these perilous criteria, I proceeded with trepidation, nurturing in the nest of my fond imaginings, the exquisitely cosy prospect of a hot meal and warm bed. With progress, anxiety slowly diminished in proportion to altitude, as I rode downhill over the waters of San Rafael, towards the blessed lights of a town that earned my gratitude for just existing – Green River.

GREEN RIVER

I had hoped to better my daily best of six-hundred miles on a motorcycle, achieved four months earlier on a 305cc Kawasaki. This bike had been loaned to me by a Long Island urologist, who accompanied me on a 750cc Hondamatic with a sidecar attached. The latter machine was, without question, the most appalling set of wheels I had ever ridden. During practice sessions I had successfully collided with a steep kerbstone whilst making a landfall at a New York deli, an experience I was in no haste to repeat. So it was, when we pulled off a flooded Pennsylvania freeway and the good doctor cheerfully speculated that I might 'like a go of the Honda,' that I gained a clearer perception of the fallibility of human rationale. The naive generosity of this offer served to emphasize the disappointing reality that even eminent physicians can be totally, but totally, wrong.

I recalled the incident in order to bolster my sodden resolve to best the six-hundred marker which collapsed at the first glimpse of an illuminated motel sign, to which I steered with magnetic enthusiasm. Five hundred and ninety miles would just have to do. I am glad that I stopped here, as I met an interesting character who was over from Australia, touring around with his wife and child trying to buy secondhand Harleys to ship home to Sydney where he had a bike business. Apparently he hadn't been able to get any worthwhile deals at all in California, and seemed to think that six-thousand dollars for a bike like mine, was pretty cheap. It was an opinion supported by a number of voices and I considered myself very lucky to have made the connection with Chip that I had back in Ohio. The Aussie, whose name was Sam, was telling me about the first time he and his mates came over the Pacific to live in Los Angeles. They didn't know anything about the area and just thumbed through the newspapers looking for the cheapest district in which to rent a house. In their innocence, they picked Watts, a notoriously strife-torn, Black neighbourhood, something like the LA equivalent of New York's Harlem. Unable to comprehend the Black landlord's reluctance to rent them the place, they insisted on trying it out, and spent a couple of fraught weeks there trying to understand the cold shouldering they experienced from a community in which they appeared just a mite conspicuous. They

282

actually thought for a while, that their neighbours did not like them because they were Australians. They didn't get mugged or robbed while they were there though, which just goes to show that with enough brass neck or naivety, you can get away with a hell of a lot.

My experience of places generally, is that nowhere is as bad as it's made out to be. In my years at sea, I was forever being warned off this bar or that bar, which made a run ashore sound about as safe as going to a mad Mullah's tea party in an 'I love New York' T-shirt. Of course if the truth had been anywhere near the tales, you wouldn't have been able to get near these bars for ambulances, and none of them could have sustained the business to survive their reputations. The only place I ever encountered that really lived up to expectations, was a sweaty little town at the Atlantic end of the Panama Canal, called Cristobal. There, the contrast between North American wealth and Central American poverty spawns a violent jealously to which many a sailor has fallen prey. It's a steaming sweaty vat of avarice, where tourists' watches are legal tender and switchblades make the contracts. Of the dozen or so of us from my ship who went ashore in various groups, everyone was mugged. That's a bad average – but they say the exception proves the rule.

In tune with that axiom was the restaurant over the road from the motel in Green River, that had run out of beer. As a rule, service in America is great. Shop service, restaurant service, you name it, people do seem genuinely interested to see you, you feel that they want your business and value your custom. What is most remarkable, is that this enthusiasm for mundane functions, like operating a checkout desk, even extends to major chain stores, where the real owner probably isn't in the same state, let alone out back keeping a listening ear out for his employee's conduct. The restaurant in question, however, was the exception. They'd run out of beer, and though there was a liquor store around the corner, no one had bothered to take a walk round to get a few bottles. They didn't mind me bringing in my own though, so I did, but I wasn't over-impressed with the hospitality. I suppose we were a little late in the evening, but when my undone bootlace got caught in the vacuum cleaner's suction, I sensed that the hints were bordering the impatient side of discretion. Every cloud has a silver lining though, and I stitched my own into this one by sparing the staff the embarrassment of a tip.

Sam was staying in the same motel as I was, I'd run into him in the motel office in fact, where the owner thought I was an Aussie. A lot of people, English people that is, have this trouble I discovered, and I found it both inexplicable and aggravating. It's not that I have anything against Aussies, but I am perplexed by the inability of many Americans to recognize the Queen's English when they hear it. I was under the impression that Americans liked to hear English accents, furthermore, that a good English accent could actually improve your prospects in America, that it provided a badge of cultural distinction, like an Eton school tie. I think a lot of people are amused by the accent, but they don't often know what it is. This ignorance of foreign accents reflects an insularity about Americans that sits strangely at odds with their global influence. Perhaps the size and diversity of the United States geographically, climatically and culturally, satiates the population's appetite for exploration, it's like a vast fun fair with every ride in the world. When wintering New Yorkers yearn for sunshine, they can board a southbound train; for Floridians, tired of the flatland heat of their home state, they can take a trip to the Rockies, and desert-dwelling Texans can join them when they want to remember what forests look like. You don't even have to trek to India to catch up on Third World poverty – just lock your car doors and take a drive downtown in most major urban conurbations. Like Linda Ronstadt said, 'Everything you want we got it right here in the USA.'

I suppose it's understandable, this confusion over accents, but there's something kind of insulting about admissions of ignorance when you feel that what those admissions reflect, is indifference. I spoke to an American biker once who guessed that there were about fifteen million people in England!

Now you may think I was being had here, but if I was, then he was one hell of an actor. The impression imparted by these admissions of ignorance is that we are just totally insignificant, which is irksome. There is no malice in the expression of the ignorance, no hint of a deliberate put down, not a trace of any superciliousness, it's just plain, incredible, innocent ignorance.

Now it's true that not everyone in America looks to this country for its roots, but damn it, we were the first major colonists of any significance. It's not coincidence that the whole bloody continent speaks English; the place has actually been governed from London for almost half of its existence, and though we had a family squabble a while back, we still play for the same team when brother Bosche goes apeshit and plans a little cross-border goose-step. The attitude of many Americans to the Old Country, resembles the bewilderment of an amnesiac son meeting his father with benign incomprehension.

'Who did you say you were?'

Maybe we British think too much of ourselves, like Cecil Rhodes who decided that, in being born British, one had 'drawn first prize in the lottery of life.' I think there's truth in that, and I like being British, but I think that if I wasn't British I'd like to have been born American. If only so I could park my arse on a stool in a New York deli and roar, 'Gimmee a salami on rye wid plenty of coleslaw, hold the pickle and go easy wid der relish,' without feeling self-conscious. Just imagine that!

THE ROCKIES AGAIN

Before I left Green River I bought a melon from a huge pile that were stacked on trestles at the roadside, bearing giveaway price tags that could scarcely be believed. In the general store where I queued to pay, I fell into conversation with an ex-serviceman whose attention had been drawn to a camper parked outside, which was adorned with a large Swiss flag. The ex-soldier had visited Switzerland in his European travels, and couldn't understand why anyone who came from such a beautiful country should bother leaving it to look at any other. I suppose everyone has trouble understanding something. I, for example, could not for the life of me understand why the American could not understand the motivation of the Swiss in the camper. Actually parts of Colorado where I had been, are a little like the Swiss Alps. There are cabins, skiing lodges and hiking lodges, even whole holiday villages built in the Swiss style, with log walls, steeply sloping roofs and timbered balconies. Aspen, the ski resort of the ridiculously wealthy, is in this part of the country. John Denver had a home here which he sang about, thus making him richer still. I never resented John Denver his wealth though; he may have been the Milky Bar Kid, super-wimp of rock, but he wrote some great melodies. Sooner his idyllic, rose-hued spectacled view of the world than the tuneless trash churned out by the get-on-down disco, house thud mechanized garbage of the musical antichrists from clubland. I'm a broad-minded chap, but when I'm exposed to this form of audible pollution, it makes me yearn for an agent of Cromwellian austerity to scour the land; a witchfinder general to wage a holy war against the defilers of human taste with a band of sturdy fellows to pulverize every manifestation of the clubbing plague from the Western world. I pondered the possibility of starting an anti-dance-music organization when I got home and even contrived a name for it – Stamp Out Dance Society, or SODS! I thought that had something of a ring to it. Cards could be printed bearing the organization's title and listing the characteristics of the pub, with boxes at the end of each feature to tick. Liked the decor, good service, good beer – pity about the filthy, stinking dance shite. SODS yes, I would see about organizing something when I got home. For the meantime, however, there were more attractive thoughts to occupy my mind, as the fabulous state of Colorado unfolded its scenic splendour to the rubber-shod progress of my mechanical horse.

I was travelling east on a more northerly latitude than the one I had followed on my westbound route, and at a later time in the season, which made for a broader variety of colour in the vegetation. Blanket green had given way to a harlequin of yellows, oranges, and intermediate hues that grew to the banks of startling blue rivers, churning their energetic paths between artistically placed boulders, like the features from an animated mural. This was a living paintbook of natural beauty, the lush opulence of which denied the notion that anything could be wrong with the world's environment. I was riding Interstate 70, a smaller highway than most which cuts the Colorado river numerous times as it writhes an eastern route toward Denver. Desperate attempts were being made to widen the road when I was there, an exercise that the rugged terrain did not happily accommodate. Engineering initiative was clearly being taxed to the hilt by the uncooperative landscape in which colossal efforts were being made to cut roads where seemingly no roads could go. Sadly, all this activity, coupled with the narrowness of the available road, prevented me from stopping. Innumerable lollipop ladies in yellow bibs, lined the route, waving the traffic on like environmental usherettes in the Rocky Mountain picture house. This was a non-stop show for transit passengers only, with no exceptions allowed. The labyrinthine character of the route dictated a funereal pace which suited me fine, as I was all eyes for this Edenesque world of wonder that was as beautiful as any place I had ever been in my life. Beauty walks in league with danger, however, the prime source of which, to me, stemmed from the lack of harmony between my line of sight, and the course of my front wheel. The pine shrouded heights held my attention one moment, their snow covered peaks protruding above the tree-line like half-clothed ice-creams. Then I was looking down, down into the luxuriant gulleys, saturated with their floral displays like over-planted nursery beds. I was looking right and left into the mosaics decorating cliffs of rock apparently too steep and uncompromising to tolerate the tenancy of root and branch, and yet managing it; great slabs of stone that titanic forces had thrust out of the subterranean world with an awesome power. With so much visually compelling scenery around me, it was nigh on impossible to keep an eye on the road ahead. This wasn't the kind of riding that gets one through the motorcycle test with a gold star, but it wasn't conducted at a pace that would have broken any lap records either, and so was not as foolhardy as might be imagined. And who cannot say that at some time, they have not compromised safety for the appreciation of beauty?

Unfortunately in a land as beautiful as this, there operates, at least for me, an aggravating agent of disenchantment that whispers seductively in the ear and muddles the mind with kaleidoscopic possibilities. Riding the bike was fine, but the voice possessed hands which opened doors onto avenues of infinite potential, suggesting alternative adventures and experiences to bewilder my over-stimulated appetite. Like Satan in the wilderness, it provoked me with a multiplicity of possibilities. Wouldn't you rather be climbing up those rocks, or sitting in that tree, or then again, swimming in the river. Wouldn't it be great to stop for some food, do a little fishing, a little hiking, walk off with a tent and camp under the pines with a coffee pot and a harmonica for company. There were so many things I could have been doing, that it seemed an insult to ride straight through and leave so many flavours untasted; a bit like going to a five-star restaurant and leaving after reading the menu and drinking a Perrier water. The joy of experience diminished by insatiable greed and the impossibility of unlimited indulgence. Life is like that; a garden with a thousand flowers, and only one nose to sniff them with. Ah, the cruel brevity of our mortal span – there has to be more, there has to be.

The last time I had felt this sensation quite so acutely was when I was eating lunch in a cafe on Plymouth Hoe. On that occasion a teenage netball team burst in and surrounded me, whereupon the helpless head swivelling to which I spontaneously succumbed earned me a nasty neck strain and I had to spend the last of my beer money on Sloane's Liniment.

BOULDER

The Rocky Mountains end very abruptly. One minute you're up there amongst all the peaks and pines, the next you're down on a great plain, interrupted by the city of Denver. The traveller who pauses up on the edge of the great divide, may visit the grave of Buffalo Bill Cody. Buffalo Bill, I learned, was an officer in the Civil War, who later made a name for himself as an Indian fighter and buffalo hunter. Buffalo hunting, or more precisely, extermination, being a tactic in the Indian wars. Notwithstanding his role in this grizzly carnage, I still thought I'd have a look at the grave of the legendary character.

Buffalo Bill ran a Wild West show in his later years, featuring an act involving a sharp-shooting girl called Annie Oakley. I bought a postcard based on an original photograph of the young woman which suggested that, besides her ballistic abilities, she wasn't exactly what you'd call ugly. I posted it to my sister in Ickenham and began the decent toward Boulder, my staging post for the night.

Back on level ground once more, I paused to take a photograph of a road sign bearing the word 'Eldorado' which just happened to be spanned by a rainbow at the time. Given the gold-hunting identity associated with the fabled name, this colourful phenomenon seemed highly appropriate, and I took it as a good omen.

Boulder felt different to any other American city I had visited or glimpsed in my travels as I circumnavigated them on the bypassing freeways. I couldn't put my finger on it at first. Was it the combination of brick-built buildings with broad-leaved trees that gave it a more European feel?

I found my friend Michael Lichter's house at the end of a quiet, leafy street full of detached wooden houses. A large ginger cat stood guard on the porch, its face so lost in its prolific fur that I took it at first for a cat with two coats, an animal uncertain of any purpose in life beyond an all-consuming obsession with appearing incomparably furry, an objective that, with no conscious thought or effort, it had achieved to its own, as to all other's, complete astonishment. It stood before me now, a whiskered concentrate of feline bewilderment. This was no suspicious doorman of hostile intent but a genial herald of hospitality, padded of paw, and damp velveted of nose.

The fearless enthusiasm of this spirited ambassador, as he trotted confidently toward me, instantly fuelled my instinctive sense of well-being about the house, whose door now opened to admit me. Once inside, an increment to the animal menagerie appeared in the form of a Spaniel equipped with ponderous, glossy-furred ears that swung and flapped about its brown face as it bounded joyfully toward me. I like animals, all animals. In fact, I have often thought I would like to be one, probably a gorilla as I could still ride a motorcycle and I'd be able to pick up litter bugs and carefully press them into large litter bins, dexterously snapping any limbs that protruded, and packing them tidily within the perimeter of the units. I always feel that there is something odd about people who don't like animals. It seems unlikely that anyone can ever find any peace in this world if they are not comfortable with animals. Then again I could be wrong as some people do.

I joined Michael and his family, which also comprised a wife and two children, for dinner. Like everything else about this place, the meal involved a variety of ingredients that suggested the operation of sensitive intellects and inquisitive appetites. I was offered a jar of home made chilli sauce, my enthusiasm for which had been instantly recognized by my hosts who urged me to take it home, an offer I felt I had, regrettably, to decline in deference to the limited volume of my saddlebags; a pity.

Outside on the street where Michael led me on a whistle-stop walking tour of Boulder, I soon understood the reason for the fundamentally different feel that Boulder had to it – it is a university town. The main street up which we walked, was pedestrianized to provide the sense of human intimacy that is tragically absent from so many of America's cities. Flower beds occupied the central reservations, separating the groups of nocturnal strollers, while trees shed their loosening autumn plumage about the feet of buskers playing in the doorways of shops, the majority of which were now closed in deference to the late hour.

There were pavement cafes and book shops, music shops, shops full of curios, posters advertising plays and meetings; all the signs of a culturally stimulating environment encouraged by active young minds. The sound of guitars flavoured the evening air, accompanied by a hum of animated chatter overflowing the doorstep of a crowded bar, which we entered in pursuit of beer. It was a trendy kind of bar, by which I mean cultured trendy, tasteful trendy in a comfortable, natural kind of way. The timber legs of the furniture scraped across wooden floorboards in a percussion section that featured rattling beer bottles and good-humoured laughter. This place had class, but not in a formal, 'no dogs or work clothes' kind of way, and definitely not in a plastic-trimmed, fruit-machined, carpeted, disco kind of way. If this place had posted hostile signs on the door they would have read, 'No Michael Jackson or RAP. No football scarves. No XR3is. And, 'The Management reserve the right to restrain anyone caught chanting "Ere we go" or saying "Get it on down," for a week of adult rock indoctrination.' The place buzzed with the cheerful vigour of young and enthusiastic patrons with taste, aspirations and standards; I liked it.

There were pretty girls all over the place, but interesting looking girls, rather than the brainless dull-witted tarts who cram their earnings into gambling machines, whilst cigarettes hang limply from speechless mouths like adult dummies. These girls looked as if they might actually have something to say, some opinions on the world, some aspirations beyond a deeper suntan from the solar centre. These are the kind of girls who wear jeans with patches because they need patches, the kind of girls who like scarves and hats which they buy from secondhand shops, the kind of girls who paint or write or act or sing, maybe even ride motorcycles. These kind of girls don't overdo makeup but they do have good teeth. I've always felt I could have a serious relationship with a girl like this. The only bad thing about girls like this, is that girls like this are never remotely interested in blokes like me. Bit of a bugger that.

Standing on the rooftop deck, looking out toward the peaks of the bordering Rockies with the energetic hum of youthful conversation in my ears, it was easy to see why Michael had moved out here from New York. As someone who has to fly to all parts of the country, its central location clearly provides a practical advantage over peripheral sites, whilst the cultured atmosphere and fabulous mountain environment close by, offer incomparable opportunities for outdoor pursuits. I could easily have spent a week here, or more sensibly a summer, perhaps longer still – pity it's so far from the sea though.

I spent the latter part of the evening watching Michael sorting out transparencies and gathering his gear together for the photo shoot he had to do at Bonneville the next day. I felt a little guilty turning up here when my host was clearly pushed for time, but only a little guilty, as I'm a selfish toad who's inclined to think that the world should shuffle its priorities to accommodate my whims.

Midnight found me making tea whilst Michael snipped away industriously at pieces of celluloid, viewing and mounting each one with a deft professionalism that earned my admiration and sympathy. Michael had a great house with a veranda out back leading into his large garden. He had his photographic studio. He had a lovely family, some great animals, and a Harley. Comparing his accomplishments to my own spartan acquisitions, he seemed pretty well set up – and, he wasn't leading a tedious life tied to some tiresome moneyspinner of a job that bored him. Michael gets flown all over the States to shoot pictures, and people pay him sensible money to do it because he is a total professional; he unfailingly delivers the goods. Like a hit man who consistently produces a corpse, Michael comes back with the definitive picture, but, and it is a big 'but', he works so damn hard. Bloody terrible business having to work hard, absolutely awful. Americans generally, take far fewer holidays than their British or, for that matter, German counterparts. A scant two or three weeks a year is commonplace, which is a terrible indictment of social mismanagement. I suppose it's all down to the Protestant work ethic that Americans will doubtless claim gives then the edge over their Russian rivals with their incurable Slavic indolence. It seems a strange thing though, that the substantial infusion of Latin blood has not tempered the general flavour of this continental pot-pourri with a stronger respect for the social stratagem of '*mañana*'. I suppose American material aspirations are higher than Mediterranean ones and set the pace. Michael's family medical insurance alone would keep a Bangladeshi village in chapattis till the next millennium, so he has to keep working.

I approached the cutting room with an iron tea pot.

'No Mutch, put it back on the gas,' ordered my host, 'boil it for a few minutes.'

'Hang on, you boil tea?' I asked, somewhat incredulously, I know Americans do a lot of things differently, but boiling tea, with the bag in the water that is ?

'We're a mile high up here,' he explained, 'up here the water doesn't boil at a hundred degrees, the tea takes a little longer.'

I put the pot back on the gas and watched as the bags danced about like bewildered windsocks. Eventually I decided it must be done; it was, and we drank it.

Michael was stuffing his bag with camera gear now, and I gawped with envy as motor-driven Nikons, flash guns, and lenses like Iraqi rocket-launchers were squeezed into the soft cases like so many spare T-shirts. All this to photograph one, admittedly not so little, motorcycle. As every photographer knows though, the one lens you don't take, is the one lens you need. At half-past two I gave up and hit the sack, leaving my host to tidy up the details.

I had meant to get away early today, I still had a thousand miles to ride to reach Indianapolis in time for the biker's convention I wanted to attend, the somewhat pretentiously titled, 'Meeting of the Minds.' But with only two days in which to complete the journey, the margins looked uncomfortably narrow. I had a call at half-past six which was when Michael was leaving for the airport, but it was no good, I was like a boxer who couldn't make the count, and I returned to the horizontal for more ZZ's. When I woke two hours later, my industrious host was already winging his way out of the state on the way to Salt Lake City and the Bonneville Salt Flats. How does he do it I wondered? Michael was gone, but his dog, cat and children were very much at home and tearing toward me at ground level with a frightening velocity. Lying flat on my back with my eyes freshly opened by the cacophony of sound was a disturbing experience. Huge ears flapped around me as padded paws landed muddily in my mouth and small hands poked me in the ears.

'Sod this,' I thought.

COPS, TURTLES AND BISON

An hour later I was skirting Denver, rolling down Highway 36 into Kansas, heading east for the city that lent its name to the eponymously titled 'Indianapolis 500.'

I now pondered the pros and cons of taking the interstate, with its sixty-five miles per hour limit, or sticking to Highway 36 with its fifty-five limit. I decided on the latter and ran down it at seventy, past a town called Last Chance – where I got pulled for speeding. I swear I'd only passed one car in the last five miles and it had to be one of those with funny flashing things on its roof. At least they became funny flashing things after I passed by going in the opposite direction. I had a feeling he was going to turn around and come after me, something about the hint of interest that I sensed behind the mirrored shades as our paths crossed, provided a subtle clue; and the way his brake lights came on as the Dodge pick-up's suspension dived like an enthusiastic Stuka. In any case, he was soon on my tail, blue lights going like sparklers in my rear view mirror. I ignored him for a while, affecting total innocence as I looked nonchalantly around at the scenery with the speedo needle welded to the highlighted fifty-five mark. There was at work here, a patent example of psychology. I like to think in these situations that they think, 'Ah, he's a decent chap. That burst of speed was an unconscious aberation, this is the speed he's actually been travelling at, and he's settled back to it even though he hasn't noticed I'm behind him.' The hope is, that the man will follow for a few hundred yards, then drop back and go his own way; clever stuff eh? It never works. I pulled over and sat guiltily as the tall, immaculately-groomed officer strode purposefully toward me. 'Good morning,' I ventured.

'Stand right there by the motorcycle sir.'

'Oh yes, sure, right here, yes.' I surrendered my documents and stood pensively, very much the boy in the corner, contemplating the motorcycle as though I'd never seen it before, whilst the dark shades surveyed me from behind the windshield of the radio-equipped pick up. How comprehensive were his checks? Did he know my MZ was parked on a public road in EC1 without a current road vehicle licence? Did he know I was living illicitly in a prefab in Bethnal Green under an assumed name? Did he know

294

that I still owed Wiltshire magistrates fifteen pounds for breaching a by-law, which forbade camping in a field occupied by cows, more than forty yards from a major road without the farmer's permission? My mind churned with the terrifying possibilities posed by the miracle of modern communications. Would I be deported from the USA and my passport marked to bar any future attempts at entry? Perhaps I'd be flung into a hard-labour camp like Cool Hand Luke, brutally provoked into escaping, and then hunted down by bloodhounds. Maybe I'd just be strapped into that nasty old chair of electric surprises, what do they call that process? Frying, yes that's it, frying. The pick-up's door opened and the tall figure strode toward me again, my documents in the hand farthest from his gun.

'The state limit is fifty-five miles per hour, you were travelling at seventy one miles per hour.' I thought about expressing incredulity for an instant, but settled for a response aimed between mild surprise and penitent resignation.

'The fine for violating the state speed limit is fifty-four dollars.' It seemed an odd figure, but I didn't feel inclined to query it, and nodded slowly in silent remorse.

'I'll just give you a warning this time,' he continued, 'but I strongly recommend that you conform to the state speed limit at all times in future.'

I offered my sincere assurance that I would, thanked him for his lenience, and climbed back on to my motorcycle. There was something novel in being chastised by an officer of the law without any reference to the fact that I was riding bareheaded. If given the choice I would far sooner have a fifty-five limit and no helmet law in Britain than the converse, though I expect I'd be in a minority.

My encounter with the law was followed by two with animals; one with a herd of buffalo, the other with a turtle. Recalling my westbound turtle encounter, and the guilt I had felt at not helping it across the road, I decided to make amends and see this one safely over the asphalt without delay. It was not as large as the one I'd seen before, which was just as well as it leaked all over me as soon as I picked it up. If I'd been sure which end was which when I took hold of it, I'd have been a happier and drier man, but as I approached the lethargic amphibian, all extraneous distinguishing appendages withdrew beneath the shell, leaving me confronted with a uniform body of indeterminate character. This presented me with more than one problem since, my uncertainty about the animal's orientation was compounded by an inability to recall in which direction the creature had been walking when I paused to expedite his migration. I was a few miles down the road when it occurred to me that I might inadvertently have negated half a morning's strenuous effort by this itinerant reptile through my misdirected efforts. I considered going back, but the need for progress prevailed over my Franciscan instincts and I continued on my eastward course.

The herd of buffalo did not, thankfully, pee on me, but they did bugger off as I scrambled down an earth bank, camera in hand, intent on recording the picture of their impressive forms. Alas it was not to be. As soon as they caught sight of my unfamiliar shape heading their way, they were off, a forest of sinewy legs kicking up a minor dust storm that shrouded the burly physiques of the retreating herd. I felt a little guilty at having disturbed these peaceful herbivores in their own territory, but I was simultaneously irritated by their timidity in view of their innate physical superiority. If I was a buffalo, with shoulders like beach balls and a neck that makes Mike Tyson's look like a pencil, then I wouldn't be scared of me. Hell, I'm me and I'm not scared of me, so what does that make them?

I lunched on enchiladas and retook the highway with a new fire in my belly and a resolve to cover some serious mileage, all at the state limit of course. The road was as straight as a die and just as empty. Many of the pick-up and truck drivers waved cheerfully as I passed, which enhanced my sense of belonging in a foreign land; I wondered if they were responding to the instantly recognisable outline of an all American motorcycle, or were simply bored; I chose to believe the former interpretation and waved back. With the road being so straight, and vehicles sighted so far off, I frequently gained the impression that oncoming travellers were on my side of the road. As I closed rapidly on a smoke-belching Peterson, the conviction grew, supported by the realisation that in this case, at least, he was. I squeezed over to my side of the single track road, leaving him adequate space to run past without totalling the Trans-am he was slowly overhauling. I spotted an apologetic wave from the driver as he steamed onward like a destroyer at full revs. Not counting New York, where motoring standards are positively Italian, this was the only occasion in seven and a half thousand miles of riding, where I could positively claim to have been the injured party in a case of motoring indiscretion, and I got an apology!

The manager of the motel I stopped at tonight directed me to a restaurant that didn't exist, but I found another where I grossed out on spaghetti bolognese with garlic bread, liberally lubricated by good old Budweiser beer, an additional quart of which, I purchased by way of a nightcap.

DRUGS

Uncapping the bottle of beer in my motel room this evening, I decided to capitalize upon the $20 investment which my room represented, by peering into that window of America, the ubiquitous television. Tonight's programme was about drugs, featuring a controlled experiment designed to explore the effects of LSD. An artist who, under supervision, had taken a quantity of the drug, was continuing to paint whilst an analytical onlooker provided a commentary on the developing behaviour and artistic expressiveness of the enthusiastic guinea pig. A TV company presenter talked with the analyst, interposing questions and issuing obligatory cautions to sustain the necessary balance between objective research and responsible discouragement of hazardous indulgences.

'Ah now see this,' said the analyst, with more than a hint of enthusiasm in his voice.

'This is a lovely effect, very nice.'

'You mean in a purely scientific way,' added the interviewer with an eagerness from which one could detect a chill breeze of warning waft from the arched eyebrows of the invisible producer as they telegraphed their anxiety.

'Oh yes, yes,' agreed the analyst, his voice betraying a feigned sincerity through which a masked bat might easily have seen. There was a little relief for the wretch with the microphone when the scene shifted to a studio for a discussion with an audience of haggard junkies, past abusers, contentious reformists and nauseating social workers, who blamed the state for everything bar their shapeless trousers and cropped hair.

In the course of the ensuing discussion, the man whose objective was to legalize everything that didn't kill you stone dead the first time you tried it, threw the director of the debate into a fresh panic. In an effort to illustrate hypocrisy at the highest level, the stirrer shouted, 'Everyone knows that Oliver North was responsible for organizing more cocaine deals then the Columbian customs.'

Struggling to retain control of the live show amidst the resultant smiles, sniggers, and nodding heads of the worldly-wise audience, the uncomfortable arbitrator squawked with a petulant urgency. 'That is disallowable, it has not been documented. Now let's have a question from over...'

As his questing clipboard hunted desperately around the unhelpful rabble of inconveniently smirking mutes, the sound of a producer's head falling heavily against the thick glass of an adjacent production room reverberated around the studio like the dull thud of an attorney's fat brief hitting a courtroom floor.

Pouring the last of the beer into my face, I retired, chuckling with wry amusement which the discomfiture of others so often affords.

RUNNING OUT OF ROAD

Today was the day I ran out of road. It wasn't as if I was flinging the bike around a series of serpentine switchbacks, or overstretching myself in inclement conditions. The weather was clear and dry, the road flat, practically devoid of traffic, and as straight as an asphalt plumb-line. I hadn't the ghost of an excuse for running off it, but I'm glad in retrospect that I did, as it fairly livened up an otherwise dull day. I'd been daydreaming, thinking about getting to Indianapolis, thinking about getting home and riding this superb machine around the rather more demanding roads of England, maybe even leaning it into a bend once in a while. It was probably this train of thought that sent me off course, and by the time I realized I was departing the straight and narrow it was too late to do much about it. Of course the armchair critics will come up with smart-arse solutions like leaning the bike back the other way. That sounds fine and simple viewed with the luxury of hindsight, but I was there, and it was then; Highway 36 visited, unvisited, and then revisited, with precious little deliberate effort on my part.

As I noted my track deviating from the straight and adequate path stretching before me, I did nothing, my body leaned involuntarily with the bike, which performed like a bicycle struck in a tram line, steering me with a resolution to the right of my intended track. I was like a rabbit caught in the paralyzing glare of a car's headlights; mysteriously motivated by unseen forces of which I was both architect and victim. The only cohesive thought I recall passing through my head as I peeled off the tarmac into the rubble was: 'I am going to crash.'

The hard-shoulder onto which I ran, was rather like a pebble beach generously mixed with dust which made for a spectacular sandstorm of Saharan proportions as I ploughed into it at a legitimate, but inadvisable, fifty-five miles per hour. I like to think that I made a successful effort to steer around the larger obstructions, though I suspect the reality was that I did nothing but hang on. Small stones clattered like meteorites into the metalwork, pebble dashing the engine as the tyres slewed about in a desperate quest for traction. I couldn't really see too well, the way the bike was bucking around, and it was all I could do to keep a hold of the handlebars and pray that I didn't ride over the bank and down the other side. It was maybe as well that I didn't have a sturdier command of events, as with a firmer hand on the tiller I might well have been tempted to brake – with tragic consequences. I imagine I travelled about fifty yards on this uncomfortable terrain before the mismanaged bronco spluttered to a halt amidst a Vesuvian cloud of airborne debris that obscured my vision and clotted my throat, already overcrowded by the unwelcome arrival of my heart. Peering through the man-made dust storm, I caught the hazy impression of an automobile cruising by, its astonished driver leaning forward against the restraining influence of his seatbelt, peering sideways toward a spectacle he was doubtless at a loss to explain. I could imagine his story.

'Hell, the guy just ran clean off the road!'

Never mind, I thought, it could have been worse, suppose it had happened up at Grand Canyon ?

Eastbound across Kansas, I spotted something I'd missed on my westbound journey a couple of hundred miles to the south. It was a statue of a man on a horse, galloping full pelt, his features set in an expression of iron determination. There was a quality to this stoic symbol that excited my interest and prompted immediate investigation. The character immortalized in bronze was one Jack Keetley, who, if I remember correctly, made the first run for the Pony Express company from Sacramento to California on April 3rd 1860, that is to say, he started the run on that date. Contrary to what might be imagined from the movies, where Pony Express riders invariably turned up looking like pin cushions, very few actually fell foul of warpath Indians, or anyone else for that matter. In reality, only one rider was ever certainly killed by Indians, one disappeared, and only one schedule was uncompleted. Looking at the impressive statue of this pioneer of the US Mail, I flattered myself by drawing comparisons between my own efforts on a twentieth-century steel horse, and the early equestrian endeavours of those hardy nineteenth-century desperados. The fact is, that riding a modern Harley-Davidson across America, with its excellent roads, innumerable motels, and friendly people, is a piece of cake. It might be verging on the self-deprecatory to say that anyone could do it, but certainly anyone in normal health who wants to do it, should find it well within their capabilities. The epidemic of violence that characterizes so many American movies is largely confined to the urban environment – easily avoided by circumnavigating cities which, geographically at least, represent a very small proportion of the American continent.

I took a look around the museum of the Pony Express, housed in a rustic stone building that had been the original starting point of the company service. The place was stuffed with musty artifacts of wood and leather which stood or hung about the cluttered confines of the old office in a manner unusually intimate for a museum, where glass cases, 'Do Not Touch' signs and watchful security men set the mood. I wondered if perhaps one day, curious tourists will shuffle across the oil-smeared floor of the last motorcycle emporium and ponder the wild and hazardous indulgence of two-wheeled transport, exhibiting the same respectful acknowledgement with which these work-worn saddles and faded sepia photographs were now treated? Probably not.

I'd indulged myself longer than I intended and fallen behind in my schedule, which seemed a good reason to speed up a little. Some miles down the road, in Missouri now, I was cruising along at seventy miles per hour when a police car passed me, travelling in the opposite direction. There was no mistaking the interest behind the dark shades as he swivelled his head, and with a sense of *déjà vu* I checked my rear view mirror for the red glow of his brake lights; none occurred and I continued for several miles with growing confidence until, at a roadside checkpoint, a corpulent stetson hatted cop strolled into the road, his hand held up palm toward me in a manner that was clearly understood.

'Where's your helmet at?' he demanded to know, in a manner more of amusement than hostility. I motioned to the sparse coconut-shell-sized dome strapped under the luggage net.

'Better put it on your head son, as long as you're in the state of Missouri,' he suggested with a convivial grin. 'State line's two miles on, you can take it off there.' We exchanged a few words about my trip and parted amicably, me with nominal head gear in place, which if the truth be known, was probably inferior in its protective potential to the cop's stetson. Three miles down the road I crossed the state line into Illinois and the helmet came off again.

My hopes of running all the way to Indianapolis tonight dwindled as drizzle turned to heavy rain. For the second time on this trip I encountered the rain that reaches the parts you bloody well don't want it to. I ran through it for almost an hour, willing civilization to appear out of the remorseless deluge. Lights did appear, but they were false messiahs, burning atop a wretched chemical complex that belched smoke and flames in defiance of the elements, like some irresistible industrialized dragon. I get very bad karma off chemical plants. I suppose some of them are necessary, but I'm sure we could make do with less, and they should definitely be put somewhere else. I was riding almost blind now, in third gear, without my glasses which simply collected water; so I rode on, one hand held across my eyes, leaving a tiny crack between two fingers to peer through. The thing about proceeding in this slightly unorthodox fashion, is that whilst you can see a lot more than might be imagined, to an oncoming motorist you appear as a suicidal maniac playing a kind of blind man's bluff cum Russian roulette; a sightless phantom of incomparable desperation. I divined these to be the sentiments of the drivers in the oncoming cars by the manner in which they hugged their side of the road. When it comes to wide berths, I was afforded the kind of respect that I, in my time as a navigation officer, used to afford Greek methanol carriers.

Blessedly the lights of a motel appeared and I pulled in. After agreeing with the old cove in the office that this was in fact the wettest night since the ark broke free from her moorings, I went in search of food. I found it in a trucker's diner a block away, where at the check-out, right in front of the table at which I had unwittingly deposited myself, squatted the world's ultimate lard arse. She was the kind of girl whom my old friend Big Dave would, somewhat hypocritically, point at and cruelly bellow, 'That's a bigun.' He'd have been right too. Strewth she was fat. Had she risen from the stool, I am sure it would have hung from between her buttocks like a straw in a burger bun. Astonished yet again by the ability of the human species to distort itself into ghastly parodies of normality, I retired to the truckstop shop where I purchased a tape of superb sixties' tracks and a baseball hat for Big Dave, bearing the legend; 'I may be fat but you are ugly and I can slim.'

Back in my motel I discovered that the tape was jammed, and the hat was clearly too small for its intended recipient. Consoling myself with a large bag of peanuts and a quart of Budweiser, I sat back to read my book about the Walapi tribe of the Grand Canyon.

THE MEETING OF THE MINDS

Thank God it's dry, I comforted myself, as I looked out next morning onto a rain-less landscape; I had a hundred and twenty miles left to travel to make the bikers' convention in Indianapolis. I was resigned to missing part of the morning session, but so long as it stays dry, I thought, I can crack along at a fair speed and be there in a couple of hours. I couldn't help noticing that the air was pretty damn sharp but I can put up with that so long as it doesn't rain, or so I told myself. Five minutes down the road I had changed my mind. Sod this I thought, I've had enough. I had spare boxer shorts stuffed down the inside of my waterproofs which were reluctantly worn as wind-breakers and embarrassment-savers as they disguised the fact that I had T-shirts stuck to my knees with insulating tape as protection from the cold. Twenty miles into the ride I was ready to trade the cold for a little rain at a higher temperature, but no one was offering a deal. Frank's diner was offering hot coffee and doughnuts, however, and I filled up to thaw out my innards before hypothermia set in. Another twenty miles up the road I was freezing, and busting to unload the recycled coffee. I solved half my problems and carried on.

At eleven-thirty, three and a half hours after leaving my motel, I cruised into Indianapolis.

I instinctively had a better feeling about this town than I'd had about Cleveland, where I had attended my last bikers' convention. It was kind of less city-like with less atmosphere of danger and hostility. I found the convention hotel, booked in, and shot up the road to get some black and white film. As I ran down to the town, I noticed a low-slung Harley coming the other way. It was ridden by a familiar looking figure, and in a moment of spontaneous recognition we realized that we knew each other, he realized that I was Ian Mutch, and I realized that he was Chip Bugansky, the man to whom I owed gratitude for setting up the Harley for me – small place America!

Inside the main theatre of activity, I spotted Pepper, sitting pensively through one of the political sessions. I plonked myself down next to her before she realized who I was, which I thought was pretty cool, particularly considering the near perfect timetabling my arrival here represented, after several other rendezvous, not to mention mountain ranges, deserts and thousands of miles since last we met.

This biker convention, somewhat pretentiously entitled the 'Meeting of the Minds,' provided an opportunity for like-thinking biker's rights activists from all over America to meet for a series of forums and socially orientated pooling of ideas, with the hope that everyone would go away better armed and encouraged to fight the good fight for libertarian and sensible attitudes to prevail, and the freedom of the road to be restored or protected.

The afternoon session ended at three-thirty, after which I killed some time hanging around the hotel before taking off with Chip for a meal of lobster which was so cheap I actually paid. I'm not given to this kind of largesse, not that I'm miserly, but I tend to spend all my money on myself. Given the help that Chip had given me with the bike that had turned up trumps, I reckoned I owed him something, and a tasty crustacean with some beer and salad was a small price to pay for over seven-thousand miles worth of superb motorcycling, with the bonus of a perfectly running machine at the end of it to take home with me like some golden handshake. Dinner over, we spent a shivering hour trying to find the field where the evening's entertainment was taking place. In fairness to the organizers, they could not have known it would be this cold in late September, but I did wonder about the wisdom of holding the do, miles from the place where everyone was sleeping, with the inevitable complications and hazards which that entails. Maybe I'm getting old but I like to know that my pit is in staggering distance of where I'm spending the evening if I am to relax. As I was on the bike, I went for softies after a single beer, but satiated my appetite for absorbing things by eating everything on offer, despite having already had a substantial meal. Corn on the cob dripping with butter, followed by kebabs, followed by more corn on the cob, and somewhere in-between all this indulgence I ran into the spectre-like form of Max. This colourful character of confused background had last been encountered in a seedy pub in East London where he used to attend the local meetings of the Motorcycle Action Group. Max is one of those desperate, incorrigible perennials who turns up like a hardy shrub that survives any injury or excess, whether self inflicted or delivered by external agents. Max is the sort of character who pops up at the scenes of the worst imaginable carnage, where all around is misery desolation and death. I am sure Max was at the Somme, at Gallipoli, at Dunkirk; Max survived the charge of the Light Brigade, scrambled from the Black Hole of Calcutta, and scuttled out of Pompeii before the mountain blew its top. In this incarnation, he was to be found, less spectacularly, leaning against a marquee pole rolling a cigarette with a laudable indifference that denied the bitterness of the night air. Max shook my hand and explained his plan to ride to California. One question hinted at a mood of uncharacteristic anxiety.

'Is there snow in the Rockies?'

Is there snow in the Rockies? Is the Pacific Ocean wet?

'Yes,' I assured him with cheerful honesty. 'There's loads of it, and it's very cold.'

Max scratched his chin and muttered something about over trousers as he pondered his preparations. About this time, a general consensus formed which favoured a return to the hotel, the band packed up its gear and we made our way back to town where I met Short Shit. Short Shit was a mate of Max who had a home in California to which Max was planning to ride. Short Shit came over to where I was sitting.

'Excuse me,' he said. 'Would you mind standing up a moment?' It was clear that his question had something to do with the crowd on the far side of the bar who were leaning toward us with obvious anticipation. I obliged him amidst a roar of laughter from the audience as my significantly superior height became apparent.

'*Orr* shit!' bellowed Short Shit. Of all the people I met in America, the one I would most like to be photographed alongside, was Short Shit. Meantime Max was off to his room with two spirited women of middle years, neither of whom struck me as being a sister of chastity.

The following morning's business at the convention featured a speech by a senator who opposed helmet compulsion. When the time came for questions from the floor, one provocative soul asked the senator how he could reconcile his libertarian attitude toward helmet compulsion with his support for the anti-abortion lobby. It was a good question, it must have been, the senator said it was. He actually said, 'That's a good question, and I'm glad you asked it.' Now I've heard that line in comedy sketches where it is used to epitomize the distress of the struggling wretch playing for time, but I don't think any British politician of note has dared to use it for quite a few years now. Perhaps, unusually, we tired of it first. Certainly on the British side of the Atlantic, its use has become confined to the satirical context, no one who wished to be taken seriously would use it, any more than a sacked politician would say he wanted to spend more time with his family. Just as the latter means, I am a has-been who has been given the boot, the former may be substituted by, 'Who invited you smart-arse, why don't you sod off?'

As it turned out, the senator talked his way around the question quite well. I did not envy him his dilemma, the abortion issue is much bigger in the USA than it is in Britain, where religious fundamentalism is less prevalent. In America, for politicians in many states, opposition to the 'pro-lifers' as the anti-abortionists are known, is political suicide.

I've never held very strong views on abortion (which may come as a relief to some readers), but one argument which the pro-abortionists frequently field does irritate me. 'A woman's right to choose – my body, my choice.' It's a simple stance that seems to ignore the obvious point that a pregnant woman is not one person, she is two people. And the call for a woman's choice frequently trumpeted by these shrill advocates of abortion, is clearly denied the unborn which they carry. If the child had been born, would a mother be exonerated for murdering it on the grounds that it was 'her child – her choice?' On what may be considered a shockingly mechanical level, however, there is always an element of my consciousness that registers relief at the fact that the world's chronic overpopulation is not exacerbated further by many thousands of unwanted children entering it. I get the same feeling when I hear that the population of Africa is being decimated by plague. It may not be a noble thought and I could no more defend complacency about such tragedy than I could defend capital punishment. I put my hand in my pocket when charity tins are rattled in my face for the sake of the Third World, but I just cannot help registering a sensation of relief when I hear of falling populations.

When one's entire life has been overshadowed by the gnawing fear that we are locked in an irreversible tailspin toward catastrophe as the environment is overstretched by its burgeoning population, how can one fail to find some compensation in the fundamental problem's solution? When every wildlife pamphlet and programme brings apocalyptic warnings about the fate of the great wild beasts of our forest and jungles being progressively threatened by human encroachment, when each day brings ever more dire warnings about ozone depletion, acid rain and melting ice caps, how can the news that the world's population is falling not bring some glimmer of hope? It is a partly selfish sentiment that owes little to compassion and everything to what is probably false optimism for the future of our species. Frankly, I think that our woes will only be resolved by divine intervention but notwithstanding this conviction, there is a facet of simple rationale that must be satisfied by any news that the big issue is being addressed, albeit by the most pernicious of agents. The inescapable reality is that man is the victim of his own success in overcoming the killer plagues by which means he has cultivated the mechanics of his own misery. This is not an entirely selfish reflection from the perspective of the industrialized world, as it is the poorest of the world's people who already suffer most from ecological mayhem. Who, for example, is more at risk from the smallest rise in sea levels than the impoverished people of Bangladesh? One can understand the indignation of the less-developed world when told that they must not aspire to Western standards of material wealth and energy consumption – but if such aspiration were satisfied, and millions perished as a result, what would it profit them?

Of course the West should do more to control its greed and utterly pointless waste, as represented by ludicrous packaging, enormous automobiles and air conditioning, for starters, but the big challenge is population. If there were only, say, half a billion people in the world then we might all drive around in Jaguars and live in fabulous homes packed with energy hungry gadgets and it wouldn't matter a damn but that just isn't the case. My Harley-Davidson, incidentally, covers over fifty miles to the gallon while being easy on tyres. Its first belt drive, I am now able to report, pulled the quarter-ton leviathan 70,000 miles before shedding its teeth, and I take the same shopping bags back to the supermarket every time I go, rather than using enough plastic carrier bags to suffocate a rhinoceros. So I am as innocent as the driven snow. Wastage and extravagance are not the same thing, and while I would rebel at the introduction of arbitrary limits on engine capacity I think huge deposits on carrier bags are a splendid idea.

I also think that the West has a responsibility to the Third World – but that all aid programmes must be complemented by population control initiatives. Finite world: infinite growth; it's as untenable as the logic is irrefutable.

The Senator's performance was followed by an emotional closing speech delivered by the Indiana ABATE president, a stocky, serious-looking chap called 'Balls'.

Balls' performance certainly supported my claim that Americans are more theatrical than we are. I didn't doubt the essential truth of the message which Balls was at pains to convey, but the vehicle employed was an oratorical equivalent of an eighteen-wheel artic rolled out to carry a hamster cage; we were talking serious over-kill. I had to applaud the man's ability, I understand he had taken lessons in public speaking, given, I would imagine, by the Royal Shakespeare Company. There were fists thumped into palms, hands held to foreheads, eyes cast upward, eyes cast downward, back turned toward the audience throughout soliloquies of Hamletian intensity. The emotional rhetoric would have nauseated most British audiences as he groaned about the love for his brother bikers and their love for freedom and their love for their motorcycles and their love for each other and their love of America and their love of their state and their love of love. Balls was a forceful character. He'd built up Indiana ABATE's membership to seventeen thousand, the highest total of any state in the union. Notwithstanding that achievement, however, I had to resist a temptation to reach for a sick bag.

TO NEW YORK

I slipped away quietly from the convention, thus avoiding the goodbyes that I don't care for, and was soon rumbling east on Interstate 70 for the Atlantic coast, now less than a thousand miles distant. It's curious how quickly you adjust to a different perspective of distance. Before I set out on this trip I was determined to get some kind of breakdown cover. The 'Triple A' motorist's organization do offer a nationwide service, but I was assured by everyone that they were of little use where motorcycles were concerned. Having made it out to the West Coast without any problems, I had developed a new confidence and become somewhat blasé about distances. 'What the hell,' I'd thought, when contemplating the eastward journey back across the country, 'it's only another three-thousand miles back to New York.'

With nightfall the temperature plummeted, and with it my optimism. I had been hoping to cover enough distance today so I could make it across New York City to Long Island before dark the following day, this now looked less likely. As the shivering increased, so to did the sense of urgency to find somewhere to stay. For the first time on this trip, I just couldn't seem to find anywhere, no friendly motel signs, no brightly-lit restaurants, no garish neon inducements, hardly any towns even. Those I did leave the highway to explore seemed to consist of nothing but houses, someone had stolen all the motels and I had become very unhappy. I was damned cold, hungry, running low on fuel and even lower on patience. As, back in the Sierra Nevada when I was desperately cold, I began to shout and scream, cursing the missing motels and highway turn-offs that didn't seem to lead anywhere. I also began to feel slightly spooked by one or two places that I pulled into. There were no people on the streets, maybe it was just the cold but I didn't like it. I was in Pennsylvania now, hilly forested country, not unlike parts of England, but the familiarity held no comfort. 'Why aren't you a motel,' I shouted at the creosoted planking of an innocent barn. 'You shit of a building, you total bastard! Sod this, sod it, sod it, all right that's enough, show me a motel; right what's this, bollocks!' A closed gas station.

I sustained this foaming dialogue for a good hour, spitting profusely into the air and cursing inanimate objects, until, to my immense relief, a motel appeared, accompanied by a very welcome 'Vacancies' sign, shining in the night like the signpost which the Israelites found after forty years of wandering in the wilderness; the one that read, presumably, 'Way Out.' Dumping my stuff in my room, I had a look at the tv. A vampire movie was showing. I didn't care for that. There is something a bit mid-European about these Eastern states that lends itself to modern day vampire like possibilities. I saw a very convincing film on this theme once, set in Pennsylvania, in which a perfectly normal middle-class mother of three was found gorging herself on the family cat – raw! Nasty business.

I was still thinking about this when, an hour later, after some indifferent pasta at a local restaurant, I crawled between fresh sheets and drifted into unconsciousness.

I was still hoping to make New York in daylight when I set out the following morning, though it was with an optimism that I would have abandoned sooner had I studied the map carefully, rather than setting off with the groundless conviction that it must be possible for no better reason than than I wanted it to be. There is an ancient school of Greek philosophy that cheerfully contends that if you say something is, then it is. I was struck by the splendid simplicity of this attitude the first time that I heard of it, and have adhered to its fundamental tenet ever since with a confidence as conscientious as it is ludicrous. When I saw signs that read, 'New York three-hundred miles,' having earlier decided that it could not be more than one-hundred and fifty, I just ignored them. 'Can't be, can't be, can't be,' I told myself, 'must be a mistake.' It wasn't.

After stopping for lunch at a roadside diner I met an old man walking slowly with the aid of a stick toward his automobile, an effort which he extended to hobble over and look at my bike. I spotted his interest and delayed my departure to await his inevitable questions. He asked me where I was going and where I'd been and I told him with a childish sense of satisfaction. He looked at me intently and then at the bike, pausing before responding.

'That's something I always wanted to do,' he said slowly. 'That's exactly what I always promised myself I'd do.'

Leaning on his stick, he stared wistfully at the Harley as one of its throw-over straps fluttered moodily in the breeze, a slim ensign of anticipation aboard a ship of dreams. I followed the old man's eyes, studying the bike with a fresh intensity. The dust of seven-thousand miles clung to the mist of oil staining the crankcase, above which, in vertical array, the singed carcasses of roasted insects were packed like corpses in the metal mausoleum of the engine finning, their bodies a grim testimony to my miles and their misfortune.

'Always wanted to do that,' repeated the old man, his eyes resting steadily on the huge machine leaning on its sidestand like a heeled schooner in a stiff sou'westerly. His wife waited patiently by the car while her spouse's eyes roamed over the motorcycle as he wallowed vicariously in the youthful dream which our encounter had rekindled.

I felt a little sorry for the old fellow as I pulled out of the parking bay. Generally I like people to feel envious of me, no home, no family, no regular job, no real ties or commitments, just this big shiny motorcycle, a fistful of dollars and a continent to play around in. The old man never had made the run he'd promised himself though, and he didn't look like he was about to do it now, which was sad. Regret is a terrible thing, failure is bad enough but regretting not trying is worse. The old man raised a hand as I pulled out of the parking lot. I waved to him but didn't look back though I knew he was watching me disappear, listening to the engine change note as I shifted gear and accelerated down the road. His words hung in my head as I rode east, my mind repeating them over and over, 'something I always wanted to do.'

A police car overtook me as I crossed the line into New York state, disturbing my reverie with a brief burst on his siren as he did so, the driver meanwhile gesturing toward his head. Assuming that this gesture did not represent a declaration of insanity, I guessed I was back in helmet land and pulled over to don the ridiculous lid.

A mile down the road I passed the same car from which an arm protruded in a friendly wave. What a good boy I was, and aren't American policemen wonderful! As I was to discover later, quite a lot of American cops ride bikes and think the helmet law sucks, which may explain the tolerant attitude, or maybe I was just lucky.

As dusk descended, an unmistakable skyline glowed in the gathering darkness, a skyline with a unique magic, a threatening magnet of obsessions, excess, indulgence and inequality. A bubbling vat of conflicting ingredients and competing desperados; a living monument to the fruits of endeavour and a grim warning to the foolhardy optimists of failure's price. The Big Apple. Viewing the giant monoliths from afar, I felt like Schwarzenegger in his barbarian movies, pausing on his horse as the sight of some nest of magnificent malevolence came into view across the expanse of the lunar landscapes which characterized those films. My sense of satisfaction was tempered with anxiety.

I had particularly wanted to avoid crossing New York City after dark, but I now had no choice. From my direction of approach I had to get across Manhattan to reach Long Island where I was heading for the home of my friend Ronald Mackenzie, a veteran helmet law campaigner and distinguished urologist.

The traffic was horrendous. It wasn't actually jammed as solidly as London's gets sometimes, but there was precious little road surface visible, and everywhere seemed to be a queue. New York, being built as it is on a collection of islands separated by various reaches of the Hudson River, you really have to plan a journey across it to make sure you arrive at the right bridges, tunnels, and ferry terminals. Navigational errors can easily leave you ending up facing a stretch of impassable water from some dubious viewpoint amidst a mass of concrete bridge pylons inhabited by human derelicts. It can be a bit like a Chinese puzzle; you see and hear the automobiles rumbling overhead on the elevated sections but you just can't understand for the life of you, how they got there. It's a bit like programming a video; you read the instructions, press all the right buttons, and go out for the evening. When you check the results next day, you find you've nothing more interesting to watch than a double bill of silent static – marvellous.

The sign that I followed for the Holland Tunnel to get me from New Jersey to Manhattan should have read, 'this way for nasty dead-end, full of oily puddles, broken bottles, alcoholics and dossers.' Fortunately I was on a 1340cc Harley-Davidson as opposed to the 305cc Kawasaki I'd been riding the last time I was lost in New York's less salubrious neighbourhoods. This made me feel a lot more confident and I accosted one of the less derelict looking citizens who was leaning for support on a wire safety barrier. I shouted to him.

'Hey!' It's always best if you start a sentence with 'Hey,' it shows you mean business, far less prissy than 'excuse me,' or an apologetic 'sorry to trouble you.' Come out with a nancyish line like that around here, I thought, and a host of grubby fingers will soon be going through your wallet, as you float face down in the East River.

'Hey,' I shouted, 'how the hell do I get to the Holland Tunnel.' New Yorkers understand this approach, and it worked. The man straightened up, took his weight off the fence and approached me as a recruit might a Sergeant Major. To my relief the advice I got was not bad, and in a matter of minutes I was nosing my way through the lattice work of Manhattan's Lower East Side. It may seem that I over-do the criticism of New York as a sewer of human derelicts, especially as I haven't really seen enough of it to make anything like a comprehensive comment on the place. It just seemed to me though, that wherever I turned I ran into another nest of destitute wretches. As I sat waiting for the lights to change, a dustbin liner moved over to my right. It then grew a head, into which it tipped the contents of a bottle, before turning back into a dustbin liner, inseparable from the others along the wall, rather like the closing scene from Bill and Ben. The shiny chrome of the Harley seemed at odds with the matt darkness of the seedy sidewalk malingerers, welded together by a common bond of desperation on a stage that has seen so many performances of human degradation.

By a series of educated guesses I worked my way up the East Side of Manhattan without straying into Harlem as I had done by mistake back in May when on the Kawasaki. Given that you know which Island you are on, and in which direction you're heading, which isn't hard given the regular nature of the roads, finding your way about is not as hard as might be imagined. Before too much time had passed I was out of the Upper East Side and skirting the Bronx on the Bruckner Expressway, from which I spotted a hoarding bearing the cheerful legend, 'We're Rebuilding The

Bronx.' Nailed as it was to the side of a grotesque tenement, one of many, I could only hope that this was not an advertisement for the architecture to which it was attached. Up ahead, a sign for the familiar 'Throgs Neck Bridge' appeared and I took it.

Riding high over Long Island Sound, I turned in the saddle to look back at the glittering towers of Manhattan, flickering between the steelwork of the great bridge as I rumbled slowly over it. I think this is the best way to see Manhattan. It's like a Rolf Harris three minute painting – you have to stand back and view it from a distance to get the right perspective. Down at street level it doesn't seem so grand. There, the skyscrapers are vastly outnumbered by buildings of comparative mediocrity. Away from the ritzy theatre land at the south end of the park, the place has a downmarket Third World feel to it. Up on the bridge though, things looked different, and not even the reality of first-hand, ground-level observation could dispel the aura of excitement and dramatic prestige which those architectural colossi convey. There's an optimism about skyscrapers which lower buildings can never possess. Their very height seems to symbolize the ambition of mankind, each tower challenges its neighbour to outreach it, like so many giants clustered together, glancing jealously over their shoulders, measuring the competition like American football players glaring through their caged faces at formidable opponents. Towers of Babel challenging the limits of mortal achievement, the skyscrapers of New York mirror the aspirations of Americans. It's an imagery that earns a poignancy from an awareness of the squalor and vice that swirls like a rancid smog about the bases of these indifferent monoliths. Excrement at the feet of giraffes. Manhattan is a living metaphor for America. No greater contrast of wealth or poverty, of achievement and failure, of splendour and squalor, so closely and dramatically co-exist anywhere on earth. The Manhattan skyline is America's crown jewels. There's a challenge posed by its lofty glitz, a challenge so appropriate to the prime point of immigration, the gateway to the New World. It's both a challenge and a warning, 'You too can have a body like mine,' say the towers, but just as you may climb onto my shoulders, so too can you fall and be trampled underfoot in the streets of New York which offer no soft landings.

I want to get to know New York better, it must have a more positive side. It is, after all, one of the great cultural centres of the world, and to dismiss it with facile criticisms of revulsion is foolishly unjust. For this trip though, I had run out of time, so it will have to wait for me. Against all odds this hive of commerce, crime and avarice, bursting at the seams with its own excesses, will just have to survive a little longer.

My thoughts were disturbed by a ripple as the front wheel mounted the steel ramp at the east end of the bridge, decanting me into the comparative safety of Long Island. I looked back one more time at the world's most celebrated skyline.

'Stay there,' I said, 'stay there.' Half fearing that if I let it out of my sight it would, like a fanciful mirage, disappear from view.

As I turned to look ahead, a motorist, stuck in traffic leaned out of his window head turned enviously toward me, eyes following my progress as the rolling icon of Americana overtook him. Leaning left under a sign for the Long Island Expressway, I twisted the throttle harder than usual, drawing a deep bellow from the huge engine and lifting the front end of the bike slightly as it hurtled past the slumbering evening rush-hour traffic.

Up ahead, the landing lights of a seven-forty-seven lit up the runway of JFK airport; somebody else had come looking for America.